"In an age of head-spinning change, Gav[in] to stand their ground and recover the theological ground already plowed by earlier generations. When the very foundations are being shaken, it is vital that churches recover their center of gravity by retrieving the past—what Bernard Ramm once called 'the evangelical heritage.' Evangelicals are not the first generation to have received the gospel. Accordingly, Ortlund here issues a manifesto about the importance of retrieving theological tradition. He then practices what he preaches in a series of astute case studies that mine the past to fund the present."

Kevin J. Vanhoozer, Research Professor of Systematic Theology, Trinity Evangelical Divinity School; author, *The Drama of Doctrine*; *Hearers and Doers*; *Biblical Authority after Babel*; and *Faith Speaking Understanding*

"Anyone convinced that *evangelical* and *ancient* are opposites should read this book. Gavin Ortlund provides a compelling case for retrieving patristic and medieval theology. Mining the premodern tradition, Ortlund reminds us of neglected and forgotten insights on the Creator-creature distinction, divine simplicity, and atonement theology. An excellent contribution to Protestant retrieval theology!"

Hans Boersma, Chair, Order of St. Benedict Servants of Christ Endowed Professorship in Ascetical Theology, Nashotah House Theological Seminary

"Ortlund argues compellingly that evangelicals can and should claim the classic theological heritage as their own. And then he actually does it, opening up the treasury of the great Christian tradition and dispensing theological wisdom with both hands. To look into this book is to look through a doorway into a world where there is such a thing as evangelical theology that is richly resourced, deeply informed, and ready for action."

Fred Sanders, Professor of Theology, Torrey Honors Institute, Biola University; author, *The Deep Things of God: How the Trinity Changes Everything*

"Gavin Ortlund, a committed evangelical, calls for a robust engagement with the first fifteen hundred years of the Christian tradition, patristic and medieval, East and West. Retrieval, not repristination, is the goal, and Ortlund shows here how this can be done—to the glory of God and the upbuilding of the church. An exciting and important book!"

Timothy George, Research Professor, Beeson Divinity School, Samford University; general editor, Reformation Commentary on Scripture

"For those who struggle with whether, how, and why to appropriate the church fathers and medieval doctors within their own theology, piety, and ministry, this book is a welcome resource. Leading us by the hand through a wide range of instructive examples, Gavin Ortlund demonstrates a principled Protestant approach to drawing upon the pastors and theologians of the past for the sake of the church's renewal in the present."

Scott R. Swain, President and James Woodrow Hassell Professor of Systematic Theology, Reformed Theological Seminary, Orlando; coauthor, *Reformed Catholicity*

Theological Retrieval for Evangelicals

Theological Retrieval for Evangelicals

*Why We Need Our Past
to Have a Future*

Gavin Ortlund

∷ CROSSWAY®

WHEATON, ILLINOIS

Library of Congress Cataloging-in-Publication Data

Names: Ortlund, Gavin, 1983- author.
Title: Theological retrieval for evangelicals : why we need our past to have a future / Gavin Ortlund.
Description: Wheaton : Crossway, 2019. | Includes bibliographical references and index.
Identifiers: LCCN 2019000335 (print) | LCCN 2019021797 (ebook) | ISBN 9781433565274 (pdf) | ISBN 9781433565281 (mobi) | ISBN 9781433565281 (epub) | ISBN 9781433565267 (tp)
Subjects: LCSH: Theology—History. | Theology—Methodology. | Evangelicalism. Reformed Church—Doctrines.
Classification: LCC BR118 (ebook) | LCC BR118 .O785 2019 (print) | DDC 230—dc23
LC record available at https://lccn.loc.gov/2019000335

Crossway is a publishing ministry of Good News Publishers.

VP		29	28	27	26	25	24	23	22	21	20	19
15	14	13	12	11	10	9	8	7	6	5	4	3	2	1

For Mom and Dad,
who are not only my wonderful parents,
but my dear friends

Contents

Even if history were judged incapable of other uses,
its entertainment value would remain in its favor.

—Marc Bloch

Preface

I can remember the day I discovered Anselm. I was sitting at the air-port, waiting with my family for our flight. Somehow I'd gotten my hands on an article by Alvin Plantinga, defending a modal version of Anselm's ontological argument. Although I had no clue what the word *modal* meant at that time in my life, I remember being utterly captivated. Could God's existence really be logically proven from the mere idea of God in the human mind? I spent about thirty minutes looking at the syllogism he provided, trying to figure out what the catch was—surely it couldn't be a sound argument! This led me to read Anselm's formulation of the argument. I spent a lot of time with it, but I couldn't figure out what was wrong with it. (Actually, I still can't.)

What I found so valuable in Anselm, however, wasn't so much the argument itself but the whole way of doing theology that I found modeled in his writing. Anselm helped me understand something of how enthralling it is to think about *God*. I had already believed there is a glory and gravitas to God, but Anselm impressed upon me that there is also a glory and gravitas to the *idea* of God. This is one basic and somewhat colloquial way to summarize the import of the ontological argument: that God's uniqueness and necessity bombard us at the realm of thought as well as at so many other levels of our existence. In this way, Anselm opened up in me an awareness that would, years later, make me sympathetic to Barth's comment that theology is the "most beautiful of all disciplines."

My interest in Anselm never left me, and when I was studying abroad a few years later in college, I somehow got my hands on the

Latin text of the *Proslogion* (the book in which Anselm advances his so-called ontological argument). I gave the argument a more careful reading in its original context, and I began to be intrigued by the spiritual intensity of Anselm's writing. Why is he writing this argument in a prayer? Why does he go on and on about *seeing God* (isn't God invisible)? And, related to this, what are all these later chapters doing, after he's proven God exists? Ultimately these interests led me to my doctoral work on the *Proslogion*.[1]

Anselm then led me elsewhere. I became more and more interested in the peculiarity of medieval theology as a whole and what I could learn from it as a contemporary evangelical. I also began to read the church fathers with greater interest. I used the coursework stage of my PhD at Fuller Theological Seminary to pursue a number of studies in theological retrieval, immersing myself in the classic texts of church history, as best as I could, for help in doing theology today. Having grown up in evangelical circles, my previous experience in historical theology had focused primarily on Protestant theologians such as Martin Luther or Jonathan Edwards. So I was stepping into a new world as I sought to engage theologians such as the Cappadocian Fathers, Pseudo-Dionysius, John of Damascus, Thomas Aquinas, and others. I can vividly recall sitting at my desk in the spring quarter of 2013, doing research for a study on patristic and medieval views of divine simplicity, and thinking, *Wow! There is a lot of treasure to be mined here. This is like discovering Anselm all over again.* (The results of that study are roughly represented by chapter 5 of this book.)

It is difficult to describe what these excursions into the classical texts of historical theology have done to me. The best I can do is compare them to getting lost in a profound piece of literature, or spending significant time in a foreign country. It has been a formative experience that has shaped not only my theological positions but my whole approach to theology. At the same time, my interest in historical theology has always seemed somewhat disconnected from my broader life and ministry in evangelical contexts. Most of the Christians I interact with

---

1. Gavin Ortlund, *Anselm's Pursuit of Joy: A Commentary on the Proslogion* (Washington, DC: Catholic University of America Press, 2020).

regularly have never heard of Anselm or struggled to understand what value there could be in studying a monk from the Dark Ages. So an abiding question in my life as an evangelical Christian and minister has been: How does my theological interest in classical theologians such as Anselm relate to my calling and context in the United States in the early twenty-first century?

Let me lay my cards on the table right up front in an effort at explaining what is basically driving this book: I think evangelical Christians can and should engage Anselm. Or Tertullian. Or Athanasius. Or Photius. And so forth. This book stems from the conviction that has been formed in me about the tremendous value of retrieving the past and broadly aims to encourage more evangelicals to join in this effort. The first section lays out an overall manifesto for theological retrieval, and the second puts it into practice with a series of case studies.

Why have I spent the larger half of the book focusing on specific retrieval efforts? My approach to engaging history emphasizes "snapshots" more than running commentary. If you are trying to get to know an unchartered jungle, it will likely be more helpful to establish three or five reliable outposts or bases from which you may make further explorations than simply to slog through from one end of the jungle to the other. So if we consider pre-Reformation church history like a dark jungle (an apt analogy for many modern evangelicals), our goal here is to carve out several outposts from which further retrieval expeditions may be made.

In this respect Joseph Ellis's *Founding Brothers: The Revolutionary Generation* has served in my mind as something of a model for the strategy of historical engagement attempted here.[2] Ellis credits the style of history telling attempted in his book—covering six particular episodes in early American history as a way to enter the whole of the Revolutionary era—to Lytton Strachey's *Eminent Victorians*, which he describes as "a combination of stealth and selectivity."[3] Strachey's quoted justification for this method may serve well as explanation of our own effort:

---

2. Joseph J. Ellis, *Founding Brothers: The Revolutionary Generation* (New York: Vintage, 2000).
3. Ellis, *Founding Brothers*, ix.

It is not by the direct method of a scrupulous narration that the explorer of the past can hope to depict that singular epoch. If he is wise, he will adopt a subtler strategy. He will attack his subject in unexpected places; he will fall upon the flank, or the rear; he will shoot a sudden, revealing searchlight into obscure recesses, hither-to undivined. He will row out over that great ocean of material, and lower down into it, here and there, a little bucket, which will bring up to the light of day some characteristic specimen, from those far depths, to be examined with a careful curiosity.[4]

Another model in this respect has been Mark Noll's brilliant book *Turning Points: Decisive Moments in the History of Christianity*, which in its preface articulates several benefits to focusing on key "turning points" as a way to narrate history.[5] I think similar principles can be at play when engaging historical theology specifically as opposed to church history more generally.

I have written with pastors, theology students, and interested lay Christians especially in mind. This is a sort of mid-level book that engages the scholarly machinery but ultimately hopes to influence a broader readership. Historically, my overall leaning has been toward those people and debates and contexts that have been particularly neglected in our own context; thus I favor patristic and medieval theology over Reformation and modern, and particularly those figures at the transition from patristic to medieval who are often neglected today, especially Boethius, Gregory the Great, and John of Damascus (in the third chapter I introduce these three figures as examples of theologians we often overlook).

Earlier versions of several chapters have appeared in the following publications:

- "Why Should Protestants Retrieve Patristic and Medieval Theology?," in *The Task of Dogmatics: Explorations in Theological Method* (Los Angeles Theology Conference Series; Grand Rapids, MI: Zondervan, 2017).

---

4. Lytton Strachey, *Eminent Victorians*, as quoted in Ellis, *Founding Brothers*, ix.
5. Mark A. Noll, *Turning Points: Decisive Moments in the History of Christianity*, 2nd ed. (Grand Rapids, MI: Baker Academic, 2000), 12.

- "Explorations in a Theological Metaphor: Boethius, Calvin, and Torrance on the Creator/creation Distinction." *Modern Theology* 33.2 (2017): 167–86.

- "Divine Simplicity in Historical Perspective: Resourcing A Contemporary Discussion," *International Journal of Systematic Theology* 16.4 (2014): 436–53.

I am grateful to the editors and publishers of these journals for their permission to republish these articles here. A few paragraphs from this preface, chapter 1, and chapter 3 are loosely related to earlier material from online writings.[6]

I want to express my thanks to Oliver Crisp and John Thompson, my professors at Fuller Theological Seminary who oversaw several of these studies in their embryonic development. Dave Lauer has also proofread several chapters and sharpened my thinking with our many theological discussions over lunch. Joel Chopp offered helpful suggestions to the first part of the book. Above all, I want to express my thanks to my precious wife, Esther, who supports me beyond what I could possibly hope for in a wife. None of my writing—indeed, very little of anything I do—would be possible without her loyalty, friendship, and encouragement.

---

6. E.g., "Gospel-Centeredness Is as Old as the Gospel," https://www.thegospelcoalition.org/article/searching-for-gospel-centered-theology-before-the-reformation; "3 Ways Our Culture Is Different From Every Other Culture in History," https://www.thegospelcoalition.org/article/3-ways-our-culture-is-different-than-every-other-culture-in-history; and "Is Christ in All of Church History,?" https://gavinortlund.com/2013/08/03/reflections-on-studying-church-history.

PART 1

A MANIFESTO FOR
THEOLOGICAL RETRIEVAL

✝ ✝ ✝

Just over a decade ago John Webster drew attention to the rising influence of "theologies of retrieval," describing them as too diverse to constitute an official movement or school.[1] If retrieval practices have grown only more diverse since that time, they are nonetheless so pervasive throughout contemporary theology that it is difficult not to conceptualize them as a kind of movement.[2] Like the turn toward theological interpretation in biblical theology, the turn toward retrieval in systematic and historical theology lacks official boundaries and resists precise definition. It is better understood as a set of shared loyalties or instincts in theological method—an overall attitude guided by the conviction that premodern resources are not an obstacle in the age of progress but a well in the age of thirst.[3]

---

1. John Webster, "Theologies of Retrieval," in *The Oxford Handbook to Systematic Theology*, ed. John Webster, Kathryn Tanner, and Iain Torrance (Oxford, UK: Oxford University Press, 2008), 584.

2. The first book-length treatment of theological retrieval as a contemporary "movement" appeared recently by David Buschart and Kent Eilers, *Theology as Retrieval: Receiving the Past, Renewing the Church* (Downers Grove, IL: IVP Academic, 2015).

3. Michael Allen and Scott R. Swain offer a more substantive description of retrieval from a Reformed perspective as stemming from the conviction "that theological renewal comes through

Of course, in one sense, theological retrieval is nothing new. A posture of reception and transmission is a basic part of Christian identity, and the church has always drawn from her past to meet the challenges of her present.[4] Nonetheless, retrieval has come to have a more specific and deliberate use in the late modern West, where the individualism and freedom from authority that characterize the secularizing culture have compelled the church to look for new sources of inspiration and synthesis. It is this cultural context, perhaps, that explains why retrieval movements are springing up in so many different traditions—from the *ressourcement* theology or *la nouvelle théologie* of Henri De Lubac and other French Roman Catholic theologians to the Radical Orthodoxy of John Milbank (Anglican), the paleo-orthodoxy of Thomas Oden (Methodist), the ecumenical labors of Donald Bloesch (UCC) or Robert Jenson (mainline Lutheran), the ancient-future movement of Robert Webber (also Anglican), and so forth.[5]

Alongside these various Catholic, Anglican, and mainline Protestant movements, retrieval is on the rise in evangelicalism. In 2015 two book-length treatments of theological retrieval came out from evangelical authors, published by evangelical presses and covered with blurbs from evangelical theologians.[6] At the same time, there remains considerable ambivalence in many Protestant circles, particularly evangelical Protestant circles in the United States, about the retrieval of patristic and medieval theology. One manifestation of our historical short-sightedness, at both popular and technical levels, is sheer ne-

---

dependence upon the generative resources of the Triune God in and through the gospel and that such dependence is best expressed in our particular historical moment by way of retrieval." See *Christian Dogmatics: Reformed Theology for the Church Catholic*, ed. Michael Allen and Scott R. Swain (Grand Rapids, MI: Baker Academic, 2016), 2.

4. Of course, different Christian traditions disagree regarding what the reception and transmission of history should look like, and such differences are among the chief causes of division within Christendom. For an overview of some of the differences within and between Protestant, Anglican, and Roman Catholic views on Scripture and tradition, with a special focus on Albert Outler's recent employment of the "Wesleyan Quadrilateral," see Edith M. Humphrey, *Scripture and Tradition: What the Bible Really Says* (Grand Rapids, MI: Baker Academic, 2013), 9–17.

5. Scott R. Swain and Michael Allen, *Reformed Catholicity: The Promise of Retrieval for Theology and Biblical Interpretation* (Grand Rapids, MI: Baker Academic, 2015), 4–12, offer a list of twelve different contemporary movements in the church characterized by retrieval.

6. Buschart and Eilers, *Theology as Retrieval*, provide an overview and guide to retrieval, focusing on six different "typologies" of what it looks like in practice; Swain and Allen, *Reformed Catholicity*, offer a "manifesto" for a specifically Reformed account of retrieval. Evidence for evangelical renewed interest in retrieval includes also the rise of various projects such as Zondervan Academic's New Studies in Dogmatics series (ed. Allen and Swain) and Baker Academic's Evangelical *Ressourcement: Ancient Sources for the Church's Future* series (ed. D. H. Williams).

glect; one wonders how many evangelical pastors or divinity students could say a single solitary thing about, say, the tenth century, or the seventh. Cardinal John Henry Newman complained in the nineteenth century that England's "popular religion scarcely recognizes the fact of the twelve long ages which lie between the Councils of Nicaea and Trent."[7] If Newman's conclusion that "to be deep in history is to cease to be a Protestant" did not strictly follow, its overall sentiment is difficult to dismiss—particularly because underneath the anti-historical bent of popular Protestantism lie deeper patterns of historical interpretation that have often marked even the most eloquent expressions of the Protestant faith.

One thinks, for instance, of the recurring identification of the antichrist with the papacy, a view that finds its way into the Westminster Confession of Faith.[8] In more recent times, Protestant interpretations of church history are often shaped by the old Enlightenment caricature of the medieval era as a "Dark Ages" of superstition and ignorance,[9] and by the Anabaptist and Restorationist[10] view of a "great apostasy" or "great fall" in the early church.[11] Today, Protestants generally affirm the ecumenical creeds; we appreciate early Christian martyrs; we approve of Augustine's *Confessions*; on rare occasions, we might even

---

7. John Henry Newman, *An Essay on the Development of Christian Doctrine*, 6th ed. (Notre Dame, IN: University of Notre Dame Press, 1989), 8.

8. Westminster Confession of Faith 15.6.

9. This characterization of medieval intellectual life is ironic in light of the fact that the modern university is essentially a twelfth-century medieval invention, deriving from the great monastic schools of the eleventh century that in turn grew out of the tenth-century cathedral schools spawned by the Carolingian Renaissance. For a recent defense of medieval Christianity against its usual caricatures and a call for evangelical Christians to humbly engage this aspect of our heritage, see Chris R. Armstrong, *Medieval Wisdom for Modern Christians: Finding Authentic Faith in a Forgotten Age with C. S. Lewis* (Grand Rapids, MI: Brazos Press, 2016).

10. The term *Restorationism* is sometimes used more generally in reference to various Christian views calling for a return to the purity of the early apostolic church and sometimes used more specifically in reference to the "Restoration Movement" or "Stone-Campbell Movement" of the early nineteenth century.

11. The "fall of the church" paradigm, usually seen as coinciding with Constantine's conversion or sometimes setting in as early as the second century, has been a classical tenet of Anabaptist theology and is carried on by many free-church and Baptist theologians into the present day, e.g., Malcolm B. Yarnell III, *The Formation of Christian Doctrine* (Nashville, TN: B&H, 2007), 150–65, esp. 157–58. Yarnell objects to the notion of the invisible church as articulated by Herman Bavinck (54–56); he believes that classical ecclesiology, including its Reformed and evangelical expressions (e.g., that of John Webster) must be rejected (*xiv*, 62–67); and he expresses concerns about other Baptist calls for ecumenicity, such as those of Timothy George (71). For a helpful critique of the notion of the fall of the church, see D. H. Williams, *Retrieving the Tradition and Renewing Evangelicalism: A Primer for Suspicious Protestants* (Grand Rapids, MI: Eerdmans, 1999), 103–72. For a briefer overview and critique, see Bryan M. Litfin, *Getting to Know the Church Fathers: An Evangelical Introduction*, 2nd ed. (Grand Rapids, MI: Baker Academic, 2016), 13–16.

quote a John Chrysostom sermon or a Bernard of Clairvaux poem. But on the whole, we tend to regard the Christianity of Caedmon and Charlemagne as more different from than similar to the Christianity of John Bunyan and Billy Graham.

This book is fueled by the conviction that one of the church's greatest resources for navigating her present challenges is her very past—indeed, her *entire* past. In this first part of the book, therefore, we argue that the affirmation of a robust Protestant identity need not prohibit, but should rather encourage, an appropriation of the wisdom of the early and medieval church.[12]

We will proceed in three movements. First, we probe different Protestant attitudes toward pre-Reformation church history, contrasting B. B. Warfield's engagement with Augustine with the retrieval practices of various earlier Protestants whom we put forth as a more helpful guide (chapter 1). Then, having established a broad framework for Protestant retrieval of early and medieval theology, we turn to explore why such a practice is particularly needed within contemporary evangelicalism in light of both cultural developments outside the church and theological developments within her (chapter 2).[13] Finally, we identify several specific ways that theological retrieval may resource evangelicals amidst their current needs, as well as several corresponding dangers (chapter 3). Here we also identify several particular theologians who may be especially helpful to retrieve, whom I have tried to rehabilitate somewhat in this book.

In sum, these chapters aim to establish that evangelicals may retrieve (chapter 1), need to retrieve (chapter 2), and should retrieve (chapter 3). Of course, retrieval is a complicated task, and there are scores of issues involved in it that are not answered or even raised

---

12. For a broader case that theological endeavor is well served by listening to the Christian tradition, see Stephen R. Holmes, *Listening to the Past: The Place of Tradition in Theology* (Grand Rapids, MI: Baker Academic, 2002), 5–36, who argues that theology must engage tradition because of our historical locatedness as temporal creatures and because of our status as members in the larger community of saints, past and present. On this latter point, see also Swain and Allen, *Reformed Catholicity*, 17–47.

13. Although I am writing primarily with an evangelical audience in mind, I would be grateful if this book could be helpful or interesting to Christians of other tribes. I should also note that here and in what follows, when I speak of evangelicalism, I am thinking primarily of evangelicalism in the Western world and especially in the North Atlantic world and to some extent the United Kingdom, not at all because I think this (relatively small) strand of evangelicalism is more important than others, but simply because I lack sufficient knowledge of global Christianity to generalize further.

in what follows. My aim is simply to establish a broad vision of the value of retrieval for evangelicalism—a brief *manifesto of sorts for theological retrieval*. It is hoped that these chapters will further this aim and prepare for the specific efforts at retrieval that follow in the subsequent chapters, even if others must come after me and say much more than I have said here.

1

Can Evangelicals Retrieve Patristic and Medieval Theology?

Whatever be historical Christianity, it is not Protestantism. If ever there were a safe truth, it is this.

—John Henry Newman

✝

On October 25, 1844, the twenty-five-year-old Philip Schaff—the German church historian and newly appointed professor in biblical literature and ecclesiastical history at the Theological Seminary at Mercersburg, Pennsylvania—opened his inaugural address with these words:

> We contemplate the Reformation in its strictly *historical conditions*, its *catholic union with the past*. This is a vastly important point, which thousands in our day appear to overlook entirely. They see in the 31st of October, 1517, it is true, the birthday of the Evangelical Church, and find her certificate of baptism in the ninety-five theses of Luther; but at the same time cast a deep stain upon the legitimacy of this birth itself, by separating it from all right relation to the time that went before. In this way all interest

is renounced in the spiritual wealth of the Middle Ages, which however belongs to us of right as fully at least as it does to the Church of Rome.[1]

Schaff published his lecture the year after as *The Principle of Protestantism*. In his introduction, John Nevin, who translated Schaff's piece from German, shared Schaff's vision of church history, lamenting "what a depressing imagination, if . . . the whole life of the Middle Ages should be relinquished to Rome, as part and parcel of the great apostasy, instead of being claimed as the catholic heritage of the Reformation itself."[2] This more catholic approach to church history, propagated by both Nevin and Schaff as one of the tenets of what would come to be called the "Mercersburg Theology," related to an ecumenical vision.[3] Schaff made clear that he was not calling for a return to Rome; he regarded Protestantism as the "legitimate offspring" of medieval Christianity and the modern Church of Rome, by contrast, as having "parted with the character of catholicity" in its continued development.[4] Nonetheless, he spoke of an "evangelical Catholicity" and "churchly Protestantism,"[5] faulting the sectarian spirit that characterized many other American Protestants of his day: "It is surely an intolerant and narrow imagination, to regard the whole Roman and Greek communions, so far exceeding us as they do in numbers, as out of the Church entirely, and only worthy of course to be blotted out of history altogether as a gigantic spiritual zero."[6]

Schaff came under fire from Joseph F. Berg, a prominent figure in the German Reformed church of which the seminary at Mercersburg

---

1. Philip Schaff, *The Principle of Protestantism*, trans. John Nevin, ed. Bard Thompson and George H. Bricker, Lancaster Series on the Mercersburg Theology 1 (Philadelphia: United Church Press, 1964), 59, emphasis original.

2. Schaff, *The Principle of Protestantism*, 48.

3. For an overview of Mercersburg Theology, see James Hasting Nichols, *Romanticism in American Theology: Nevin and Schaff at Mercersburg* (Chicago: University of Chicago Press, 1961); and W. Bradford Littlejohn, *The Mercersburg Theology and the Quest for Reformed Catholicity* (Eugene, OR: Wipf & Stock, 2009). Darryl G. Hart, "The Use and Abuse of the Christian Past: Mercersburg, the Ancient Church, and American Evangelicalism," in *Evangelicals and the Early Church: Recovery, Reform, Renewal*, ed. George Kalantzis and Andrew Tooley (Eugene, OR: Cascade, 2012), 85–103, offers a critical analysis of Nevin and Schaff's effort. Douglas A. Sweeney, "Mercursburg Theology as a Double-Edged Sword: A Response to Darryl G. Hart," in *Evangelicals and the Ancient Church*, 104–7, provides an insightful response.

4. Schaff, *Principle of Protestantism*, 73–74.

5. Philip Schaff, "What Is Church History? A Vindication of the Idea of Historical Development," in *Reformed and Catholic: Selected Historical and Theological Writings of Philip Schaff*, ed. Charles Yrigoyen and George M. Bricker (Pittsburgh, PA: Pickwick, 1979), 114.

6. Schaff, "What Is Church History?," in *Reformed and Catholic*, 139.

was a part. In a sermon presented only eight days prior to Schaff's address, at the opening of the Synod that concluded to hear Schaff's address, Berg had sought to trace the history of the German Reformed church through the Waldensians back to the second century. The Waldensians, Berg maintained, were the descendants of a group of second-century disciples of Polycarp in southern Gaul who had fled into the Alps during the persecution of 177.[7] It was necessary to seek historical continuity only in separatist movements because, Berg maintained, "if we admit that the Church of Rome has ever been the Church of Christ, you concede the entire ground."[8] Given that these two different conceptions of church history—expressed within eight days of each other in connection to denomination's gathering—are diametrically opposed to one another, it is not surprising that a controversy ensued. Berg himself led the charge, in fact, accusing Schaff of heresy—though the charges were dismissed and the examination resulted in praising both Nevin and Schaff for their efforts to "build up and honor the welfare of the church."[9]

In addition to this ongoing dispute within the German Reformed Church, the Mercersburg theology came under further criticism from the Princeton theologian Charles Hodge. In his review of *The Principle of Protestantism*, Hodge expressed a number of serious concerns, but unlike Berg, he did not dispute Schaff's basic historical interpretation of the Reformation as neither a revolution nor a mere restoration: "The middle ages were no doubt pregnant with the Reformation; the church lived through all those ages, and Protestantism was the revival, through the word and Spirit of God, of a backslidden church, and not a new creation."[10] Nonetheless, Hodge criticized Schaff's portrayal of American Protestantism as sectarian and, although admitting there was much in the book he did not understand, emphasized the book's dependence on German philosophy and national outlook.[11]

---

7. As cited in Schaff, *Principle of Protestantism*, 13.
8. As cited in Schaff, *Principle of Protestantism*, 14.
9. As cited in David R. Bains and Theodore Louis Trost, "Philip Schaff: The Flow of Church History and the Development of Protestantism," *Theology Today* 71.4 (2015): 425. Bains and Trost also offer a helpful overview of the theology espoused in Schaff's *Principle of Protestantism* (417–23).
10. Charles Hodge, "Schaff's Protestantism," *The Biblical Repertory and Princeton Review* 17 (1845): 627.
11. Hodge, "Schaff's Protestantism," 634–36.

Hodge's subsequent writings against the Mercersburg theology, particularly against Nevin's *The Mystical Presence*, would become more polemical,[12] and he would put more focus on the Hegelian foundations of Schaff's philosophy of history.[13] Ultimately, while Hodge would agree that the Reformation was not a rebirth of the church, he would nonetheless construct a contrasting account of doctrinal development to that of Schaff (and naturally, in turn, that of Newman):

> Christianity is a system of doctrines supernaturally revealed and now recorded in the Bible. Of that system there can be no development. No new doctrines can be added to those contained in the word of God. No doctrine can ever be unfolded or expanded beyond what is there revealed. The whole revelation is there, and is there as distinctly, as fully, and as clearly as it can ever be made, without a new supernatural revelation. Every question, therefore, as to what is, or what is not Christian doctrine, is simply a question as to what the Bible teaches.[14]

This historical vignette raises the question of Protestant identity in relation to church history and draws attention to some of the other issues that are bundled up together with this question. What is the proper Protestant attitude toward the pre-Reformation history of the church and the Protestant identity in relation to her? Is the vision of Princeton or Mercersburg more authentic to the original Protestant effort?

We can clarify this question by envisioning opposite possible answers. In the one direction, we might emphasize *Protestant* over and against *catholic*: we are (mainly) Protestant and (in a subsequent, secondary way) catholic. Thus our consciousness of tradition is primarily a half millennium old, with some scattered precursors. In the extreme, this view tends to operate as though little good happened in the church during the span of time between John the apostle's visions on Patmos and Martin Luther's epiphany about Romans 1:17, locat-

---

12. See the overview in Littlejohn, *The Mercersburg Theology and the Quest for Reformed Catholicity*, 25–55.
13. Charles Hodge, *Systematic Theology*, 3 vols. (Grand Rapids, MI: Eerdmans, 1982), 1:118–19.
14. Charles Hodge, "Dr. Schaff's Apostolic Church," *Biblical Repertory and Princeton Review* 26 (1854): 274.

ing (with Berg) the true church only in separatist movements or not at all. (Of course, a special challenge is involved in knowing which separatist movements to include, since most are either heretical or only came about roughly a few centuries prior to Luther.[15] It is noteworthy, in this connection, that when Pope Francis called the Waldensians "evangelical" during his June 2015 apology, he also called them the *oldest* evangelical church.)[16] In the other direction, we might emphasize *catholic* over *Protestant*: we are (mainly) catholic Christians who also happen to be vaguely involved in some kind of ongoing protest. In its stronger varieties, this emphasis tends to correspond with an extreme embarrassment over the Reformation, as though the medieval era was a time of richness and abundance until the Reformation came along and ruined everything.

It is not hard to see how our answer to this question will ripple outwards to influence other areas of theology, such as our historical interest and ecumenical posture. We might attempt to answer it in a variety of ways, but in this chapter we will approach it historically— in essence, seeking to "retrieve retrieval" by considering how previous generations of Protestants have appropriated the early and medieval church. If the Reformers understood themselves to be operating within a catholic heritage, modern views of Protestantism that downplay catholicity become more difficult to justify. Thus here we will consider B. B. Warfield's appropriation of Augustine as a representative of certain modern views before looking at the views and practices of the Reformers, alongside other early Protestants, as a better model to us. Although there are many additional questions about retrieval that this chapter does not address, hopefully what is said here will broadly contribute to the notion that Protestants can function as vitally connected

15. Kenneth J. Stewart, *In Search of Ancient Roots: The Christian Past and the Evangelical Identity Crisis* (Grand Rapids, MI: IVP Academic, 2017), 23–40, argues that evangelical movements have been "perennial and recurring" throughout church history. To the extent that the term *evangelical* becomes decoupled from any denominational and institutional moorings and functions as a more generic descriptor of certain spiritual or theological qualities, the claim of longevity becomes less relevant to the challenge of departures from Protestantism today, which Stewart seeks to address. Nonetheless, Stewart's broader concern that Protestant Christians can and should appropriate the past is helpfully articulated, and his book helpfully documents how previous generations of Protestants were not as historically shortsighted as many modern evangelicals.

16. Sarah Eekhoff Zylstra, "Pope Apologizes to 'First Evangelicals' for Persecution," *Christianity Today* (July 7, 2015), accessed December 15, 2017, http://www.christianitytoday.com/news/2015/july/pope-apologizes-to-first-evangelicals-for-persecution.html.

to the entire stream of church history without thereby compromising their Protestant convictions.

Extracting the Leavened Bread: Warfield on Interpreting Augustine

Some of the eccentricities of modern Protestant interpretation of patristic and medieval theology can be observed in B. B. Warfield's appropriation of Augustine's theology.[17] Warfield argues that the doctrine of *grace* is Augustine's greatest legacy and the truest center of his thought. He locates Augustine's significance as being the first of the church fathers to give adequate expression to "evangelical religion"— that is, the religion of faith as opposed to the religion of works.[18] For Warfield, "a new Christian piety dates from [Augustine]," as well as "a new theology corresponding to this new type of piety," such that Augustine may be termed the author of grace as well as the father of evangelicalism.[19]

Warfield is not, however, blind to the aspects of Augustine's theology that seem to stand at odds with this interpretation: his complex sacramentology, complete with doctrines of baptismal regeneration, a sacrificial understanding of Mass, and an *ex opere operato* understanding of sacramental efficacy; his hierarchical ecclesiology, complete with an affirmation of the papacy, the magisterium of the church, and an understanding of the visible church as God's kingdom on earth; as well as his doctrines of saintly intercession, purgatory, penance, merits, and the perpetual virginity of Mary. With these aspects of his theology in mind, Warfield calls Augustine "the founder of Roman Catholicism" who "called into being a new type of Christianity" in which the church is the center of religious feeling.[20]

Ascribing to the same person the titles "father of evangelicalism" and "founder of Roman Catholicism" conjures up a sense of ambivalence that may usefully describe Warfield's broader attitude toward the whole of medieval Christianity stemming from Augustine. Indeed,

---

17. Benjamin Breckinridge Warfield, *Calvin and Augustine*, ed. Samuel G. Craig (Philadelphia: Presbyterian & Reformed, 1956).
18. Warfield, *Calvin and Augustine*, 319–20.
19. Warfield, *Calvin and Augustine*, 320–21.
20. Warfield, *Calvin and Augustine*, 313.

he suggests, "the problem which Augustine bequeathed to the Church for solution, the Church required a thousand years to solve."[21] Warfield describes these two sides of Augustine's thought—his "evangelical" doctrine of grace and his Roman Catholic ecclesiology—as "two children . . . struggling in the womb of his mind." But for Warfield, Augustine's doctrine of grace is the "child of his heart."[22] Thus in Warfield's interpretation, the *real* Augustine is the desperate and prayerful Augustine of the *Confessions*, the anti-Pelagian Augustine who can pray, "Command what you will, and give what you command."[23] In his doctrine of the church, by contrast, we get the vestiges of Cyprian and Tertullian, taken on unthinkingly by Augustine, and gradually diminishing throughout his life. In Warfield's metaphor, the leaven of Augustine's doctrine of grace was working through the dough of his doctrine of the church, but "death intervened before all the elements of his thinking were completely leavened."[24] Thus had Augustine only lived longer, he would have handed down "a thoroughly worked out system of evangelical theology" rather than the contradictions that would instead rend the church for a millennium.[25] That these perceived tensions in Augustine become Warfield's rubric for engaging the medieval church as a whole is evident in his definition of the Reformation as "the triumph of Augustine's doctrine of grace over Augustine's doctrine of the Church."[26]

Warfield's interpretation of Augustine poses challenges. One wonders, for instance, whether Augustine was quite so decidedly on his way toward becoming a proto-Protestant, had he only lived longer. But underneath these interpretational matters lies a more basic methodological issue regarding how we do retrieval as Protestants. In Warfield's method of retrieval, Augustine's theology seems to get sifted through the grid of the Reformation such that the good in Augustine's theological legacy is distinguished from the bad basically by its sixteenth-century consequence. Warfield's approach could give the impression that a modern Protestant's primary theological community

---

21. Warfield, *Calvin and Augustine*, 322.
22. Warfield, *Calvin and Augustine*, 322.
23. Warfield, *Calvin and Augustine*, 322.
24. Warfield, *Calvin and Augustine*, 321.
25. Warfield, *Calvin and Augustine*, 322.
26. Warfield, *Calvin and Augustine*, 383.

is the last five hundred years of Protestant history, and then from this community one makes a secondary, more tentative step into the previous fifteen hundred years of church history. To construct a metaphor, Protestant theology is the castle in which we safely live: patristic and medieval theology is a dark forest surrounding the castle into which we may occasionally venture.

Of course, there is nothing wrong with Warfield reading church history as a Protestant, with Protestant convictions intact under an overall commitment to *sola Scriptura*. But affirming Protestant distinctives is not the same as using them as a filter, and a principial *sola Scriptura* can easily slide into a practical *sola reformatione*. Approaching the early church indirectly, through the intermediate link of Reformation theology, poses the danger of failing to appreciate patristic and medieval theology on its own terms and in its own context and thus of hindering our ability to learn from it. After all, there are many doctrines that the Reformers held in continuity with the early and medieval church but did not engage since they were not in dispute in the sixteenth century. There are many other doctrines that the Reformers affirmed with the early and medieval church but did so with less eloquence or detail. And there are still other doctrines where the Reformers' approach was different from that of earlier generations, and yet we may not be convinced that their efforts are the final word on the matter. In Warfield's account, it never seems to come into view where Protestant theology might be profitably stretched or challenged by Augustine. A figure so sharply divided against himself (indeed, in Warfield's account, an entire millennium so sharply divided against itself) would need to be disentangled more than heard.

Returning to Patristic Purity: Calvin and Luther on the Reformation as Retrieval

But there are good reasons for favoring a more inclusive approach in which all two thousand years of church history function as our most basic theological community, and Scripture alone stands above as our authoritative norm. Indeed, the practice of the Reformers would suggest that such an approach is not only more practically beneficial but actually more rigorously Protestant. As severe as the Reformers' criticisms of medieval Roman Catholicism could be, they always distinguished themselves from the Anabaptists, making clear that their intention was to reform, not recreate, the true church of God. To this end they not only regularly retrieved the theology of the early church but in large measure cast their entire reform effort *as* its retrieval.

John Calvin, for instance, in his prefatory letter to King Francis in the *Institutes*, defended the Reformation cause against the charge of novelty by grounding the Protestant claim to antiquity in "the right of recovery" (*postliminii iure*)—a technical legal term referring to the recovery of lost property or privilege.[27] Rather than overthrowing tradition, Calvin compiled an extensive list of issues—ranging from eating meat during Lent to transubstantiation to ministerial celibacy—on which church fathers stood with the Reformers and against their Roman Catholic opponents.[28] Calvin made this appeal repeatedly in various disputations with Roman Catholic opponents. At Lausanne in October 1536 he reproduced a series of lengthy quotations from the church fathers, taken from memory.[29] Later, in his 1539 dispute with Cardinal Sadoleto, he claimed: "Our agreement with antiquity is far greater than yours, but all that we have attempted has been to renew the ancient form of the church . . . [that existed] in the age of Chrysostom, and Basil, among the Greeks, and of Cyprian, Ambrose, and Augustine, among the Latins."[30] With the other magisterial Reformers, Calvin affirmed the ecumenical creeds and councils, stating that words like *ousia* and *hypostasis* were necessary to confront heresy. In the section on the Trinity in his draft of the *French Confession* he wrote, "We receive what was determined by the ancient councils, and we hate all sects and heresies which were rejected by the holy doctors from the time of St. Hilary and Athanasius until St. Ambrose and Cyril."[31]

---

27. John Calvin, "Prefatory Address to King Francis," in *Institutes of the Christian Religion*, ed. John T. McNeill, trans. Ford Lewis Battles (Louisville, KY: Westminster John Knox, 2006), 16. As the editors note, *postliminium* literally means "behind the threshold," i.e., safe, and refers to the recovery of property or privilege so as to be secured.

28. Calvin, "Prefatory Address to King Francis," 19–23.

29. For an overview, see Anthony N. S. Lane, *John Calvin: Student of the Church Fathers* (Grand Rapids, MI: Baker, 1999), 25–28.

30. John Calvin, "Reply to Sadolet," as quoted in Robert Letham, *The Holy Trinity: In Scripture, History, Theology, and Worship* (Phillipsburg, NJ: P&R, 2004), 266.

31. As quoted in Letham, *The Holy Trinity*, 266.

Like Calvin, Martin Luther opposed Roman Catholic doctrine on patristic grounds as well as apostolic. The sharpness of his distinction between the "holy fathers" and the earlier Roman tradition over and against later medieval corruptions is evident in a letter to the Christians at Halle:

> I shall not cite here the sayings of the other saintly fathers, such as Cyprian . . . or Irenaeus, Tertullian, Chrysostom, etc. Rather I wish to confine myself solely to the canon law of Popes and the Roman church, upon whose ordinances, usages, and tradition they so mightily depend and insist. They have to admit that they stand in contradiction to God's word, Christ's ordinances, Paul's teachings, and the usages of earlier popes and the usages of the early Roman church, and all the holy fathers and teachers.[32]

It is striking that Luther set his Roman Catholic opponents over against not only Christ and Paul, and not only Christ and Paul and the church fathers, but also against the earlier positions of Popes and the Roman church herself. Luther also affirmed the four earliest councils and their creeds (Nicene, Constantinople, Ephesus, and Chalcedon), and he defended the use of technical Trinitarian terminology employed by the church fathers (like *homoousios*) against Martin Bucer, who protested that we must use strictly biblical language.[33] Luther did draw a sharp distinction between the church fathers and the apostolic writings, perhaps not always altogether fairly.[34] Nonetheless, Luther's insistence on Holy Scripture as the highest authority for faith and life did not entail a complete rejection of tradition and creed, as it is often construed today.[35] Thus, in his *On the Councils and the Church*, Lu-

---

32. As quoted in D. H. Williams, *Evangelicals and Tradition: The Formative Influence of the Early Church*, Evangelical *Ressourcement: Ancient Sources for the Church's Future* (Grand Rapids, MI: Baker Academic, 2005), 121.

33. Cf. D. H. Williams, *Retrieving the Tradition and Renewing Evangelicalism: A Primer for Suspicious Protestants* (Grand Rapids, MI: Eerdmans, 1999), 185, who quotes Luther on the Apostles' Creed particularly as writing, "Here you find the whole essence of God, his will and his work beautifully portrayed in a few but comprehensible words."

34. Jaroslav Pelikan, *The Vindication of Tradition* (New Haven, CT: Yale University Press, 1984), 9–10, e.g., questions Luther's view that Tertullian was the first significant Christian writer after the apostles, which made it possible to distinguish between Scripture and tradition on *chronological* grounds.

35. Keith A. Mathison, *The Shape of Sola Scriptura* (Moscow, ID: Canon, 2001), 237–53, offers a critique of modern misunderstandings of *sola Scriptura* as out of alignment with the original intent of this doctrine in the context of the Reformation. I have discussed the meaning

ther argued that "the decrees of the genuine councils must remain in force permanently, just as they have always been in force."[36] Luther would even publish in 1538 his own edited versions of the Apostles' and Athanasian Creeds, along with the *Te Deum* with the Nicene Creed appended to it.[37]

Later Lutherans followed Luther in this regard, placing the Apostles', Nicene, and Athanasian Creeds at the front of the Book of Concord (as Anglicans would with the Thirty-nine Articles).[38] The Augsburg Confession, the primary Lutheran confession and arguably perhaps the most important sixteenth-century Protestant confession, would conclude by affirming the continuity of Lutheran doctrine with the true church: "In doctrine and ceremonials among us there is nothing received contrary to Scripture or to the Catholic Church, inasmuch as it is manifest that we have diligently taken heed that no new and godless doctrines should creep into our Churches."[39]

Even from this very brief survey, it is clear that there are some significant differences between early Protestant views of church history represented by Calvin and Luther and those modern Protestant views represented by Warfield. Warfield saw the early church, most basically, as a fall to be recovered from—he could even claim that "to pass from the latest apostolic writings to the earliest compositions of uninspired Christian pens is to fall through such a giddy height that it is no wonder if we rise dazed and almost unable to determine our whereabouts."[40] Luther and Calvin, by contrast, saw the early church as a resource to be utilized and spoke of the goal of the Reformation as its retrieval.

Now, granted, the Reformers tended to be cooler in their attitude toward medieval theology than toward patristic. Here we must neither

---

and implications of *sola Scriptura* and its frequent misconstrual today in Gavin Ortlund, "*Sola Scriptura* Then and Now: Biblical Authority in Late Medieval and Patristic Context," *Credo* 6.4 (December 2016): 26–31.

36. As quoted in Jaroslav Pelikan, *Obedient Rebels: Catholic Substance and Protestant Principle in Luther's Reformation* (New York: Harper & Row, 1964), 75.

37. As noted by Williams, *Retrieving the Tradition and Renewing Evangelicalism*, 187–88.

38. See the discussion in Carl L. Beckwith, "The Reformers and the Nicene Faith: An Assumed Catholicity," in *Evangelicals and Nicene Faith: Reclaiming the Apostolic Witness*, ed. Timothy George (Grand Rapids, MI: Baker Academic, 2011), 65–70.

39. Augsburg Confession, trans. Charles Krauth (Philadelphia: Caxton, 1869), 60.

40. As quoted in Scott R. Swain and Michael Allen, *Reformed Catholicity: The Promise of Retrieval for Theology and Biblical Interpretation* (Grand Rapids, MI: Baker Academic, 2015), 1–3.

downplay the Reformers' critiques of medieval Christianity nor fail to appreciate their nuance. If we wonder, for instance, what exactly Calvin means when in his prefatory letter to King Francis he refers to Protestant doctrine as "laid long unknown and buried,"[41] we get some clue later in the *Institutes* when he refers to the church of Gregory I's day (at the turn of the seventh century) as "well-nigh collapsed" since it "had deteriorated much from its ancient purity."[42] Later he appears to regard the agreement between Pepin the Short and Pope Zachary in 751 as marking a new era of papal temporal power.[43] That Calvin regarded the papacy as falling further into apostasy and corruption from that point is clear from his assertion that the institution was in his own day "a hundred times more corrupt than it was in the times of Gregory and Bernard, though even then it greatly displeased those holy men."[44] The rise of the papacy was accompanied by other errors. Lane marshals evidence indicating that Calvin thinks the heights of papal power were reached only four hundred years prior to the Reformation and compulsory confession for only three hundred—while belief in the carnal presence of Christ in the Lord's Supper had prevailed for six hundred years.[45] What emerges is that Calvin appears to regard the medieval church's decline into corruption as progressive and incremental.

At the same time, unlike "fall of the church" narratives characteristic of the Anabaptist tradition, Calvin staunchly denied that this decline ever resulted in death. In the context of developing his doctrine of the invisible church, Calvin rejected the possibility that the church "has been lifeless for some time," affirming from Matthew 28:20 that Christ preserves and defends the true church in every generation: "The church of Christ has lived and will live so long as Christ reigns at the right hand of the Father. It is sustained by his hand; defended by his protection; and is kept safe through his power."[46] What separated Calvin from the Anabaptists, therefore, was not simply a different construal of *sola Scriptura* but a different vision of church history, rooted in Calvin's affirmation

---

41. Calvin, "Prefatory Address to King Francis," 16.
42. Calvin, *Institutes of the Christian Religion* 4.4.3.
43. Calvin, *Institutes of the Christian Religion* 4.7.17.
44. Calvin, *Institutes of the Christian Religion* 4.7.22.
45. Lane, *John Calvin*, 42.
46. Calvin, "Prefatory Address to King Francis," 24.

of the preservation of the church.[47] In light of this, it is not surprising to find how much energy Calvin spent in the *Institutes* retrieving medieval theology as well as patristic. He is especially appreciative of Gregory the Great (who is the fourth most-cited theologian throughout his writings), Peter Lombard, and Bernard of Clairvaux.[48] Many scholars have also drawn attention to the Scotist elements in Calvin's thought.[49]

Luther also, for all the harshness of his attacks on Rome, always affirmed the preservation of the true church amidst seasons of corruption. Writing in the 1530s, he declared that the errors of the Church of Rome, though severe, did not nullify her holiness, and the testimonies to the gospel within her:

> Today we still call the Church of Rome holy and all its sees holy, even though they have been undermined and their ministers are ungodly. . . . It is still the church. Although the city of Rome is worse than Sodom and Gomorrah, nevertheless there remains in it Baptism, the Sacrament, the voice and text of the Gospel, the Sacred Scriptures, the ministries, the name of Christ, and the name of God. . . . Therefore the Church of Rome is holy.[50]

In keeping with this vision, Luther would occasionally temper his acerbic antipapal rhetoric to speak with nuance of the Protestant heritage: "We do not reject everything that is under the dominion of the Pope. For in that event we should also reject the Christian church. Much Christian good is to be found in the Papacy and from there it descended to us."[51]

Our Church Was in the Papacy: Turretin on the Preservation of the Church

Later Protestants would affirm and develop this doctrine of the preservation of the church. Francis Turretin, to pick just one example,

47. This point is emphasized by Stephen R. Holmes, *Listening to the Past: The Place of Tradition in Theology* (Grand Rapids, MI: Baker Academic, 2002), 15–17.
48. For a list of theologians most frequently cited by Calvin, see Lane, *John Calvin*, 41. For an overview of Calvin's engagement with Bernard, see Lane, *John Calvin*, 87–114.
49. See the discussion in Willem J. van Asselt and Eef Dekker, "Introduction," in *Reformation and Scholasticism: An Ecumenical Enterprise*, ed. Willem J. van Asselt and Eef Dekker (Grand Rapids, MI: Baker Academic, 2001), 30.
50. Quoted in Beckwith, "The Reformers and the Nicene Faith," 63–64.
51. As quoted in Timothy George, *Theology of the Reformers* (Nashville, TN: B&H, 1988), 81.

developed a nuanced, careful response to the criticism of his Roman Catholic contemporary opponents that the Reformed church did not exist before Luther and Zwingli, and it may be helpful to consider his points. In the first place, he protested the tenuousness of the charge on several initial grounds, including that it reasons "from the ignorance of a thing to its negation, as if it was necessary for a thing not to be because it is not known."[52] This is a basic point, but it is often overlooked in historical study. Its importance can be seen in a thought experiment: suppose that five hundred years from now a historian were attempting to describe evangelical Christianity in the United States in the early twenty-first century. What broad picture would he gather? Unfortunately, the most visible and large expressions of Christianity (and therefore generally those most likely to be available to the historian) are often among the least healthy. One can well imagine a historical sketch of twenty-first-century evangelicalism, written five hundred years from now, discussing Benny Hinn and Donald Trump but leaving out Russell Moore and Tim Keller—even though many of us who go by the name "evangelical" would be embarrassed to be associated with the former and honored to be associated with the latter. We must remember this point when we envision medieval Christianity: there may be much good that is simply unavailable to, or at least not in the foreground of, historical knowledge.

Back to Turretin. After his initial cautions, Turretin proceeds to answer the charge that the Protestant church is historically rootless by considering this claim in relation to four points: the doctrine and faith of the elect; their persons and condition; their place; and the form of government of their external worship. Several important points that surface in the discussion that follows may be helpful to reference here to develop our understanding of a Protestant view of pre-Reformation church history. First, Turretin distinguishes "the substance of the faith from the corrupting accidents in doctrine and worship."[53] He identifies this substance of the faith as evident in the Scriptures, the Apostles' Creed, the law (more specifically, the Decalogue), the Lord's Prayer,

---

52. Francis Turretin, *Institutes of Elenctic Theology*, ed. James T. Denniston, trans. George M. Giger (Phillipsburg, NJ: P&R, 1997), 18.10.4.
53. Turretin, *Institutes of Elenctic Theology* 18.10.10.

and the sacraments, which he argues "by a special providence (God) willed to preserve always in the church for sustaining the elect."[54] Through these means, Turretin insists, God never allowed the knowledge of the true gospel to be extinguished, even in times of greatest doctrinal and spiritual corruption.

How, specifically, did God preserve the true church amidst seasons of greatest darkness? Turretin proposes four ways. First, God the Holy Spirit continued to work through the ordinary public ministry of the church.[55] Thus, even amidst "deadly errors" added onto the truth, the "principal heads of Christianity" were taught and known. Here Turretin emphasizes that this could the more easily be done because corruptions were not introduced into the church into direct and open opposition to the Christian faith as handed down by apostolic teaching but rather by the "conjunction and mixture of falsehood with the truth."[56] This enabled many believers, enabled by the Holy Spirit, to embrace the truth and repudiate the falsehood, such that "the hearts of hearers were often more holy than the mouths of priests and teachers."[57]

Second, Turretin proposes that God used the private ministry of colleges and monasteries to advance the knowledge of the gospel. He points to the example of many of the Reformers themselves, who "in cloisters and convents learned religion, whether by the reading of the Scriptures and of the purer fathers and other writings of this kind in which the rays of truth shone, or by the instruction of those who knew how to separate pure Christianity from the papal errors."[58] The obvious example of this is Luther, and Turretin also points to Zwingli, Bucer, Peter Martyr, and Oecolampadius. He then adds that the private and domestic instruction in family life, through family prayer and reading used in the course of the instruction of children, also preserved the knowledge of the gospel.[59]

Third, Turretin points, in addition to the ordinary ministry of the church, to the extraordinary ministry of various witnesses whom God raised up to bear witness to the truth. He compares this to the ministry

---

54. Turretin, *Institutes of Elenctic Theology* 18.10.10.
55. Turretin, *Institutes of Elenctic Theology* 18.10.25–26.
56. Turretin, *Institutes of Elenctic Theology* 18.10.26.
57. Turretin, *Institutes of Elenctic Theology* 18.10.26.
58. Turretin, *Institutes of Elenctic Theology* 18.10.27.
59. Turretin, *Institutes of Elenctic Theology* 18.10.27.

of Old Testament prophets.[60] As examples, he cites Charlemagne's opposition to the worship of icons, and the condemnation of this practice at the Council of Frankfurt in 794, as well as the opposition to transubstantiation by Ratramnus in the ninth century and later by Berengar of Tours in the tenth.[61] Turretin regards these two men as the "two witnesses" of Revelation 11:3 and affirms that others also were called to this sacred ministry of protest. Fourth, Turretin argues that God preserved the true church by slowing the growth and official sanction of various errors so that many believers were able to maintain an unstained conscience in worship.[62]

Earlier in his treatment of the "place" of the church, Turretin expounds the third of the points raised above at greater length. Here he argues that the true church existed in various separatist and/or protest movements against the Church of Rome, both in the east and west. He identifies the Waldensians and Albigenses specifically, pointing to their public assemblies in Bohemia, parts of England, and parts of France, and after their persecution as remnant groups in various places, particularly in the Pyrenean forest and in the valleys of the Alps. Turretin calls these groups "purer Christians" and maintains that they "held the same faith with us in essentials."[63] Later Turretin goes further, asserting that "there were innumerable persons who professed our faith and protested publicly against the papal errors," including here not only the Waldensians and Albigenses but "the Hussites, Wyckliffites, Lollards and Picards," referencing here several historiographical works to substantiate this claim.[64] In a later list of such examples, Jerome of Prague is added, and he references "very many others."[65] It is clear that Turretin regards the movement sparked by Luther as grounded in a significant tradition of antecedent voices of dissent against Rome.

But then Turretin develops a further argument for a Protestant basis in history from the ecclesiological notion of a *remnant*. Here Turretin

---

60. Turretin, *Institutes of Elenctic Theology* 18.10.28.
61. Turretin, *Institutes of Elenctic Theology* 18.10.28. Turretin calls Ratramnus "Bertram" and Charlesmagne "Charles the Great."
62. Turretin, *Institutes of Elenctic Theology* 18.10.29.
63. Turretin, *Institutes of Elenctic Theology* 18.10.14.
64. Turretin, *Institutes of Elenctic Theology* 18.10.20.
65. Turretin, *Institutes of Elenctic Theology* 18.10.28.

writes, "But we further add that our church was in the papacy itself, inasmuch as God always preserved in the midst of Babylon a remnant for himself according to the election of grace."[66] These Christians groaned under various corruptions in the church, according to Turretin, panting for spiritual deliverance. To develop this notion of a remnant ecclesiology, he adduces a number of proof texts, introduces several new historical works, and provides four biblical precedents of a remnant: the church in Egypt after Joseph's death; the church in Elijah's time under King Ahab; the church in Samaria after the ten tribes had been carried off to Assyria; and the Jewish church in the Babylonian captivity.[67] The second of these examples, and specifically God's reference to the seven thousand who have not bowed the knee to Baal after Elijah's complaint that he alone is left (1 Kings 19:18), features recurrently throughout his argumentation.[68] This notion of a remnant preserved amidst seasons of corruption, drawn specifically from 1 Kings 19, was also an important feature of Calvin's defense of the Protestant cause against the charge of novelty in his letter to King Francis prefacing the *Institutes*.[69]

Turretin acknowledges that "the church which was in the papacy before the Reformation" (in distinction from the Eastern church, and the various separatist movements he has surveyed) lacked among its articles of faith the doctrine of justification by faith alone and was beset by other various doctrinal corruptions, such as worship of icons, invocation of the saints, etc. Nonetheless, he argues that "it does not follow that believers did not have in the doctrine received for that time the necessary food for salvation."[70] In this respect he distinguishes the doctrine of the late medieval Western church from that of Socinianism—whereas the latter directly attacks the foundation of Christianity by denying the Trinity and the deity of Christ, the former merely added on new doctrines that are incompatible with it. While both contain grievous errors, according to Turretin, the guilt of Socinian errors is greater, such that under a Socinian ministry it is impossible to work out one's salvation.[71] Turretin goes on to argue that despite

---

66. Turretin, *Institutes of Elenctic Theology* 18.10.15.
67. Turretin, *Institutes of Elenctic Theology* 18.10.16–18.
68. E.g., Turretin, *Institutes of Elenctic Theology* 18.10.11, 18.10.30.
69. Calvin, "Prefatory Address to King Francis," 25.
70. Turretin, *Institutes of Elenctic Theology* 18.10.31.
71. Turretin, *Institutes of Elenctic Theology* 18.10.32.

differences of form and government, there is a fundamental continuity in the essential truth and unity of the Protestant church and the pre-Reformation Roman church.[72] In his own day, however, "secession" from the Roman Catholic Church was necessary because the errors had reached such a height.[73]

We Don't Breed with Monsters: Other Protestant Appeals to Historical Continuity

In developing these ecclesiological considerations Turretin was by no means a lone voice among those following in the footsteps of the Reformers. Rather, in the generations following the Reformation, Protestants found themselves increasingly compelled to ground their religion within the catholic tradition in order to combat charges of heresy and novelty. John Jewel's 1562 *An Apology for the Church of England* grounded Anglican (and more generally, Protestant) doctrine on points such as Scripture or the church in a litany of patristic sources.[74] For instance, in the context treating Roman Catholic versus Protestant views of the Lord's Supper, Jewel claimed:

> We, for our parts, have learned these things of Christ, of the apostles, of the devout fathers; and do sincerely and with good faith teach the people of God the same. Which thing is the only cause why we this day are called heretics of the chief prelates (no doubt) of religion. O immortal God! hath Christ himself, then, the apostles, and so many fathers, all at once gone astray? Were then Origen, Ambrose, Augustine Chrysostom, Gelasius, Theodoret, forsakers of the catholic faith? Was so notable a consent of so many ancient bishops and learned men nothing else but a conspiracy of heretics? Or is that now condemned in us which was then commended in them?[75]

Jewel then laments, along with the earlier heresies, the birth of "certain new and very strange sects, as the Anabaptists, Libertines,

---

72. Turretin, *Institutes of Elenctic Theology* 18.10.34.
73. Turretin, *Institutes of Elenctic Theology* 18.10.36.
74. John Jewel, *An Apology of the Church of England*, ed. John E. Booty (New York: Church, 2002). Jewel's treatment of the Eucharist on 31–36 is especially noteworthy. Cf. the discussion of Jewel's points in Stewart, *In Search of Ancient Roots*, 31–34.
75. Jewel, *An Apology of the Church of England*, 41.

Menonians, and Schwenkfeldians," protesting that "we neither have bred, nor taught, nor kept up these monsters."[76] Jewel's effort to link the Anglican view with that of the church fathers along with Christ and the apostles, together with his eagerness to distance the magisterial Reformation from the Radical Reformation, testifies to the extent to which he maintained protest against Rome on a historical basis, not merely a biblical or theological one.

Similar appeals were made in the second generation of the Lutheran tradition, for instance, in Martin Chemnitz's four-volume *Examination of the Council of Trent* or in the Augsburg Confession, which claimed that "the Churches among us dissent in no article of faith from the Catholic Church, and only omit a few of certain abuses, which are novel."[77] Carl Braaten and Robert W. Jenson trace this catholic impulse throughout the history of Lutheranism, from Luther himself up to more recent theologians such as Friedrich Heiler, Paul Tillich, and Gustaf Aulén.[78] Heiler, for instance, would claim, "It was not Luther's idea to set over against the ancient Catholic Church a new Protestant creation; he desired nothing more than that the old Church should experience an evangelical awakening."[79] Among the Puritans, William Perkins would write his famous work *A Reformed Catholike*, which affirmed a Protestantism that holds the same "heads of religion" with the Roman Catholic church, but simply "pares off and rejects all errors in doctrine, whereby the said religion is corrupted."[80]

This emphasis on continuity between the Protestant cause and earlier generations of the church makes it less surprising to find that the best of the later Protestant tradition continued to retrieve both patristic and medieval theology. In some respects the Reformed scholastic tradition, particularly extending into the seventeenth and eighteenth centuries, displayed greater acquaintance and interaction with the

---

76. Jewel, *An Apology of the Church of England*, 42. Booty notes here that the Libertines were a Flemish sect of Antinomians; Menonians is another term for Mennonites; and Schwenkfeldians were followers of Caspar Schwenkfeld (d. 1561).

77. Augsburg Confession, 30. Swain and Allen, *Reformed Catholicity*, 13, identify Chemnitz's work alongside Jewel's as providing the best framework for a project of Protestant retrieval.

78. Carl E. Braaten and Robert Jenson, "Preface," in *The Catholicity of the Reformation*, ed. Carl E. Braaten and Robert Jenson (Grand Rapids, MI: Eerdmans, 1996), *viii–x*.

79. Braaten and Jenson, "Preface," in *The Catholicity of the Reformation*, *viii*.

80. William Perkins, *A Reformed Catholike* (Cambridge, UK: John Legat, 1600), 905.

medieval tradition than the Reformers did.[81] The Puritan theologian John Owen, for instance, drew heavily from the logic, technical language, and metaphysical tradition of medieval theology, particularly that of Thomas Aquinas.[82] Carl Trueman notes that Thomas influenced Owen on topics such as divine knowledge, divine providence, divine simplicity, election, and sin, and that from the earliest times in his career Owen drew upon Thomistic trajectories of thought (particularly as developed in the subsequent Dominican tradition) for polemical purposes in his arguments against Jesuits, Arminians, and Socinians.[83] While Owen certainly does not engage Thomas uncritically, he shows a penetrating grasp and respectful utilization of his theology.

It is also interesting to note, in this connection, that many classic points of dispute within the Protestant tradition—disputes we often perceive as original to Protestantism—are actually extensions of earlier patristic and medieval discussion. Disagreements about the extent of election in the Reformed tradition, for instance, are remarkably reminiscent of the firestorm generated by the ninth-century theologian Gottschalk of Orbais.[84] Gottschalk affirmed that divine foreknowledge and foreordination are simultaneous because both occur in God's eternal present.[85] He affirmed an unflinching account of double predestination in which God "predestined the devil himself, the head of all the demons, with all of his apostate angels and also with all reprobate human beings, namely, his members, to rightly eternal death.[86] Anticipating a similar move to be made by many of his Calvinistic descendants, Gottschalk defended the notion of reprobation by linking it

---

81. For a magisterial account of the development of Protestant theology in the Reformed tradition after the Reformation, see Richard A. Muller, *Post-Reformation Reformed Dogmatics*, 4 vols. (Grand Rapids, MI: Baker Academic, 1987–2003). On continuities between medieval scholasticism and Reformed scholasticism, see also Willem J. van Asselt and Eef Dekker, "Introduction," in *Reformation and Scholasticism*, 11–43.

82. As observed by Carl R. Trueman, *John Owen: Reformed Catholic, Renaissance Man*, Great Theologians (Burlington, VT: Ashgate, 2007), 21, who notes that "the quest for historical precedent in Reformed Protestantism, so important to a church keen to allay any suspicions that it was introducing novelties of any kind, was not restricted to a canon of authors who wrote before the sixth century, even though such early authors might in general be given slightly more weight than those writing after the great period of Trinitarian and Christological creedal formulation and the dramatic rise to papal power."

83. Trueman, *John Owen*, 23.

84. Cf. the discussion in Victor Genke and Francis X. Gumerlock, *Gottschalk and a Medieval Predestination Controversy: Texts Translated from the Latin*, Medieval Philosophical Texts in Translation 47 (Milwaukee, WI: Marquette University Press, 2010).

85. Genke and Gumerlock, *Gottschalk and a Medieval Predestination Controversy*, 56.

86. Genke and Gumerlock, *Gottschalk and a Medieval Predestination Controversy*, 54–55.

to the power of divine grace, arguing that if God does not sovereignly direct his grace, then that grace is not truly omnipotent, free, and effectual. As he puts it, going so far as to identify God with his grace, "is not grace God and omnipotent, which gratuitously saves and sets free whomever it wants?"[87] It is difficult not to draw comparisons between Gottschalk's treatment of predestination and its later treatment in the Reformed tradition. Similar historical comparisons come to mind in this regard, e.g., the debate between Luther and Erasmus about the human will and the earlier dispute between Augustine and Pelagius, or Protestant disputes about the presence of Christ in the Supper and the ninth-century disagreement between Radbertus and Ratramnus. Leaving room for various differences in these respective debates, we may still say that, in general, it is difficult to find any significant Protestant theological disputes that are unanticipated in the broader catholic tradition. Protestant theology should not be, and ultimately cannot be, abstracted from the broader tradition that preceded it.

On the whole, the attitude toward patristic and medieval theology modeled by the Reformers, and later Protestants such as Turretin and Jewel and Owen, is more careful and generous than that entailed by Warfield's metaphor of extracting leavened bread from the unleavened. The magisterial Reformers (and their successors, for the most part) affirmed the preservation of the church in every generation; they drew widely from the wisdom of earlier generations, and they summed up their own goal as returning to the purity of the early church. The last thing in the world they intended was a wholesale rejection of the thirteen centuries separating John the apostle from John Wycliffe. As D. H. Williams put it, the mission of the Reformers was to point "not to themselves as the begetters of a new 'protestantism' but to the establishment of a proper catholicism—anti-Roman perhaps but not anti-catholic."[88] Or, as Kevin Vanhoozer puts it, "the Reformation was less about starting a new church than retrieving the one and ancient true church. . . . The Reformers' main objection to Roman Catholicism was not its catholicity but its narrow focus on Rome."[89] Thus,

---

87. Genke and Gumerlock, *Gottschalk and a Medieval Predestination Controversy*, 58.
88. Williams, *Evangelicals and Tradition*, 120.
89. Kevin J. Vanhoozer, "A Mere Protestant Response," in Matthew Levering, *Was the Reformation a Mistake? Why Catholic Doctrine Is Not Unbiblical* (Grand Rapids, MI: Zondervan, 2017), 229.

contrary to Newman's claim that "to be deep in history is to cease to be Protestant," the best of Protestantism has always been "deep in history." In this connection, it is worth mentioning, as Ken Stewart recently pointed out, that Newman made this claim while he was still an Anglican, in the context of a larger book and argument that were hardly uncontroversial among Roman Catholic authorities.[90]

Thus far all this has been to establish just this end, that Protestant Christians can retrieve patristic and medieval theology as a part of their own catholic heritage. To say that we *can* do this, however, is not yet to establish that we *should*. In the next two chapters we turn to consider what makes such an endeavor not merely permissible but valuable.

---

90. Stewart, *In Search of Ancient Roots*, 188.

2

Why Evangelicals Need Theological Retrieval

How shall we labour with any effect to build up the Church, if we have no thorough knowledge of her history, or fail to apprehend it from the proper point of observation? History is, and must ever continue to be, next to God's word, the richest fountain of wisdom, and the surest guide to all successful practical activity.

—Philip Schaff

Sometimes the best way to go forward is, paradoxically, to go backward. This is true in solving math problems, executing military operations, navigating relational conflict, and (here I suggest) doing theology. That is to say, contemporary evangelical theology can be enriched and strengthened in her current task by going back to retrieve classic theological resources. But of course, as we have already said, the basic idea of theological retrieval—what we may broadly define as resourcing contemporary systematic/constructive theology by engaging historical theology—is nothing new. The church has always looked backward to learn from the insights of previous generations for help in moving forward. John of Damascus summed up much of the earlier Eastern tradition, Anselm maintained and furthered much of Augustine, Calvin appealed to the church fathers for the Reformation cause, Warfield drew heavily upon the Reformers in a modernist context, and so forth. And yet several complementary factors make retrieval theology an especially worthwhile project today—particularly in evangelical circles in the modern West. Retrieval may not be new, but it is newly needed.

In this chapter we explore two indicators of our need for retrieval: a thirst among younger evangelicals for historical rootedness and the cultural pressures we face in our late modern context. Retrieving the past, we suggest, is one way to touch both this angst within the church as well as the pressure upon her.

The Evangelical Ache for History

In early 2017, Hank Hanegraaff, the famous "Bible answer man" who has authored more than twenty books and hosted a nationally syndicated radio broadcast, converted to Eastern Orthodoxy. In his appreciative response, Rod Dreher—a fellow Orthodox Christian whose book *The Benedict Option* was widely discussed among evangelicals—cast Hanegraff's decision in relation to the larger issue of evangelical thirst for historical depth: "Many evangelicals seek the early church; well here it is, in Orthodoxy."[1]

This isn't the first time Protestants have been confronted with a relatively late-life, high-profile defection from their ranks. One thinks of G. K. Chesterton turning to Roman Catholicism in 1922, a good fourteen years after he published his influential *Orthodoxy*; or Malcolm Muggeridge's conversion to Catholicism in 1982, at age seventy-nine; or the reception of Jaroslav Pelikan (prominent church historian and longtime Lutheran) into the Eastern Orthodox Church in 1998, toward the end of his career.

But today, evangelical conversions to Roman Catholicism or Eastern traditions seem to be happening at an increasing rate.[2] Back in

---

1. As cited in Sarah Eekhoff Zylstra, "'Bible Answer Man' Converts to Christianity," *Christianity Today* (April 12, 2017), accessed December 31, 2017, http://www.christianitytoday.com/news/2017/april/bible-answer-man-hank-hanegraaff-orthodoxy-cri-watchman-nee.html.

2. In what follows I focus on Eastern Orthodoxy particularly, but we should keep in mind that there are a conglomeration of other Eastern traditions as well (Oriental Orthodox churches, Assyrian Church of the East, etc.).

1993, in his foreword to Scott and Kimberly Hahn's *Rome Sweet Home: Our Journey to Catholicism*, Peter Kreeft described the testimony they recount in their book as "one of increasingly many such stories that seem to be springing up today throughout the Church in America like crocuses poking up through the spring snows."[3] This trend should not be exaggerated or regarded with alarmism. Globally, more people are converting to Protestantism from Roman Catholicism than vice versa.[4] Nonetheless, there is enough movement toward Rome or Constantinople from places such as Wheaton College or Willow Creek Community Church that the phenomenon cannot be simply ignored—particularly as it often occurs in relation to relatively well-known, influential leaders in the church. When Francis Beckwith converted back to the Roman Catholic heritage of his youth, for example, he had been elected president of the Evangelical Theological Society just four months prior;[5] and many evangelicals had been long familiar with the sociologist Christian Smith's diagnosis of "moralistic therapeutic deism" before they encountered his book *How to Go from Being a Good Evangelical to a Committed Catholic in Ninety-Five Difficult Steps.*[6]

In a few cases, the allure of Orthodoxy or Catholicism seems to take hold within an entire Protestant institution or setting. The first paragraph of the back cover of the 2016 book *Evangelical Exodus: Evangelical Seminarians and Their Paths to Rome* narrates a fascinating story:

> Over the course of a single decade, dozens of students, alumni, and professors from a conservative, Evangelical seminary in North Carolina (Southern Evangelical Seminary) converted to Catholicism. These conversions were notable as they occurred among people with varied backgrounds and motivations—many of whom did not share their thoughts with one another until this book was

---

3. Peter Kreeft, "Foreword," in Scott and Kimberly Hahn, *Rome Sweet Home: Our Journey to Catholicism* (San Francisco: Ignatius, 1993), *vii*.

4. As noted by Kenneth J. Stewart, *In Search of Ancient Roots: The Christian Past and the Evangelical Identity Crisis* (Grand Rapids, MI: IVP Academic, 2017), 256.

5. Francis J. Beckwith, *Return to Rome: Confessions of an Evangelical Catholic* (Grand Rapids, MI: Brazos, 2009).

6. Christian Smith, *How to Go from Being a Good Evangelical to a Committed Catholic in Ninety-Five Difficult Steps* (Eugene, OR: Wipf & Stock, 2011).

produced. Even more striking is that the seminary's founder, long-time president, and popular professor, Dr. Norman Geisler, had written two full-length books and several scholarly articles criticizing Catholicism from an Evangelical point of view.[7]

In the book's introduction, Douglas Beaumont observes that "this movement from conservative Evangelicalism to Catholicism is not limited to this school; in fact, some refer to the phenomenon as an exodus."[8] If the term *exodus* is too strong, at the same time we cannot deny a phenomenon that begs for exploration and listening.

So what is causing the trend? Obviously, every person's story is unique, and we must leave room for a wide array of different kinds of factors in each case.[9] However, one of the recurring themes among these denominational migrations is related to how Dreher interpreted Hanegraff's conversion: the desire for historical depth.

In Smith's *How to Go from Being a Good Evangelical to a Committed Catholic in Ninety-Five Difficult Steps*, the very first of the ninety-five steps toward Catholicism is "begin to feel rootless."[10] Smith describes this feeling of rootlessness as comparable to "living on the edge, carrying a low balance in life's checking account, being stuck in the present."[11] He counsels his readers not to ignore this sensation, because "there are good reasons for your feeling this way. This intuition is telling you something important. Something is missing. You need to find out what it is."[12] Many of Smith's subsequent steps develop this perception of rootlessness, for instance, #11: "read some church history," or #28: "start wondering when the supposed 'great apostasy' happened and where the true Christian church was for the 1,000–1,400 years between then and the Reformation." It is in the context of developing this latter point that Smith presses the historical claim that there was no "black hole" in church history prior to the

---

7. *Evangelical Exodus: Evangelical Seminarians and Their Paths to Rome*, ed. Douglas M. Beaumont (San Francisco: Ignatius, 2016).

8. Beaumont, ed., *Evangelical Exodus*, 16.

9. Scot McKnight, "From Wheaton to Rome: Why Evangelicals Become Roman Catholic," *Journal of the Evangelical Theological Society* 45.3 (September 2002): 451–72, discusses a number of "prototypical" evangelical conversions to Roman Catholicism and explores some of the most commonly involved.

10. Smith, *How to Go from Being a Good Evangelical*, 26.

11. Smith, *How to Go from Being a Good Evangelical*, 27.

12. Smith, *How to Go from Being a Good Evangelical*, 27.

Reformation: "Had the Holy Spirit fallen asleep on the job? Had the gospel gone into hibernation?"[13]

The sense of rootlessness and the desire for historical depth come up again and again in the testimonies of those moving out of evangelicalism. Often, in fact, the movement toward Catholicism or Orthodoxy is *equated* with the discovery of church history. This is the impression given by many of the stories listed on websites chronicling this phenomenon, such as *Why I'm Catholic*[14] and *Called to Communion*[15] and *Journey to Orthodoxy*.[16] Similarly, David Palm, after referencing his discovery of the doctrine of the "Real Presence" of Christ in the Eucharistic elements in the church fathers, testified: "I could no longer swallow our Protestant assertion that millions upon millions of Christians, including some who knew the apostles personally, had been misled by the Holy Spirit until Calvin and Zwingli came along to set everybody straight."[17] In line with this, those seeking an ancient tradition frequently express dissatisfaction with the typical evangelical posture toward church history. In his fascinating story of moving from pastoring First Baptist Church in Wheaton, Illinois, to ministering at Holy Transfiguration Antiochian Orthodox Church in Warrensville, Illinois, Wilbur Smith notes, "One of my strongest impressions in my journey from the Baptist vision of the Christian faith to Orthodoxy is how little the actual life of the Church during its two-thousand-year history really marks present-day thinking in the Evangelical church."[18] Marcus Grodi, a former Presbyterian pastor who converted to Catholicism and now serves as founder and president of The Coming Home Network,[19] summed up this sentiment vividly: "The more I read church history and Scripture the less I could comfortably remain Protestant."[20] Many similar testimonies could be adduced.[21]

---

13. Smith, *How to Go from Being a Good Evangelical*, 61.

14. http://www.whyimcatholic.com/.

15. http://www.calledtocommunion.com.

16. http://journeytoorthodoxy.com/.

17. Quoted in McKnight, "From Wheaton to Rome," 465.

18. Wilbur Smith, "A Journey to Eastern Orthodoxy," in *Journeys of Faith: Evangelicalism, Eastern Orthodoxy, Catholicism, and Anglicanism*, ed. Robert L. Plummer (Grand Rapids, MI: Zondervan, 2012), 48.

19. https://chnetwork.org/.

20. Quoted in McKnight, "From Wheaton to Rome," 464.

21. Perhaps the largest stream of literature within this field is stories about conversion to Roman Catholicism. To provide just a few examples: Marcus Grodi, *Journeys Home* (Goleta, CA:

Several broader ecclesiological convictions often coincide with this desire for historical rootedness. One is a desire for unity in the contemporary church. For instance, involvement in ecumenical dialogue is a significant feature of the six conversions from Protestantism to Roman Catholicism recounted by Jason Byassee: "Three Lutherans—Reinhard Hütter and Bruce Marshall, theologians at Methodist seminaries (Duke and Southern Methodist), and Mickey Mattox, a Luther scholar at Marquette; two Anglicans—Rusty Reno of Creighton and Douglas Farrow of McGill University; and a Mennonite—Gerald Schlabach of St. Thomas University."[22] Related to this is a respect for the claim of institutional and historical primacy made by the Roman and Eastern traditions. For instance, in his own testimomy Francis Beckwith references Carl Trueman's review of *Is the Reformation Over?*, in which Trueman describes Roman Catholicism as the "default position" in the West because of its historical and institutional pedigree, such that Protestants require a good reason not to be Catholic, lest they be participating in schism. Beckwith claims that "after reading that paragraph, I felt as if I had been punched in the nose," and identifies this as the moment he knew he had to return to Catholicism.[23] Related to both of these factors (the ecumenical urge and the recognition of Roman/Eastern priority) is the frequent perception of evangelicalism as a kind of eccentric new oddity—a new aberration whose existence must be somehow explained. Thomas Howard's older book opens with something like this sentiment, expressing admiration for evangelicalism's vigorous commitment to the ancient faith yet asserting at the same time that its *flavor* differs from the one, holy, catholic, and apostolic church.[24]

Within this larger picture, Anglicanism plays an interesting role. Obviously a movement from, say, an evangelical Baptist or free church

---

Queenship, 1997); Steve Ray, *Crossing the Tiber: Evangelical Protestants Discover the Historical Church* (San Francisco: Ignatius, 1997); David Currie, *Born Fundamentalist, Born Again Catholic* (San Francisco: Ignatius, 1996); *Surprised by Truth: 11 Converts Give the Biblical and Historical Reasons for Becoming Catholic*, ed. Patrick Madrid (Strathfield, AU: Basilica, 2016). Some representative books about the journey to Eastern Orthodoxy include Frederica Matthewes-Green, *Facing East: A Pilgrim's Journey into the Mysteries of Orthodoxy* (New York: HarperCollins, 1997); and Peter E. Gillquist, *Becoming Orthodox: A Journey to the Ancient Christian Faith* (Brentwood, TN: Wolgemuth & Hyatt, 1989).

22. Jason Byassee, "Going Catholic," *Christian Century* 123 (August 22, 2006): 18.
23. Francis J. Beckwith, "From 'Historic Christianity' to the Christianity of History," in *Evangelical Exodus*, 9–10.
24. Thomas Howard, *Evangelical Is Not Enough* (Nashville, TN: Thomas Nelson, 1984), 3–4.

into the Anglican communion is a different animal than the stories described above, since it is a movement within Protestantism and not necessarily a movement out of evangelicalism (some of the leading twentieth-century evangelicals, such as J. I. Packer and John Stott, are Anglican). But in light of Anglicanism's historical status as the so-called *via media* ("middle road") between the alternative perceived extremes of Christendom, Canterbury is often considered as a "safer" way to attain a more liturgical, historically conscious expression of worship and spirituality. It is striking, for instance, that in *Journeys of Faith* it is included alongside Roman Catholicism, Eastern Orthodoxy, and evangelicalism.[25]

And, doubtless, this same yearning for historical rootedness is at play in evangelical interest in Anglicanism. In his *Evangelicals on the Canterbury Trail*, published back in 1985, Robert Webber identified the desire for historical rootedness as one reason behind many conversions to Anglicanism, including his own. He describes feeling like an "ecclesiastical orphan looking for spiritual parents" in his upbringing in a fundamentalist Baptist context, while now as an Anglican discovering a spiritual identity "with all God's people throughout history."[26] Later he narrates how, after taking a course on the apostolic fathers, "the dawning sense of a link with primitive Christianity was exhilarating. . . . I felt like I had found my family tree in the attic."[27] Many since then and today can relate to Webber's experience, and many, within and without the Anglican communion, share his vision for returning to classical Christianity to help uphold the Christian faith in a postmodern context.[28]

Now, this desire for historical depth is not exclusively manifested by denominational migrations, of course. Many evangelicals are seeking

---

25. In the book's introduction, Robert Plummer recognizes that "at this point, a few readers are surely wondering if it is appropriate to include Anglicanism alongside Eastern Orthodoxy and Catholicism—especially since Anglicanism—in some expressions—espouses a thoroughly Evangelical theology." Plummer grants that this perception is true but nonetheless suggests that "the history of prominent 'free church' Evangelicals walking 'the Canterbury trail' is a phenomenon which fits naturally in this conversation." *Journeys of Faith*, 15.

26. Robert E. Webber, *Evangelicals on the Canterbury Trail: Why Evangelicals Are Attracted to the Liturgical Church* (Waco, TX: Word, 1984), 15–16.

27. Webber, *Evangelicals on the Canterbury Trail*, 61–62.

28. See Robert E. Webber, *Ancient-Future Faith: Rethinking Evangelicalism for a Postmodern World* (Grand Rapids, MI: Baker, 1999); cf. his earlier work, *Common Roots: A Call to Evangelical Maturity* (Grand Rapids, MI: Zondervan, 1978).

to "beef up" their liturgy and historical consciousness while remaining in their current context. Increasingly, one hears of evangelicals observing Lent, even in Baptist, free church, and nondenominational settings. Some churches are returning to historic practices of worship and art; for instance, in 2010 a *Christianity Today* interview drew attention to a church in Rock Harbor, Massachusetts, incorporating carved stone, cast bronze, mosaic, fresco, and stained glass into its sanctuary, in the conviction that these elements assist in the church's worship.[29] Many evangelicals are interested in monasticism and are utilizing classic devotional and spiritual literature, such as Thomas à Kempis's *The Imitation of Christ*.

Reactions to a Real Problem

What shall we make of this movement and seeming restlessness within evangelical Christianity? Amidst other observations we might also make, one strong impression that arises is of *a deep thirst for historical rootedness* that evidently is not being met in many current evangelical contexts. Particularly among the younger generation of evangelicals today, there seems to be a profound sense of emptiness and dislocatedness and consequent malaise. We are aching for the ancient and the august, for transcendence and tradition, for that which has stability and solidity and substance. And many of us simply aren't finding that in our evangelical churches and institutions.

Let me say at the outset that I believe that evangelicals can cultivate a sense of historical placement without abandoning evangelicalism. Much of my overarching burden throughout the rest of this book is to further the intuition that *evangelical* and *ancient* are far from antonyms, just as *catholicity* and *Catholicism* are less than synonyms. As Swain and Allen put it, "we can and should pursue catholicity on Protestant principles."[30] But here we can briefly ask: Given all the problems in evangelicalism, why *not* go to Rome, or the East?

I have great admiration for my friends in the Roman and Eastern traditions, and I can understand the appeal these churches offer. I have

---

29. David Neff, "The Art of Glory," *Christianity Today* (October 2010), 34–36. Stewart, *In Search of Ancient Roots*, 266, drew my attention to this article.

30. Scott R. Swain and Michael Allen, *Reformed Catholicity: The Promise of Retrieval for Theology and Biblical Interpretation* (Grand Rapids, MI: Baker Academic, 2015), 13.

always found it easy to appreciate the intellectual rigor of the Catholic tradition in particular, since within her are nearly all my favorite writers—Chesterton, Tolkien, Muggeridge, and Pascal. This book is not the place to explain why I identify as an evangelical Protestant Christian, but in passing I would observe one tiny point that relates to the topic at hand: it is not clear to me whether a return to either Rome or Constantinople is more of a movement *toward* or *away from* an ancient, mainstream Christianity. C. S. Lewis (my other favorite writer) had a similar intuition: "The Roman Church where it differs from this universal tradition and specifically from apostolic Christianity I reject. . . . The whole set-up of modern Romanism seems to me to be as much a provincial or local variation from the ancient tradition as any particular Protestant sect is."[31] Nonetheless, although I am not advocating for a return to Catholicism or Orthodoxy, I believe that evangelicals have much to learn from these other branches of Christendom. We must engage these traditions respectfully and graciously, in a posture that recognizes the significance of our theological differences without failing to appreciate and cultivate our common ground.

At the same time, I want to affirm that the restlessness that is throbbing in evangelical circles—what some have called "the evangelical identity crisis"[32]—is a reaction to a real problem. On the one hand, I do not think of evangelicalism as some shoddy, ragtag eccentricity that must apologize for itself. It is currently somewhat hip to knock on low-church expressions of worship and "piety" (often a term of derision), and I am eager to defend evangelicalism to the extent that these criticisms rest upon caricatures. Nor do I accept that the regrettable historical shallowness that characterizes much of American evangelical faith and practice is a *necessary* feature of evangelical theology, in the ways Christian Smith seems to believe. And yet, on the other hand, I believe that the phenomenon of evangelical departures reflects real weaknesses in evangelicalism and that those of us who go by the name "evangelical" must listen to and learn from this phenomenon.

---

31. C. S. Lewis, "Letter to Lyman Stebbins, May 8, 1945," in C. S. Lewis, *The Collected Letters of C. S. Lewis*, vol. 2, *Books, Broadcasts, and the War, 1931–1949*, ed. Walter Hooper (New York: HarperSanFrancisco, 2004), 646–47.

32. D. H. Williams, *Retrieving the Tradition and Renewing Evangelicalism: A Primer for Suspicious Protestants* (Grand Rapids, MI: Eerdmans, 1999), 24–26; Stewart, *In Search of Ancient Roots*, 6.

There are a variety of indicators of evangelical shallowness that we could point to, for instance, the alarming number of high-profile fallen pastors in recent years and the increasing sense that we need a more developed pastoral theology, or the current political scene and the desire among many younger evangelicals for a more robust public theology and social ethic. But since this book is about *theological* retrieval specifically, let me just observe one area where our need for historical depth has become conspicuously evident—recent disputes about the doctrine of God among evangelicals.

Perhaps the most prominent example that leaps to mind is the dustup about the Trinity that swept through the evangelical blogosphere during the summer of 2016 in relation to the notion of "eternal functional subordination." This idea, which several prominent evangelical theologians (including Wayne Grudem and Bruce Ware) had used to ground a complementarian view of gender roles, came under fire as a departure from Trinitarian orthodoxy—interestingly, largely from other theologians who were themselves complementarian (e.g., Carl Trueman, Liam Goligher). Whatever position one takes on the issue, it is difficult to read through the various relevant posts and not gather the impression that a lack of general historical/creedal consciousness is not plaguing the progression of the discussion somewhat.[33]

Much could be said to develop this point simply from this Trinity debate, but let me here draw attention to an episode about a year after this that generated less noise but was just as instructive, or perhaps more so: evangelical reactions to the publication of James Dolezal's *All That Is in God: Evangelical Theology and the Challenge of Classical Christian Theism.*[34] Drawing from his earlier work on divine simplicity,[35] in this book Dolezal defended the classical Christian conception of God as involving his simplicity, pure actuality, immutability, aseity, impassibility, eternity, and the substantial unity of the divine persons (contra social

---

33. Carl Trueman repeatedly drew attention to this concern in his responses. E.g., "Motivated by Feminism? A Response to Recent Criticism," *Mortification of Spin*, June 14, 2016, accessed January 3, 2018, http://www.alliancenet.org/mos/postcards-from-palookaville/motivated-by-feminism-a-response-to-a-recent-criticism#.Wk0gOt-nGM8: "I understand that many hold these views sincerely, without realizing the historical/theological/creedal implications."

34. James Dolezal, *All That Is in God: Evangelical Theology and the Challenge of Classical Christian Theism* (Grand Rapids, MI: Reformation Heritage, 2017).

35. James Dolezal, *God without Parts: Divine Simplicity and the Metaphysics of God's Absoluteness* (Eugene, OR: Pickwick, 2011).

Trinitarianism). But he also went on the offensive, criticizing what he called "theistic mutualism," an alternative way of thinking about God that holds that God in some sense changes in response to creatures, which Dolezal perceives to be widely held throughout evangelicalism. Dolezal distinguished between hard and soft versions of theistic mutualism but regarded them both as a threat to a classical and biblical doctrine of God, and he cast his book as a polemical effort against this position.

The prominent evangelical theologian John Frame wrote a critical review of Dolezal's book, which in some respects mirrored an earlier interaction between Frame and Richard Muller in the 1990s in the *Westminster Theological Journal*.[36] Frame himself drew associations with Dolezal's "scholasticism" with the theological method of Richard Muller, criticizing their prioritization of "historical theology" over "systematic theology" as inconsistent with the doctrine of *sola Scriptura*: "Like Muller, then, [Dolezal] tries to make systematic theology totally subordinate to historical theology. But this is to put the cart before the horse. We can learn much from the theologians who have preceded us in history, but *sola Scriptura* requires us to test everything they say by the direct study of Scripture."[37] Frame criticized Dolezal for treating people such as Thomas Aquinas as infallible and warned of the dangers of leaning too heavily on tradition in theology: "Total alignment with a historical tradition leads to spiritual shipwreck."[38]

Frame's response raises a number of questions. For instance, is it possible to separate systematic theology from historical theology, as though there were some ahistorical vantage point from which one can engage in a "direct study" of Scripture?[39] Frame's concern that

---

36. John Frame, "Muller on Theology," *Westminster Theological Journal* 56 (Spring 1994): 133–51; Richard A. Muller, "The Study of Theology Revisited: A Response to John Frame," *Westminster Theological Journal* 56 (Fall 1994): 409–17; John Frame, "In Defense of Something Close to Biblicism: Reflections On *Sola Scriptura* and History in Theological Method," *Westminster Theological Journal* 59 (Fall 1997): 269–91; David F. Wells, "On Being Framed," *Westminster Theological Journal* 59 (Fall 1997): 293–300; Richard A. Muller, "Historiography in the Service of Theology and Worship: Toward Dialogue with John Frame," *Westminster Theological Journal* 59 (Fall 1994): 301–10; John Frame, "Reply to Richard Muller and David Wells," *Westminster Theological Journal* 59 (Fall 1997): 311–18.
37. John Frame, "Scholasticism for Evangelicals: Thoughts on All That Is in God by James Dolezal," November 25, 2017, accessed December 20, 2017, https://frame-poythress.org/scholasticism-for-evangelicals-thoughts-on-all-that-is-in-god-by-james-dolezal.
38. Frame, "Scholasticism for Evangelicals."
39. As observed by Stephen Wedgeworth, "Against 'Historical Theology,'" *The Calvinist International*, December 5, 2017, accessed December 20, 2017, https://calvinistinternational.com/2017/12/05/against-historical-theology.

Dolezal's view amounts to Docetism, and his apparent belief that the incarnation is at odds with divine immutability, also raises the question of how Frame regards the huge swath of the Christian tradition that has roughly held to the same view. Keith Mathison suggests that Frame's response on this point, as well as on his critique of scholasticism as a theological position rather than a method, pays too little attention to the historical record: "Our orthodox forefathers in the faith were aware of these challenges centuries ago, and they provided biblically faithful and thoughtful answers to all of them."[40] All this raises the question: How should evangelicals who hold to *sola Scriptura* think about the role of *historical theology*? Is it possible to settle a challenge like the relation of the incarnation to divine immutability without referencing the tradition's way of dealing with it? How lightly can we depart from a classic view, and when we do so, should we not make it clear to our readers that this is what we are doing?

My interest right now is not to settle all the issues raised in this debate (in chapter 6 I take up a view of divine simplicity to resonant with Dolezal's), but more with what it reveals about the state of American evangelical theology. One broad impression that arises is of a general underdevelopment among evangelicals on the doctrine of God, or theology proper. Many of those evangelical readers following along a debate like this appear to be stretching into new territory, as though concepts like impassibility and simplicity are altogether new. Next to this underfamiliarity there seems to be a general undersensitivity to the *significance* of many classical doctrines—how else can we understand the casualness with which doctrines as important and mainstream throughout church history as, say, the eternal generation of the Son, or divine simplicity, are often jettisoned by evangelicals today?[41] Timothy George is surely right to lament that "evangelicals have paid too little attention to the sum total of the Christian heritage handed down from previous generations."[42]

---

40. Keith A. Mathison, "Unlatched Theism: An Examination of John Frame's Response to All That Is in God," *Tabletalk*, November 30, 2017, accessed December 20, 2017https://tabletalkmagazine .com/posts/2017/11/unlatched-theism-an-examination-of-john-frames-response-to-all-that-is-in-god.

41. For a recent treatment of eternal generation, see *Retrieving Eternal Generation*, ed. Fred Sanders and Scott R. Swain (Grand Rapids, MI: Zondervan, 2017).

42. Timothy George, *Reading Scripture with the Reformers* (Downers Grove, IL: IVP Academic, 2011), 25.

Tradition O - Kyle
Church

To the extent that evangelicals adopt a kind of "me and my Bible" theological method, as though theology can be done without appropriation of the battles and settlements of earlier generations, we diminish and destabilize our theological witness.[43] Christopher Hall's rebuke to efforts to construct the doctrine of the Trinity on the basis of the Bible alone, without reference to tradition, may serve as a broader warning to us:

> We inevitably reinvent the wheel, but too often with missing or cracked spokes. Not infrequently we fall into the very heresies the church rejected after much toil, tribulation, and yes, spilled blood. Our inattentiveness to ancient sources undercuts our ability to mine the riches of the Scripture well, with the unhappy result that poorly catechized evangelical teachers produce poorly catechized students.[44]

We can and should strengthen the vitality of evangelical Protestantism by thinking about our historical identity with greater scrutiny and self-awareness and doing theology with more self-conscious engagement with the classical creeds, confessions, and theological texts of the church.

A Better Way to Be Protestant

The restlessness we have recounted here is not, of course, the *whole* story of evangelical Protestantism. Happily, many evangelical leaders today are calling for a more catholic and more historically rooted vision of Protestantism. Kevin J. Vanhoozer, for instance, explores the five *solas* of the Reformation to envision "mere Protestantism" as a renewal movement for the church in the twenty-first century. For Vanhoozer, the five *solas* provide "not an alternative to orthodox tradition but rather a deeper insight into the one true gospel that undergirds

---

43. George Kalantzis and Andrew Tooley, "Introduction," in *Evangelicals and the Early Church: Recovery, Reform, Renewal*, ed. George Kalantzis and Andrew Tooley (Eugene, OR: Cascade, 2012), 8–10, examine the evangelical tendency to neglect the early church and discuss several factors contributing to it. Further exploration of this theme is provided in the same volume by Christopher A. Hall, "Evangelical Inattentiveness to Ancient Voices: An Overview, Explanation, and Proposal," 31–39. Williams, *Retrieving the Tradition and Renewing Evangelicalism*, 18–23, explores some of the roots of American evangelicalism's antitraditionalism and anticredalism.

44. Hall, "Evangelical Inattentiveness to Ancient Voices," in *Evangelicals and the Early Church*, 51.

that tradition."[45] Accordingly, Vanhoozer argues that "the Reformation was a *retrieval*, first and foremost of the biblical gospel, particularly the Pauline articulation, but also, secondarily, of the church fathers."[46] Vanhoozer and others have drawn together a Reforming Catholic Confession.[47] This document acknowledges that Protestants have sometimes been divisive and sectarian but denies that such a posture is necessary to Protestantism as such. It seeks to recover the "unitive Protestantism" that was originally expressed in the five *solas*.

This more balanced approach to Protestant identity is able to acknowledge the lamentable divisiveness that has sometimes resulted from Protestant attitudes and practices, without thereby succumbing to the popular tendency to lay all the ills of modern society at the feet of Protestantism. This, of course, is a common criticism. Brad Gregory has notoriously argued, for instance, that the ultimate domino effect of the Reformation has been the secularization of the West: "The Reformation is the most important distant historical source for contemporary Western hyperpluralism with respect to truth claims about meaning, morality, values, priorities, and purpose."[48] Within the ranks of Protestantism as well, it is increasingly common to hear laments of the Reformation's divisiveness. In particular, the doctrines of *sola Scriptura* and the priesthood of all believers are often singled out as leading toward interpretative anarchy that has rent Western Christendom and society. Alister McGrath uses the label "Christianity's dangerous idea" for this precarious notion that all Christians should read and interpret the Bible for themselves, since it "created space for entrepreneurial individuals to redirect and redefine Christianity."[49]

If we cannot accept that Protestantism is quite to blame for all this, the critics nonetheless have a point. Protestants often have been divisive. But what to do about this? Peter Leithart, for one, has called for an "end" to the kind of Protestantism that is defined by opposition to

---

45. Kevin J. Vanhoozer, *Biblical Authority after Babel: Retrieving the* Solas *in the Spirit of Mere Protestant Christianity* (Grand Rapids, MI: Brazos, 2016).

46. Vanhoozer, *Biblical Authority after Babel*, 22–23, emphasis original.

47. https://reformingcatholicconfession.com.

48. Brad S. Gregory, *The Unintended Reformation: How a Religious Revolution Secularized Society* (Cambridge, MA: Belknap Press of Harvard University Press, 2012), 369.

49. Alister McGrath, *Christianity's Dangerous Idea: The Protestant Revolution—A History from the Sixteenth Century to the Twenty-First* (New York: HarperOne, 2007), 4.

Roman Catholicism.[50] In his earlier online article by the same name, Leithart distinguished between "Protestantism" that is defined by its opposition to Roman Catholicism and "Reformational Catholicism" that is more ecumenical. Among his other points of contrast between these two outlooks are their respective views of church history:

> A Protestant's heroes are Luther, Calvin, Zwingli, and their heirs. If he acknowledges any ancestry before the Reformation, they are proto-Protestants like Hus and Wycliffe. A Reformational Catholic gratefully receives the history of the entire Church as his history, and, along with the Reformers, he honors Augustine and Gregory the Great and the Cappadocians, Alcuin and Rabanus Maurus, Thomas and Bonaventure, Dominic and Francis and Dante, Ignatius and Teresa of Avila, Chesterton, de Lubac and Congar as fathers, brothers, and sisters. A Reformational Catholic knows some of his ancestors were deeply flawed but won't delete them from the family tree.[51]

Leithart concludes his article by stating that "Protestantism has had a good run," but the world is a different place today, and it is no longer needed. Instead, he wants to affirm the more ecumenical vision of "Reformational Catholicism" as the future of the church and as more in line with the original vision of the Reformers themselves.

I appreciate Leithart's ecumenical desire, and I understand what he is reacting against. Like him, I want to see evangelical Protestants breaking out of a parochial and defensive posture and engaging the church catholic. However, since Leithart does not advocate for a return to Rome, it is unclear in what sense there must be an "end" to Protestantism for the achievement of this aim. In a pungent response to Leithart's piece, Fred Sanders objects to how Leithart has invested the word *Protestant* with "a new, private meaning," pointing out that "the whole point of actual Protestantism (when it's not having a new meaning forced on it as a term of abuse) is to claim the full heritage of the church while making necessary adjustments in recent

---

50. Peter J. Leithart, *The End of Protestantism: Pursuing Unity in a Fragmented Church* (Grand Rapids, MI: Brazos, 2016).
51. Peter J. Leithart, "The End of Protestantism," *First Things*, November 8, 2013, accessed December 19, 2017, https://www.firstthings.com/web-exclusives/2013/11/the-end-of-protestantism.

deviations."[52] Sanders's response reminds us that what is good about Leithart's appeal for catholicity has actually *always* been a part of the Protestant tradition.[53] As we have urged, the vision for a more catholic Protestantism reflected in a document such as the Reforming Catholic Confession is no recent rarity but rather joins a chorus of voices stemming from the Reformers themselves. J. I. Packer sums up this way of understanding the Reformation well: "At the Reformation skewed understandings of the church, the sacraments, justification, faith, prayer and ministry were, as I believe, corrected; but the correction took place within the frame of the great tradition and did not break it."[54] Timothy George agrees: "For all their critique of the received doctrines of medieval Catholicism, the reformers saw themselves in basic continuity with the foundational dogmas of the early church."[55]

Getting the Cultural Picture

Before moving on, it might be helpful to step back and ask a larger question: Where is this sense of rootlessness coming from in the first place? To understand this, we must gain some sense of the broader cultural picture and in particular the *abruptness* of the transition we are currently walking through in the late modern West. The world around us is rapidly changing. We face many challenges that are unprecedented in the entire history of the church. Athanasius stood *contra mundum*; Aquinas synthesized Aristotle; Luther strove with his conscience; Zwingli wielded an axe; but probably none of them ever dreamed of a world in which people could choose their gender. Secularizing late modernity is a strange, new animal.[56]

---

52. Fred Sanders, "Glad Protestantism," *The Scriptorium Daily*, November 11, 2013, accessed December 19, 2017, http://scriptoriumdaily.com/glad-protestantism. See also Sanders's review of Leithart's 2016 book, "Does Protestantism Need to Die?," *Christianity Today* (November 2016), 70–71.

53. Leithart himself gestures toward the catholic nature of the Reformation at the end of his article and also makes this very point elsewhere. E.g., Peter J. Leithart, "Foreword," in W. Bradford Littlejohn, *The Mercersburg Theology and the Quest for Reformed Catholicity* (Eugene, OR: Wipf & Stock, 2009), *xi*: "In its origins and at its core, Protestantism is, as Philip Schaff saw and many recent students of the Reformation have confirmed, a thoroughly catholic enterprise."

54. J. I. Packer, "On from Orr: Cultural Crisis, Rational Realism, and Incarnational Ontology," in *Reclaiming the Great Tradition: Evangelicals, Catholics, and Orthodox in Dialogue*, ed. James S. Cutsinger (Downers Grove, IL: InterVarsity Press, 1997), 156.

55. Timothy George, *Theology of the Reformers* (Nashville, TN: B&H, 1988), 308.

56. I here follow those who prefer the term *late modern* rather than *postmodern* insofar as the threefold premodern/modern/postmodern schema can be taken to imply that postmodernism is roughly as significant a change from modernism as modernism was from premodernism. In most

We might say that modernity is to human cultural and intellectual history what the Cambrian explosion is in fossil history or what a sudden mutation is in the evolution of a species. In other words, human history does not develop at an even pace but subsists in vast stretches of relative stasis suddenly punctuated with radical mutation in the space of just a few centuries. A few hundred years ago, people had just begun to use last names. Now, just a few centuries later, almost a quarter of the world is connected via Facebook. And we tiny portion of humanity here in the twenty-first century live on the far side of this great change.

The changes involved with the advent of modernity affect all areas of human existence, and we can stack up a lot of abstract words to try to capture them: industrialization (in which Europe and North America become less agrarian and more focused on the manufacturing of goods and services); urbanization (in which human populations migrate to the cities); pluralism (in which ideas and cultures may coexist within one society rather than assimilate to the whole); individualism (in which society emphasizes the individual, and her rights and equality, instead of the community); technological modernization (bringing you from the printing press, through the steam engine, telegraph, electricity, mass production of steel, paper currency, eventually up to the atomic bomb and color TV, and finally—thank you, Al Gore—the Internet); economic modernization (from feudalism to capitalism and the market economy with a corollary division between the public and private spheres); globalization (in which the human cultural, economic, and political intercourse becomes more internationally connected); and the development of the modern nation-state with its constituent institutions (e.g., representative democracy, public education, etc.).

But for our purposes, towering above these respective industrial, cultural, social, technological, economic, global, and national/political

---

disciplines, however, postmodernism involves a change more of "mood" than of substance— a chastened and perhaps cynical posture toward finding the answers more than a fundamentally new set of questions. To give a metaphor: if premodernism is a peaceful morning at home, and modernism is a fire breaking out in your neighborhood at 7:00 p.m., then postmodernism is a changing of strategy for how to put the fire out around 7:45. Here, as with Western intellectual and cultural history, there is ultimately one most pivotal and decisive change, and the second is more of a modification than equal response.

changes is the reality of secularization, in which people begin to look to individual reason as the final arbiter of truth rather than tradition or authoritative texts or figures, and in which progress and science are emphasized over the mysticism and superstition of the past.

Now, it is highly disputed what exactly this process of secularization involves and how quickly it is occurring. The noted sociologist Charles Taylor tells the story of secularization particularly in terms of "a move from a society where belief in God is unchallenged and indeed, unproblematic, to one in which it is understood to be one option among others, and frequently not the easiest to embrace."[57] Taylor disputes the notion of science and reason simply replacing religion and superstition—what he calls "the modern subtraction story of the Enlightenment."[58] In the story he traces, the modern secular age is more complex—indeed, "schizophrenic, or better, deeply cross-pressured."[59] Thus, after recounting the incentives that modern society provides for unbelief and hedonism, Taylor continues:

> All this is true, and yet the sense that there is something more presses in. Great numbers of people feel it: in moments of reflection about their life; in moments of relaxation in nature; in moments of bereavement and loss; and quite wildly and unpredictably. Our age is very far from settling in to a comfortable unbelief.[60]

The recent history of the United States, at least, would seem to support this picture of secularization as making religious belief more complicated rather than stamping it out altogether. Ross Douthat, for example, describes the "slow-motion collapse of traditional Christianity" in the United States over the last several decades but notes that this collapse has not resulted in a pure secularism, but rather "the rise of a variety of destructive pseudo-Christianities in its place."[61]

Nonetheless, in this "schizophrenic" age in which we now live, there can be no question that for a huge swatch of humanity, morality has tilted toward self-expression, meaning has been reduced to a

---

57. Charles Taylor, *A Secular Age* (Cambridge, MA: Harvard University Press, 2007), 3.
58. Taylor, *A Secular Age*, 273.
59. Taylor, *A Secular Age*, 727.
60. Taylor, *A Secular Age*, 727.
61. Ross Douthat, *Bad Religion: How We Became a Nation of Heretics* (New York: Free Press, 2012), 3.

personal construct, and life has been drained of much of its former transcendence. In most ancient cultures, by contrast, life and meaning were relatively stable. You didn't have too many people like Albert Camus contemplating whether the absurdity of human existence necessitated suicide among the ancient Mongols, Mayans, or Vikings. The premodern mind-set is better captured by Brother Lippo Lippi from Robert Browning's poem, "This world's no blot for us, nor blank; it means intensely, and means good: to find its meaning is my meat and drink."

Many today lack this sense of objective meaning; we are starved of transcendence, community, stability; we're aching to find something big to live for; we feel listless, adrift, barren. Think of Nietzsche's anguish in proclaiming the death of God in the late nineteenth century—in a milder, semiconscious way, this is how many feel today. Our standard of living has risen but so have our suicide rates; we are smarter but more uncertain, surrounded with pleasure but less fulfilled, able to do almost anything but uncertain whether to do anything. As Taylor puts it, modernity has produced "a wide sense of malaise at the disenchanted world, a sense of it as flat, empty, a multiform search for something within, or beyond it, which could compensate for the meaning lost with transcendence."[62]

Similarly, certain basic instincts regarding personal identity and morality that all premodern cultures (for all their diversity) together took for granted are now increasingly questioned. In most cultures throughout history it was assumed that external reality is fixed and that the basic point of life is to conform ourselves to it in some way. Buddha and Plato agree on this point; they only differ on what the conforming process looks like. Our culture, by contrast, tends to exalt human desire and aspiration such that the point of life is for external reality to be conformed to it. As C. S. Lewis put it, "For the wise men of old the cardinal problem had been how to conform the soul to reality, and the solution had been knowledge, self-discipline, and virtue. For magic and applied science alike the problem is how to subdue reality to the wishes of men; the solution is a technique."[63]

---

62. Taylor, *A Secular Age*, 302.
63. C. S. Lewis, *The Abolition of Man*, in *The Complete C. S. Lewis Signature Classics* (repr. New York: HarperCollins, 2002), 728.

Thus truth has been reduced to a relative construct, and we have lost confidence in reason's ability to access external reality. Plato could have at least understood Buddha's four noble truths; Buddha would have comprehended Plato's advocacy for reason and justice—both would be only perplexed and exasperated with the modern mantra "be true to yourself."

Secularization has also expanded a phenomenon that has been quite rare for most of human history—religious skepticism. In premodern eras, religion was institutionalized everywhere and pretty universally assumed to be a worthy part of society. You might disagree on whom and where and how to worship but generally not on whether to worship. There are a few scattered examples of atheism in premodern times, but it is strikingly rare. For every one Lucretius or Democritus, you can find entire centuries and nations that know only of priests, monks, imams, lamas, shamans, sages, or sorcerers. C. S. Lewis put it well in *Mere Christianity*:

> The first big division of humanity is into the majority, who believe in some kind of God or gods, and the minority who do not. On this point, Christianity lines up with the majority—lines up with ancient Greeks and Romans, modern savages, Stoics, Platonists, Hindus, Mohammedans, etc., against the modern Western European materialist.[64]

Now, the historical and global isolation of our culture does not, of course, automatically discredit it. "Weird" is not always "wrong." But seeing our culture in a broader historical context may go a long way to explaining the deep restlessness and search for rootedness that characterizes so much of the modern malaise. More than that, it may help us appreciate why theological retrieval holds promise in helping us respond to the crises of our particular moment. In many respects, the story of theological retrieval begins with the turn toward postliberalism, as the critical methods of mainstream liberal theology, in which Christian theology is perceived to be one particular instantiation of a more general phenomenon of human religion and culture, ultimately reducible to human knowledge and interpretation,

---

64. C. S. Lewis, *Mere Christianity*, in *The Complete C. S. Lewis Signature Classics*, 39.

were increasingly felt to be a dead-end. As John Webster has noted, those initiating the turn to classical theological resources have tended to be simultaneously turning away from (for instance) "theological construction by correlation" (think Paul Tillich) or immanentist approaches to theology that "subsume historical and dogmatic theology under social pressures" (think Ernst Troeltsch).[65] Those receiving the past are, in certain ways if not all, rejecting the present. One thinks of Oden, for instance, or, in his own way, Barth.

Evangelicals have a somewhat distinct relation to this turn, as they never fully bought into the liberal project to begin with. But obviously it would be a mistake to think that evangelicals have not been influenced by the broader assumptions of modernity. We therefore may find theological retrieval to function in relation to our current cultural moment somewhat like a map does for a man alone in the woods. That is, if modernity is like a traveler who, after years of plodding along in the same general direction, suddenly turns off the path in pursuit of a new goal, to study the past is to look back on the path from which we came. It provides context, perspective, and guidance. It gives you bearings.

Buschart and Eilers develop this point in their helpful book on retrieval. As they point out, at the heart of the ethos of modernity is "emancipation from authority, from transcendence, from prejudgments, and naturally then from tradition."[66] Thus, in modern theology, there exists a host of bifurcations and stalemates (text vs. meaning, Bible vs. theology, church vs. academy, intellectual vs. spiritual, etc.) that premodern theology did not face. Now, exactly how retrieval might help us navigate these challenges will depend on how we interpret modernity more precisely (more on this in chapter 3). But the point remains: since our culture tends toward an isolation from the past, we must be all the more alert to our need to learn from it, and we may find it to be an especially useful corrective. Indeed, we may find retrieving our ancient roots to be precisely the guide that can help

---

65. These terminologies are employed by John Webster, "Theologies of Retrieval," in *The Oxford Handbook to Systematic Theology*, ed. John Webster, Kathryn Tanner, and Iain Torrance (Oxford, UK: Oxford University Press, 2008), 593, 596, to describe various kinds of theological method generally declined by those operating in the mode of retrieval.

66. David Buschart and Kent Eilers, *Theology as Retrieval: Receiving the Past, Renewing the Church* (Downers Grove, IL: IVP Academic, 2015), 23.

us envision a healthier and deeper evangelicalism in our increasingly fragmented world.

To speak from my own experience, retrieval has functioned not only like a map amidst wandering but like water amidst thirst. The rest of this book extends from this conviction and hope and approaches classical theology, in Webster's words, "as resource rather than a problem."[67] In the next chapter, we lay out several ways that retrieval may play this role specifically for contemporary evangelical Christianity.

---

67. Cf. Webster, "Theologies of Retrieval," 585.

3

Benefits and Perils of Retrieval

We set forth our confession as those who stand on the shoulders of our Reformation forbears and their Catholic and Orthodox ancestors (i.e., patristic and medieval theologians), and ultimately on the only enduring foundation of the faith: the written Word of God that attests the good news of the living Word of God made flesh, who dwelt among us (John 1:14), died for us, and lives in us.

—A Reforming Catholic Confession 20

In the early 1970s, while teaching at Drew University, Thomas Oden experienced a profound personal renewal by immersing himself in the classical texts of Christianity. He describes his experience reading each morning in the library carrel:

> Every question I previously thought of as new and unprecedented, I found had already been much investigated. . . . As I worked my way through the beautiful, long-hidden texts of classic Christianity, I reemerged out of a maze to once again delight in the holy mysteries of the faith and the perennial dilemmas of fallen human existence. It was no longer me interpreting the texts but the texts interpreting me.[1]

---

1. Thomas Oden, *A Change of Heart: A Personal and Theological Memoir* (Downers Grove, IL: IVP Academic, 2014), 138–39.

Elsewhere Oden reflects on the role of "classical Christianity" in his theological pilgrimage as a kind of food and as a kind of home:

> Looking back, I know God has accompanied me on a long, circuitous path in order to help me arrive finally on the narrow road to experience the reliability of classic Christianity. My major learning has been the rediscovery of Christmas (incarnation) and Easter (resurrection).
>
> I did not become an orthodox believer or theologian until after I tried out most of the errors long rejected by Christianity. If my first forty years were spent hungering for meaning in life, the last forty have been spent in being fed. If the first forty were prodigal, the last forty have been a homecoming.[2]

Thus far we have seen that contemporary evangelical theology may benefit from historical deepening and that Protestantism (the particular stream of Christianity in which evangelicalism is located) has a significant history that is part of its legitimate heritage. Now we turn to consider more specifically how this identified heritage can help meet this identified need. How might evangelicals today, facing the specific challenges we face today, benefit from the kind of library readings that Oden conducted? Might the spiritually hungry among us, or the theologically wandering among us, find food and shelter in classical Christian theology, as he did?

In this chapter we identify three particular benefits of retrieval, articulated metaphorically as going to school, traveling to a foreign country, and seeing a counselor. We also draw attention to several potential perils of retrieval. Then, with a view to the case studies coming in subsequent chapters, we provide some examples of theologians in particular need of retrieval and say something about the excitement of the task at hand.

How Patristic and Medieval Theology Can Resource Contemporary Protestants

It is difficult to quantify exactly what benefits retrieval can hold, and they may vary widely from one situation to another. Nonetheless, we

---

2. Oden, *A Change of Heart*, 56–57.

might conceptualize three broad ways that patristic and medieval theology is particularly well positioned to interact with modern evangelical theology, without intending to preclude other additional benefits. First, patristic and medieval theology can help bulk up contemporary Protestant theology in areas where it is historically weak and/or underdeveloped. A good metaphor for this benefit of retrieval might be a student attending a school or a child learning to talk by listening. Retrieval is a valid means of theological education, in part because each era of church history faces different theological controversies, and it is usually in the context of controversy that doctrinal precision tends to develop, often along with a shared technical vocabulary. Thus one need not regard church tradition as infallible or comprehensive to recognize that each generation of the church has a unique contribution to offer all the others.[3] In the case of our patristic and medieval forbearers, there are many doctrinal battles over which they agonized and even shed blood, and yet we think about comparatively little today.

One example would be the doctrine of angels. The medieval era represents perhaps the richest period of reflection on angelology in the history of the church. Whereas modern Protestants generally have little use for angels beyond, in certain charismatic circles, an interest in angels' supernatural involvement in our lives, medieval theologians found great consequence in questions concerning the creation of angels, the nature of angels, the fall of angels, the role of angels in redemption, and the relation of angels to material creation. Many a page of Thomas Aquinas's *Summa Theologica* is spent seeking to establish that angels inhabit this universe as part of God's creation, that they have a stewardship role over other material created bodies, that two angels cannot occupy the exact same place at the same time, that one angel cannot occupy two places at the same time, that the movement of an angel from one place in God's creation to another is not instantaneous but requires a duration of time, that angels are capable of assuming a physical body—and other views such as these.[4] These were not idle, "ivory tower" questions for him, as often cast today, but integrally

---

3. For an eloquent expression of the benefit of reading from different historical eras, see C. S. Lewis, "Introduction," in Athanasius, *On the Incarnation*, trans. a religious of C.S.M.V., Popular Patristics 3 (Crestwood, NY: St. Vladimir's Seminary Press, 1977), 3–10.
4. Thomas Aquinas, *Summa Theologica* I, Q. 50–64, trans. Fathers of the English Dominican Province (Notre Dame, IN: Christian Classics, 1948), 259–324.

related to deeper theological matters concerning the nature of God's creation and the relation of the spiritual and physical realms. Modern Protestants may develop more satisfying ways of thinking theologically about created realities such as space and time and matter—particularly this side of Einstein—by cultivating curiosity for these questions that drove medieval angelology.

To mention another example, John Duns Scotus's "formal distinction" is an often forgotten construct that may have a broad utility in contemporary theology. Because it is stronger than a merely conceptual distinction and yet weaker than a real distinction that implies metaphysical separation,[5] the formal distinction enabled Scotus to differentiate both the divine persons and divine attributes from the divine essence without compromising divine simplicity.[6] Scotus held that divine attributes such as omnipresence or omnipotence are identical with the divine essence, but *formally* (unlike, say, divine unity). The formal distinction also enabled Scotus to develop a unique account of individuation that shaped his view of the nature of angels and other created objects. The Scotist view (often called *haecceitas*, a Latin neologism meaning "thisness") attributes each object's uniqueness radically to itself. While Scotus was a realist and believed in universals, he nevertheless taught that each object possesses individuality by its unique instantiation of properties and not merely by its participation in the form of a universal. Marcia Colish provides a helpful comparison: "We might compare it to the way that 'dogness' or 'collieness' inhere in Lassie, in contrast with the way they inhere in Lad and other collies, including those in Lassie's immediate gene pool."[7] Although some evangelicals are starting to give Scotus more attention, it is often in

5. Mary Beth Ingham and Mechthild Dreyer, *The Philosophical Vision of John Duns Scotus: An Introduction* (Washington, DC: Catholic University Press of America, 2004), 34, explain that "the formal distinction is based upon an existing aspect of the object (Scotus calls it a distinction *a parte rei*) and so is not merely mental, yet the aspect in question is not capable of existing independently from the object in which it is found." Peter King, "Scotus on Metaphysics," in *The Cambridge Companion to Duns Scotus* (Cambridge, UK: Cambridge University Press, 2004), 22, identifies the "core intuition" that lies behind the formal distinction as the notion that "existential inseparability does not entail identity in definition."

6. For a discussion of Duns Scotus's formal distinction in relation to the Trinity and divine simplicity, see Thomas H. McCall, "Trinity Doctrine, Plain and Simple," in *Advancing Trinitarian Theology: Explorations in Constructive Dogmatics*, ed. Oliver D. Crisp and Fred Sanders (Grand Rapids, MI: Zondervan, 2014), 52–53.

7. Marcia L. Colish, *Medieval Foundations of the Western Theological Tradition 400–1400*, Yale Intellectual History of the West (New Haven, CT: Yale University Press, 1997), 310.

relation to the historical interpretations of radical orthodoxy. There is further benefit to be had, I would suggest, in putting these Scotist categories to more constructive usage. Scotus is a good example, in fact, of the kind of theologian who could help us derive greater nuance and precision in areas where we as evangelicals tend to be rather flat-footed and uncreative, such as ontology and doctrine of God (I write this as someone who does not finally agree with Scotus's view of univocity.)

This educational benefit is in some ways the most basic of theological retrieval, but it should not for that reason be considered necessarily the most valuable. Almost invariably theological retrieval serves a more catalytic role of deepening our sensitivities to theological concerns we do not already feel and cultivating theological values we do not already possess. To construct a metaphor, visiting the Sistine chapel does more than conceptually advance your knowledge of Michaelango's view of final judgment, as visiting the Grand Canyon does more than provide you information about the history of the Colorado River. There are sensibilities and emotions that are shaped by the whole experience. So also patristic and medieval theology can function to shape theological values and inclinations we will likely lack so long as we work narrowly within Reformation and modern theology alongside the Bible. It is an enriching, formative experience, comparable to traveling to a foreign country and being immersed in the culture and geography.

Chapters 4 and 5 of this book, dealing with the doctrine of God, will provide an example of this kind of retrieval. In our treatment of both the Creator/creation distinction as well as divine simplicity, we aim to draw attention not merely to how early and medieval theologians treated the doctrine of God itself but to the values and instincts that undergirded their whole approach. In the case of divine simplicity, for instance, it is worth pointing out that this doctrine was nearly universally affirmed throughout all of church history, East and West, while today it is increasingly ignored or rejected within modern Protestantism. More than that, modern theologians and philosophers tend to critique divine simplicity for reasons that all too often did not even come into view in its premodern articulations. How do we account for this discrepancy? Retrieving the doctrine of God in its patristic and medieval context will help explain these differing instincts by calling attention to the deeper ontological differences at stake and thereby sensitize us to the values that drove ancient formulations of divine simplicity. If retrieving medieval angelology results in something like education, retrieving divine simplicity in its patristic and medieval context feels something like traveling to a new country to see the historical sites. It not only imparts categories; it shapes values. The doctrine of God (theology proper) appears to be an area of theology in which modern evangelicals may especially experience this benefit in the retrieval of patristic and medieval theology.

A third example of how the retrieval of patristic and medieval theology can resource contemporary Protestant theology is reframing modern debates by providing a premodern perspective. Specifically, because it operates in a premodern context where there was no "liberal versus conservative" spectrum as such, pre-Reformation theology can helpfully redirect us away from some of the limiting features that tend to characterize our more polarized contexts. As John Webster puts it, describing the "decentering" role of retrieval in exposing the assumptions of modernity, "the Christian past . . . precisely because it is foreign to contemporary conventions, can function as an instrument for the enlargement of vision. Classical sources outweigh modern norms."[8]

If our previous metaphors have been going to school and traveling to another country, our metaphor for this benefit of retrieval is going to see a counselor to get an outside perspective on one's family history. Just as a counselor gives you a self-perspective you might not otherwise have, so contact with the broader Christian tradition can be an illumining influence that exposes modern eccentricities of different kinds. Both a nineteenth-century liberal and a twentieth-century fundamentalist would find their theological method seriously challenged if they could travel back in a time machine to, say, the ninth century.

The goal of most counselors, however, is not simply to provide perspective but generally to facilitate healing and reconciliation of some sort. Chapter 6 of this book provides a more ambitious example of

---

8. John Webster, "Theologies of Retrieval," in *The Oxford Handbook to Systematic Theology*, ed. John Webster, Kathryn Tanner, and Iain Torrance (Oxford, UK: Oxford University Press, 2008), 590.

this "therapeutic" benefit of retrieval: previous doctrine is being applied to current theological disagreements specifically for the purpose of reconciling two estranged parties. This chapter opens by observing that contemporary atonement theology tends to be organized around either a renunciation or reaffirmation of a so-called objective model of the atonement, particularly those involving the notion of penal substitution. It seeks to bring about rapprochement between *recapitulation* models of atonement (traditionally ascribed to Irenaeus and Athanasius) and *satisfaction* models (traditionally ascribed to Anselm) by emphasizing points of convergence between them in their historical articulations. The chapter then draws implications for contemporary discussion regarding the atonement, particularly in relation to the importance of parsing out the varying soteriological contributions of Christ's birth, life, death, resurrection, ascension, and second coming.

Perils of Retrieval

But, of course, retrieval can go wrong. Having seen some of the ways retrieval might be beneficial, it may also be useful to briefly articulate several dangers here, though this list is by no means exhaustive, and these comments are not intended to resolve these challenges so much as flag them for attention.

In the first place, we must be wary of the danger of *distortion*, in which we move too quickly to the present issue without sufficiently "doing our homework," such that the historical resource being retrieved is somewhat caricatured or misconstrued. To the extent that our retrieval of the past is motivated to confirm a present opinion or advance a polemical purpose, we may be especially in the way of this danger. Theological retrieval is not a piecemeal ransacking and deploying of whatever quotes or concepts from church history we happen to find useful. Rather, at its best it will involve a deep respect for the original context and concerns of the resources being retrieved, a sensitivity to how easily they can be warped by too quick an application, and a judicious employment of all the rigors of historical scholarship in engaging them.

A second danger is *artificiality*, in which past resources are pressed into the service of present needs in a way that is forced or inauthentic.

If systematic theologians are more likely to fall into the previous error, this one may be especially tempting to historians. Thoughtful retrieval should show restraint, even a kind of modesty, in working from the historical source to the constructive usage. There is, of course, no obvious set of guidelines for how the past best touches the present. But (as I have mentioned elsewhere) if we start getting books on how Basil of Caesarea's sacramentology can solve all of Greece's financial problems, or how Kierkegaard's notion of the self redefines our ecological situation, or how Zacharias Ursinus's doctrine of predestination is the answer to urban overcrowding, then we may be justified to suspect that the procedure has outpaced the purpose.[9]

This danger is all the more lively because retrieval seems to be becoming, in some circles, something of a fad in theology. We must always check and reorient our motives toward substance and truth, away from style and trend. Douglas Sweeney is right to lament, "It is sad that evangelicals often look to the tradition only because its smells and bells render our services more chic and intensify our spiritual subjectivism."[10]

A third danger is *repristination*, in which retrieval becomes merely an exercise in restating the past, under the impression that classical sources represent some kind of grand, immovable, final verdict on all matters they address. Among other problems, this kind of retrieval tends to leapfrog over the problems associated with modernity, as though premodernity offered us a way out of these challenges simply by preexisting them. In relation to this concern, Buschart and Eilers wisely warn against the dangers of retrieval resulting in mere retrenchment.[11] As they note, such postures of retrieval "fail to appreciate the holy strangeness of the past and thereby the opportunity to be constructively decentered by it."[12] If in our efforts at retrieval we never or rarely find ourselves in disagreement with the resources

---

9. I have articulated this concern previously in connection to my review of Buschart and Eilers, *Theology as Retrieval*, at The Gospel Coalition, July 21, 2015, https://www.thegospelcoalition.org /reviews/theology-as-retrieval-receiving-the-past-renewing-the-church.

10. Douglas A. Sweeney, "Mercursburg Theology as a Double-Edged Sword: A Response to Darryl G. Hart," in *Evangelicals and the Early Church: Recovery, Reform, Renewal*, ed. George Kalantzis and Andrew Tooley (Eugene, OR: Cascade, 2012), 107.

11. David Buschart and Kent Eilers, *Theology as Retrieval: Receiving the Past, Renewing the Church* (Downers Grove, IL: IVP Academic, 2015), 272.

12. Buschart and Eilers, *Theology as Retrieval*, 270.

we engage, we must be especially on the alert as to whether we have fallen into this danger.

A final danger is *minimalism*, in which all the difficult or cacophonous elements of the past resources are flattened out in the search for a common denominator of unity. This danger is particularly lively when we approach the past with an ecumenical concern (itself, of course, a laudable goal). We must remember that cause of genuine unity is better served by respectfully engaging our differences within the body of Christ than by ignoring or suppressing them. In this regard, theological retrieval would do well to bear in mind the powerful observation of Father Richard John Neuhaus, itself made in the context of ecumenical effort, that "our unity in the truth is more evident in our quarreling about the truth than in our settling for something less than the truth."[13]

These dangers must be taken to heart. However, none of them, so far as I can see, are intrinsic to retrieval. They urge caution in the task but not its avoidance.

Some evangelicals worry that if we display too much interest in theologians such as Thomas Aquinas, we will end up becoming Roman Catholic. I do not take this to be a real danger of retrieval. To be sure, an interest in church history does often coincide with a movement toward Rome or the East, as we noted in chapter 2. Many of the stories in the recent book *Evangelical Exodus* make for fascinating case studies in evangelical retrieval of medieval theology, since a fascination with Thomas Aquinas preceded many of the conversions to Catholicism recounted in the book. This was a somewhat exceptional situation, however, insofar as Thomas appears to have been singled out as the *primary* theologian who shaped the school's ethos and method. One of the book's contributors claims that "for all intents and purposes, Saint Thomas Aquinas was [Southern Evangelical Seminary's] 'patron saint,' though no one would ever dare frame it in such terms."[14] Norman Geisler, who cofounded the institution, recognized

13. Quoted in James S. Cutsinger, "Introduction," in *Reclaiming the Great Tradition: Evangelicals, Catholics, and Orthodox in Dialogue*, ed. James S. Cutsinger (Downers Grove, IL: InterVarsity Press, 1997), 8.

14. Joshua Betancourt, "Rome: The True Church and Refuge for Sinners," in *Evangelical Exodus: Evangelical Seminarians and Their Paths to Rome*, ed. Douglas M. Beaumont (San Francisco: Ignatius, 2016), 53.

Thomas's notorious reputation among evangelicals but nonetheless claimed, "As for myself, I gladly confess that the highest compliment that could be paid to me as a Christian philosopher, apologist, and theologian is to call me 'Thomistic.'"[15] Protestant retrieval need not and generally will not assign so powerfully authoritative a role to any single theologian or tradition being retrieved.

But more basically, I would suggest that denominational changes usually involve a wide variety of factors and that retrieval in and of itself generally reveals, rather than causes, a vulnerability of denominational identity. In fact, I would wager that it is precisely the cultivation of a more catholic and historically rooted evangelical identity that will equip us to interact with our Roman Catholic (and Eastern) friends more preparedly, more respectfully, and more capably. At any rate, what is the alternative to retrieving the past? Ignoring it? If that is so, must we also avoid the study of Luther, lest we become Lutherans, or Marx, lest we become socialists, or Gandhi, lest we become pacifists?

Exploring Neglected Figures

Throughout this book we will emphasize that those neglected periods of church history can be of special help in theological retrieval, and so here we can introduce three early medieval figures, in particular, whom we will engage more thoroughly in the later parts of the book. These three figures stand out not only because modern Protestants tend to neglect them but also because they were hugely influential in previous generations of the church. In other words, we are eccentric within the church catholic for *not* retrieving them.

The first example is Boethius, whom we will engage especially in chapters 4 and 5. Boethius's *The Consolation of Philosophy*, written in the early sixth century as he was in prison awaiting execution, became arguably the single most translated and most influential text outside the Bible throughout the medieval and into the modern era, such that in the twentieth century C. S. Lewis could declare, "Until about two hundred years ago it would, I think, have been hard to find an educated man in any European country who did not

---

15. Norman Geisler, *Thomas Aquinas: A Critical Appraisal* (Grand Rapids, MI: Baker, 1991), 14.

love it."[16] And yet today Boethius is often regarded as an unoriginal thinker, a conduit from the classical to the medieval world, a transmitter of Aristotelian logic and the music and arithmetic of antiquity who had little of his own to say. It is Boethius the translator, Boethius the commentator—not Boethius the thinker.[17] Moreover, where Boethius's own thought is engaged, the prominence of *The Consolation of Philosophy* in relation to his other writings has tended to generate interest in the literary and philosophical aspects of his thought at the expense of the theological.[18]

In earlier generations, Boethius's reputation and influence was not so limited. It was *The Consolation of Philosophy*, together with his broader work of translation and commentary on Aristotle, that made him "second only to the Bible in popularity" throughout the medieval era, so that C. S. Lewis could write, "To acquire a taste for it is almost to become naturalised in the Middle Ages."[19] Nonetheless, Boethius's own theology also had a huge influence in the medieval era. Many of the themes of the *Opuscula Sacra*, for instance, are picked up in Alcuin, Erigena, Anselm, and Aquinas; in the twelfth century, John of Salisbury would distinguish Boethius as "profound in doctrine."[20] Moreover, in their own day, as John Marenbon has pointed out, the *Opuscula Sacra* were distinctly innovative in their approach to

---

16. C. S. Lewis, *The Discarded Image: An Introduction to Medieval and Renaissance Literature* (Cambridge, UK: Cambridge University Press, 1964), 75. Boethius's work was translated by figures as diverse as King Alfred in the ninth century (into Old English), Geoffrey Chaucer in the fourteenth century (into Middle English), and Queen Elizabeth I in the sixteenth century (into Early Modern English). For further discussion of Boethius's influence, see Margaret Gibson, ed., *Boethius: His Life, Thought, and Influence* (Oxford, UK: Basil Blackwell, 1981).

17. In an extreme case, James Shiel went so far as to claim that Boethius in his logical commentaries has done nothing other than translate an existing body of material into Latin. See the discussion in John Marenbon, "Introduction: Reading Boethius Whole," in *The Cambridge Companion to Boethius*, ed. John Marenbon (Cambridge, UK: Cambridge University Press, 2009), 3.

18. Some have even posited that Boethius abandoned his Christian faith at the end of his life, since *The Consolation* (written during his imprisonment while awaiting execution) contains little explicitly Christian content. But for Boethius, Lady Philosophy functions as a handmaiden for Boethius's faith in God, not an alternative to it. In fact, at several points in the book she explicitly acknowledges her limitations and directs Boethius to God (e.g., 139). Her presence indicates not the absence of God but the presence of such a high view of God that he cannot be dialogued with directly, in the way Boethius wants to do. As C. S. Lewis, *Discarded Image*, 77–78, put it, "If we had asked Boethius why his book contained philosophical rather than religious consolations, I do not doubt that he would have answered, 'But did you not read my title?'"

19. Lewis, *Discarded Image*, 75. Lewis also wrote, "Until about two hundred years ago it would, I think, have been hard to find an educated man in any European country who did not love it" (75).

20. For further discussion of Boethius's theological influence, see Edmund Reiss, *Boethius*, Twayne's World Authors Series (Boston, MA: Twayne, 1982), 160–61.

theology;[21] and *The Consolation of Philosophy* offered an original treatment of the problem of divine foreknowledge and human free will that would define the Western church's treatment of this problem for centuries.[22]

Boethius may be a particularly helpful figure for modern Protestants to engage in sharpening their doctrine of God, particularly with a view to the nature of the Creator/creation distinction, divine simplicity, divine foreknowledge, and the relation of eternity and time. Boethius also affirms a doctrine of human happiness that may counterbalance the more austere outlook that often characterizes the Puritan strand of the Protestant tradition.[23] Furthermore, because of its profoundly formative role upon the medieval church, *The Consolation* may function for modern Protestants as a helpful introduction to that whole era. As Lewis put it, "To acquire a taste for [*The Consolation*] is almost to become naturalised in the Middle Ages."[24]

A second example is Gregory the Great, whose *Book of Pastoral Rule* is our subject of interest in chapter 7. An important pope at the turn of the seventh century, Gregory was a capable administrator whose reforms and initiatives marked the church for centuries. But Gregory regarded himself as primarily a religious leader, and his greatest influence was arguably upon the church's liturgy, monastic organization, and theology. Like Boethius, his influence was particularly felt by the medieval church, and he was respected by the Reformers as well.[25] Chris Armstrong claims no Western father was read more by the medieval church, suggesting that "if Augustine of

---

21. John Marenbon, *Boethius*, Great Medieval Thinkers (Oxford, UK: Oxford University Press, 2003), 4–6; Marenbon, "Introduction," in *Cambridge Companion to Boethius*, 1–2.

22. Marenbon, *Boethius*, 128, 130, 143, explores various influences on Boethius's argument and concludes that while he certainly drew from various elements of Greek philosophical thought as early as Parmenides, he combines them in a way that is original to himself. Robert Sharples, "Fate, Prescience, and Free Will," in *Cambridge Companion to Boethius*, 207, argues that Boethius's treatment of this issue is "the most persuasive attempt in Greco-Roman antiquity to solve the problem, and the basis for subsequent medieval discussion."

23. On this point, cf. Chris R. Armstrong, *Medieval Wisdom for Modern Christians: Finding Authentic Faith in a Forgotten Age with C. S. Lewis* (Grand Rapids, MI: Brazos, 2016), 168–69.

24. Lewis, *Discarded Image*, 75.

25. Gregory is recognized as a saint by the Anglican church and many Lutheran churches, and as we noted in chapter 2, Calvin regarded him as a "holy man." In the *Institutes* he notes with appreciation on several occasions Gregory's opposition to any bishop claiming "universal" jurisdiction. E.g., John Calvin, *Institutes of the Christian Religion*, ed. John T. McNeill, trans. Ford Lewis Battles (Louisville, KY: Westminster John Knox, 2006), 4.7.22. It is frequently claimed that Calvin called Gregory the "last good pope," but I have not been able to find any proper documentation

Hippo was the father of medieval theology, then Gregory was the father of medieval spirituality."[26] But Gregory was also a profound theologian who himself appropriated and extended much of Augustine's thought.[27] Mark Noll describes his *Book of Pastoral Rule* as "for nearly a thousand years . . . the Western church's principal guide to pastoral counseling."[28] Moreover, in Gregory's capacity as papal representative to the Byzantine emperor, he lived in a Latin district of Constantinople for almost seven years, and thus his theology was uniquely shaped by, and interactive with, the theology of the Eastern church. As George Demacopoulos notes, after reading *The Book of Pastoral Rule*, the Byzantine Emperor Maurice ordered that the book be translated and disseminated to every bishop in his empire.[29] Gregory is the only Latin father whose works were translated into Greek within his own lifetime.

The *Book of Pastoral Rule* argues that pastoral ministry requires a delicate balance of inner and outer qualities—theory and practice, contemplation and activity, holy detachment from the affairs of the world and practical skill at engaging those affairs. This dual focus reflected Gregory's own life, in which he had been drawn into various administrative and leadership roles despite his constant desire for the contemplative life. As a result, Gregory's *Rule* has a particularly practical thrust. Comparable works of pastoral theology in the Protestant tradition tend to focus on qualifications for pastoral ministry and godliness in ministry (one thinks of Baxter's *The Reformed Pastor*, for instance, or Spurgeon's *Lectures To My Students*). While these are emphases of Gregory's also (parts 1 and 2 of his book, respectively), the greater portion of Gregory's text is on pastoral *skill* and practice;

of where this occurs; it is generally cited without page number from book 4 of the *Institutes*, ed. F. L. Cross (New York: Oxford University Press, n.d.).

26. Armstrong, *Medieval Wisdom for Modern Christians*, 146.

27. Gregory is sometimes seen as most basically a transmitter (like Boethius), but his utilization of Augustine's theology did not exclude his own innovations. For a brief overview of some areas in which Gregory left his own stamp on the Augustinian legacy that would shape medieval theology and spirituality, see Justo A. González, *The Story of Christianity*, vol. 1: *The Early Church to the Dawn of the Reformation*, 2 vols. (San Francisco: HarperSanFrancisco, 1984), 246–48.

28. Mark A. Noll, *Turning Points: Decisive Moments in the History of Christianity*, 2nd ed. (Grand Rapids, MI: Baker Academic, 2000), 115.

29. George E. Demacopoulos, "Introduction," in St. Gregory the Great, *The Book of Pastoral Rule*, Popular Patristics 34 (Crestwood, NY: St. Vladimir's Seminary, 2007), 10. As Demacopoulos notes, this rubs against the common notion that Gregory is fundamentally a transmitter of Augustine.

its treatment of how a pastor should teach different kinds of people differently in part 3, the lengthiest section of the book, is particularly full of wisdom, and Protestants may find this book supplementing the emphases of their typical literature on pastoral theology, particularly as it is generally neglected among modern Protestants.

A final example is John of Damascus's various writings on the iconoclast controversy. Living in the East in the eighth century, John follows and sums up early Eastern theology, especially that of the Cappadocian fathers, such that Andrew Louth calls him the "pre-eminent representative of the Byzantine theological tradition."[30] Yet Louth notes that "there has been little attempt to reflect on the theology of the Damascene,"[31] and that he has "generally been dismissed, either explicitly or implicitly, as an unoriginal thinker, a mere compiler of florilegia."[32] In particular, John's thought has often been isolated from the Western theological tradition. Apart from a few references in florilegia, he was basically unknown in the West until his *Exact Exposition of the Orthodox Faith* was translated into Latin in the twelfth century, which was then heavily utilized by Peter Lombard and Thomas Aquinas. Its subsequent influence was significant, such that Peter Toon characterizes it as "important in the creation of Western medieval theology."[33] Nonetheless, John's broader writings on the iconoclast controversy, arguably his greatest theological legacy, continued to be unknown, and later Protestant iconoclasm (particularly in the tradition following Calvin's vigorous denunciation of icons) further distanced John from Protestant consciousness.

Retrieving John's theology thus brings modern Protestants into contact with a whole stream of Christianity that is all too often completely lost to us. The sheer size and diversity of this slice of Christendom begs for retrieval, and John's writings on the iconoclast controversy are perhaps the most sensible entry point into it, since it was this dispute that dominated the Eastern church in the eighth and first half of the ninth centuries. John's defense of the use of icons against the charge

---

30. Andrew Louth, *St John Damascene: Tradition and Originality in Byzantine Theology* (Oxford, UK: Oxford University Press, 2002), 16.
31. Louth, *St John Damascene*, vii.
32. Louth, *St John Damascene*, viii.
33. Peter Toon, "John of Damascus," in *The New International Dictionary of the Christian Church*, ed. J. D. Douglas (Grand Rapids, MI: Zondervan, 1974), 542.

of idolatry was grounded above all in the doctrine of the incarnation, emphasizing that Christ's flesh was not a mere garment but was truly united to incorruptible divinity even while it retained its fleshly status.[34] Moreover, John maintained that all human thought about the divine is inherently pictorial. As a result, rejecting the use of images did not simply threaten one particular devotional practice but confused the whole task of theology.[35]

As a result of this controversy, the Eastern church was compelled to develop a rich theology of art and a high view of the material world, grounded in theological reflection about the nature of the incarnation. For evangelicals, who often have a very shallow view of the arts, and who tend to pit the spiritual and the physical against each other, John's writings may prompt deeper reflection on what our status as embodied creatures entails for the nature of theology. We engage John's insights throughout the following chapters, particularly chapter 5, although his writings on the iconoclast controversy await further, more comprehensive treatment.

Navigating the Hugeness of History as an Evangelical Protestant

This reference to John of Damascus raises one final consideration that may help us feel something of the excitement of retrieval: the sheer immensity of church history. It is this quality of history that, in part, explains why retrieval is so useful for helping us to move forward past the barrenness that characterizes so much of the intellectual world of late modernity. There are few better ways to melt away cynicism than getting lost in a deep story (how many of us have experienced this with reading *The Lord of the Rings* or a Dostoevsky book?).

And church history is an incredibly deep, complex, and fascinating story. Our labels for the periods of church history particularly in view in this book—patristic and medieval—give the impression of two distinct, recognizable periods of time. A geographical metaphor may help us appreciate the hugeness of what actually lies underneath these labels.

---

34. E.g., John of Damascus, *Three Treatises on the Divine Images*, trans. Andrew Louth, Popular Patristics 24 (Crestwood, NY: St. Vladimir's Seminary, 2003), 22: "I venerate together with the King and God the purple robe of his body, not as a garment, nor as a fourth person (God forbid!), but as called to be and to have become unchangeably equal to God."

35. Cf. Andrew Louth, *Greek East and Latin West: The Church AD 681–1071*, The Church in History 3 (Crestwood, NY: St. Vladimir's Seminary, 2007), 51–54.

Before moving to Washington, DC, I thought of it vaguely as a city in the Northeast. Having spent most of my life in the South and Midwest, it was in my mind loosely associated with Boston, New York, Philadelphia, and Baltimore, as one of those northern cities in which people are a bit more direct and the culture a bit more progressive. Then, after I moved to Washington, DC, I realized that I had lumped together a number of things that are really quite distinct. Washington, DC, is actually a part of the Mid-Atlantic region, which is quite distinct from the New England region farther north. In addition, Washington, DC, is quite culturally distinct from the surrounding areas in the Mid-Atlantic region, and within DC, one neighborhood differs widely from another. What looks from a distance as a unity turns out, when you get closer, to be as complex and diverse as can be imagined.

A similar thing happened when we subsequently moved from Washington, DC, to Southern California. I remember being excited to explore the west. Somehow, having lived on the eastern half of the United States for most of my life, everything beyond Oklahoma and Nebraska got lumped together in my mind as one united region. But, of course, as soon as you start actually driving around Wyoming or New Mexico or Oregon, you realize how different each part of the western US is from all the others. Even within the state of California, you can find cold and hot, conservative and liberal, skyscraper and desert, palm tree and redwood forest, Disneyland and Yosemite.

This has been my increasing discovery with respect to patristic and medieval church history. These labels—"medieval" and "patristic"— are as vague and superficial as "northeast" or "west." As soon as you dig into the material, you realize that the Northumbrian renaissance is as different from the Carolingian renaissance as Wisconsin is different from Arizona, and post-Charlesmagne European Christianity is as different from pre-Charlesmagne European Christianity as Boston is from New York.

Take the Eastern Orthodox church(es), for example. We tend to think of early Eastern Christianity as uniformly Greek in contrast to the Latin West. But upon closer examination we find in the East a conglomeration of Greek, Syriac, Coptic, Ethiopic, Georgian, and

Armenian churches as well an emerging Arab Christianity existing under the domination of Islam and various Slavic churches starting in the ninth century.[36] Amidst this diversity, the sheer size of this sector of Christendom is overwhelming. During the High Middle Ages, Constantinople (formerly Byzantium, now Istanbul), the seat of the Byzantine Empire, was the greatest city in Europe. Within her history lies a whole world of emperors and intrigue, of theological decisions and disputes, of political dynasties and military disasters, of missions efforts to India and China, of advance, retreat, death, recovery, and death again. This empire stood for more than a millennium, twice the time that such a thing called "Protestantism" has existed.

We contemporary Protestants are doubly disconnected from this world. We are a branch on a branch—an offshoot of Western, Roman Christianity, which itself had already long drifted away from her Eastern sister. To step into the writings of Maximus the Confessor or Didymus the Blind or Photius I is therefore, to my mind, as rich and exciting an adventure as exploring a once important but long forgotten world. By analogy, suppose that archeologists discovered that Atlantis had really existed. Imagine the flood of energy and initiative that would be devoted to researching and studying this lost civilization—the *excitement* in the discovery of a lost world. This is how I feel about retrieval. There is a whole world back there, waiting to be explored—a world that helps us understand our own story and purpose as the people of God.

Much of church history will doubtless feel quite foreign—like Seattle feels when you've lived in Alabama all your life. And, of course, there will be much to reject as unhelpful or unbiblical (since, after all, we are engaging church history as *Protestants*). And yet amidst all the strangeness and at times corruption, I believe that Christ can be found throughout church history, including Eastern and medieval church history. It is difficult to accept that his promise—"I will build my church, and the gates of hell shall not prevail against it" (Matt. 16:18)—was suspended from the sixth to the sixteenth century, as though the church sank into the mud during the eras of castles and

---

36. For a helpful introduction to Eastern Christianity during its development away from the Western church, see Louth, *Greek East and Latin West*.

cathedrals, monks and monasteries, only then to suddenly reemerge with Luther's ninety-five theses. No, I believe that there is a steady stream of Christianity subsisting from the missionary labors of Boniface in the eighth century to the spiritual theology of Bonaventure in the thirteenth, from the pioneering efforts of Patrick in Ireland to the theological discussions in the Carolingian court. Through many advances and retreats, corruptions and renewals, Jesus has not broken off from advancing his mission. "He will not grow faint or be discouraged till he has established justice in the earth; and the coastlands wait for his law" (Isa. 42:4).

Now, to be sure, it is possible to so emphasize "mere Christianity" (what C. S. Lewis calls "a standard of plain, central Christianity"[37]) that we lose our Protestant distinctives. But it is also possible so to bask in our particular denominational enclave that we lose touch with the entire Christian tradition. We contemporary Protestants need a *balanced* historical identity. We should engage both the last five hundred years and the previous fifteen hundred, discerning areas of discontinuity as well as appreciating points of overlap, being careful not to give the impression that the former is our *real* tradition. A good image is a family photo album. In any such album there may be pictures that embarrass us, and we may be more proud to be related to one great uncle than to another. But warts, blemishes, and all, our family is still *our family*—and it would be foolish to cut ourselves off. After all, we wouldn't even be here without them.

In fact, the great exciting thing is, amidst the grand diversity in church history, to seek out a unity. To return to the geographical metaphor, there is something that unites Mount Rushmore, the Mississippi River, and the Mojave Desert. For all their diversity, they are all part of the same country. They are within the same national borders, they share a common language and culture and history, and they are overseen by the same federal government. Likewise, there is an underlying current that, for all its diversity, unites Bernard and Barth, Tertullian and Tolkien, Polycarp and Pentecostalism.

C. S. Lewis spoke eloquently of the irreducible core of Christianity throughout the ages when describing his own conversion:

---

37. Lewis, "Introduction," in Athanasius, *On the Incarnation*, 4.

Measured against the ages "mere Christianity" turns out to be no insipid interdenominational transparency, but something positive, self-consistent, and inexhaustible. I know it, indeed, to my cost. In the days when I still hated Christianity, I learned to recognize, like some all too familiar smell, that almost unvarying *something* which met me, now in Puritan Bunyan, now in Anglican Hooker, now in Thomist Dante. It was there (honeyed and floral) in Francois de Sales; it was there (grave and homely) in Spencer and Walton; it was there (grim and manful) in Pascal and Johnson; there again, with a mild, frightening, Paradisial flavor, in Vaughn and Bohme and Traherne. . . . It was, of course, varied; and yet—after all—so unmistakably the same.[38]

As evangelical Protestants we must read early and medieval church history with our convictions about, say, the doctrine of salvation by grace firmly intact. We should engage in retrieval critically, with Scripture as our supreme authority at every moment. And yet, simultaneously, we may read the entirety of church history with a sense of personal identity—this is *our* story. The remark of an early African Christian captures this instinct well: "I am a Christian, and nothing which concerns Christianity do I consider foreign to myself." So can we evangelicals say, as we wade into the vast annals of our past.

---

38. Lewis, "Introduction," in Athanasius, *On the Incarnation*, 6.

PART 2

CASE STUDIES IN
THEOLOGICAL RETRIEVAL

✝ ✝ ✝

Books about method are dangerous. You start talking about *how* to do something, and before you know it, you have lost your interest in actually doing it. The *talking about* gets rather abstract and tiresome. It diminishes what you loved in the first place.

I have always felt sympathetic, for this reason, to Karl Barth's prioritization of exegesis over hermeneutics (though of course there are dangers in pushing this prioritization too far).[1] In a similar way, I have always felt that the best shorthand way to commend theological retrieval is simply to do it. The process explains the procedure.

In the remainder of this book, therefore, we conduct a series of case studies in theological retrieval, focusing on some of the topics and figures we have already drawn attention to, in particular, the doctrines of God (chapters 4 and 5) and atonement (chapter 6), and Gregory the Great's *Book of Pastoral* Rule (chapter 7). We have selected the doctrines of God and atonement because they appear to be

---

1. On this point, see Richard E. Burnett, *Karl Barth's Theological Exegesis: The Hermeneutical Principles of the Römerbrief Period* (Grand Rapids, MI: Eerdmans, 2004), 14–23.

two particularly ripe areas for retrieval, since they are simultaneously well served by premodern theology and often neglected and/or beset among evangelicals. The overriding conviction that drives chapters 4 and 5 is that many of our current eccentricities within the doctrine of God stem from a diminished emphasis on God's ontological uniqueness and that premodern theology may help us cultivate instincts to correct this deficiency. In this vein, chapter 4 offers a constructive metaphor in relation to the Creator/creation distinction; chapter 5 offers a defense of divine simplicity from various current critiques. What is decisive in both cases is a renewed emphasis, in line with classical ways of approaching theology, on God's sheer otherness. Chapter 6 addresses the polarized state of contemporary evangelical treatment of the atonement, exploring how the retrieval of three classical accounts of Christ's atoning work may open up new pathways forward. Chapter 7 then makes a more specific effort with respect to Gregory the Great's *Book of Pastoral Rule*, which we suggest is a prime example of a text in need of retrieval among evangelicals.

Obviously this is a very limited sampling. But recall Lytton Strachey's strategy of effective historical narration, which we referenced in the preface:

> It is not by the direct method of a scrupulous narration that the explorer of the past can hope to depict that singular epoch. If he is wise . . . he will row out over that great ocean of material, and lower down into it, here and there, a little bucket, which will bring up to the light of day some characteristic specimen, from those far depths, to be examined with a careful curiosity.[2]

In this spirit, think of what follows as tiny specimens from a vast ocean, the value of which lies not so much in themselves but in encouraging others to explore the waters.

---

2. Lytton Strachey, *Eminent Victorians*, as quoted in Joseph J. Ellis, *Founding Brothers: The Revolutionary Generation* (New York: Vintage, 2000), *ix*.

4

Explorations in a
Theological Metaphor

Boethius, Calvin, and Torrance on
the Creator/Creation Distinction

The Incarnation of God is an infinitely greater thing than anything I would dare to write.
—J. R. R. Tolkien, letter to Michael Straight, early 1956

✝

Albert Einstein famously relied on "thought experiments" to seek intellectual breakthrough.[1] Guided by an instinctive sense that the structure of reality must be harmonious, beautiful, and (above all) simple,
he stipulated, "When I am judging a theory, I ask myself whether, if
I were God, I would have arranged the world in such a way."[2] He
compared his motivation for science to that of a poet: "It's a sudden

1. Walter Isaacson, *Einstein: His Life and Universe* (New York: Simon & Schuster, 2007),
esp. 548–51.
2. Isaacson, *Einstein*, 551.

illumination, almost a rapture. Later, to be sure, intelligence analyzes and experiments confirm or invalidate the intuition. But initially there is a great leap forward in the imagination."[3] His strong emphasis on the role of imagination also led him to speak of himself as an artist: "I'm enough of an artist to draw freely on my imagination. Imagination is more important than knowledge. Knowledge is limited. Imagination encircles the world."[4]

If imagination can have such a role in theoretical physics, what use might it serve in theology? This chapter is animated by this curiosity. It attempts its own "thought experiment," comparing God and creation to an author and story in order to explore the nature of the Creator/creation distinction. An author/story metaphor for God/creation has been a topic of exploration in recent theological discourse, though typically it has been approached from a constructive/systematic angle.[5] This chapter approaches this metaphor from a historical route, in an effort at theological retrieval, bringing it into dialogue with three doctrines from church history: Boethius's doctrine of divine foreknowledge, the so-called *extra Calvinisticum*, and Thomas Torrance's account of Christ's ascension. We have chosen these three theologians partly for their diverse representation from church history and partly for the relative neglect of their respective doctrines (discussed below), but mainly because the complexity of the Creator/creation relationship is particularly visible in them. In other words, there is a common

---

3. Isaacson, *Einstein*, 549.

4. Isaacson, *Einstein*, 387.

5. Frederick Christian Bauerschmidt, "God as Author: Thinking through a Metaphor," *Modern Theology* 31 (October 2015): 573–85, acknowledges some difficulties inherent in the metaphor but draws attention to its power to emphasize God's role in bestowing meaning on the world. He notes the relative dearth of the use of this metaphor throughout the Christian tradition, suggesting that this is due to the relatively recent emphasis on authorly creativity and the development of realistic narratives (he thinks of "story" in terms of the genre "novel" and later suggests "magical realism" as a potential subgenre). A classic engagement with this metaphor was offered by Dorothy L. Sayers, *The Mind of the Maker* (San Francisco: Harper & Row, 1941), who used it to explore a range of Christian doctrines, including the Trinity, free will, and the image of God. For Sayers, the doctrine of creation ex nihilo is best understood as an act of divine imagination, and thus "this experience of the creative imagination in the common man or woman and in the artist is the only thing we have to go upon in entertaining and formulating the concept of creation" (29–30). The story metaphor also impinges on some species of "narrative theology"; cf., e.g., Robert W. Jenson's narratival approach to the identification of God, *Systematic Theology, vol. 1: The Triune God* (Oxford, UK: Oxford University Press, 1997), 42–60. Francesca Aran Murphy, *God Is Not a Story: Realism Revisited* (Oxford, UK: Oxford University Press, 2007), offers a critical analysis of Jenson's narrative theology, as well as narrative theologies associated with the "Yale school" (George Lindbeck, Hans Frei, Stanley Hauerwas, etc.), drawing upon the theology of Hans Urs von Balthasar as well as modern film theory for an alternative constructive proposal.

thread among Boethius's account of created time as an imitation of eternity, Calvin's affirmation of the incarnate Christ's existence *extra carnem* (beyond the flesh), and Torrance's emphasis on the ascension as a bodily, space-time event; namely, all require an infinite distance, as well as a dynamic involvement, between Creator and creation.

To try to capture something of this curious blend of immense distance and intimate proximity, we will imagine God and creation in terms of a specific author and book, J. R. R. Tolkien and *The Lord of the Rings*.[6] Thus, with respect to Boethius's view of foreknowledge, we will imagine Tolkien flipping ahead in the book to read of Sauron's defeat; with respect to the *extra Calvinisticum*, we will imagine Tolkien writing himself into Middle-earth as a character; with respect to Torrance's doctrine of Christ's ascension, we will imagine Tolkien transporting the space-time of Middle-earth back with him to Oxford. The story metaphor, like all metaphors, has limitations and ultimately breaks down when we get to the ascension. But if we approach it as a heuristic device, a kind of Einsteinian thought experiment, it may nonetheless induce reflection about the Creator/creation relationship, particularly with respect to (1) God's ontological priority over creation, and (2) the determinative significance of Christ's incarnation and ascension for anchoring their relationship.

If imagination has intellectual capabilities that knowledge lacks, as Einstein intimated, then perhaps there are arenas within theology that can be accessed only by the imagination—like mountain peaks that

---

6. J. R. R. Tolkien, *The Lord of the Rings* (1954–1975; repr. New York: Houghton Mifflin, 2004). Novels that involve the author writing himself into the story (as possibly occurs in the Peter Wimsey novels) might seem a more natural choice, given their anticipation of my comments with respect to the incarnation. But Tolkien will prove the better choice, partly because his story is better known; partly because the distinction between Middle-earth and earth is thicker and thus more useful than that involved in other stories; and partly because Tolkien's own rich doctrine of subcreation will impinge upon my account. Within Tolkienology, *subcreation* is a technical term that interprets human storytelling and myth building in light of God's original work of creation. It attaches metaphysical significance to the ability of rational beings for intellectual exploration and invention, especially within the realm of fiction, seeing this tendency as mirroring something of the original ex nihilo act. In his famous poem "Mythopoeia," Tolkien places "man" and "subcreator" in apposition, and the human ability for subcreation appears to be his chief indication that humanity, though fallen, retains the lordship of the *imago Dei*. The poem concludes by correlating God's creative work with human art, especially in the realm of fantasy (elves, goblins, etc.): "Though all the crannies of the world we filled / with elves and goblins, though we dared to build / gods and their houses out of dark and light, / and sow the seed of dragons, 'twas our right / (used or misused). The right has not decayed. / We make still by the law in which we're made." For Sayers as well, the most fundamental characteristic common to both God and humanity, and thus the core of the *imago Dei*, is "the desire and the ability to make things." *The Mind of the Maker*, 22.

cannot be scaled by climbing but must be viewed from a height above the mountain (say, from a helicopter). The theologian, then, like the theoretical physicist, may occasionally think like a poet or an artist, following the imaginative instinct and asking questions like, "What if . . . ?" and "What would I do?"

Tolkien Reading Ahead: Boethius on Divine Foreknowledge

Boethius's account of divine foreknowledge in *The Consolation* is noteworthy not only for its originality and influence but for its honest, full-blooded tone.[7] While many treatments of human freedom and divine foreknowledge/sovereignty have a somewhat speculative feel, for Boethius his entire consolation in the face of death and ruin hangs upon this question. It arises in Book 5 as the climax of his dialogue with Lady Philosophy regarding suffering, fortune, divine justice, and happiness. Unjustly imprisoned and awaiting execution, Boethius reasons his way to the conclusion that an understanding of God's government of the world is the key to happiness in any situation. Having found refuge in the consideration of divine providence, however, Boethius is then drawn into a subsequent dilemma: if God's providence entails his foreknowledge of all things, how can human actions be free?[8]

Boethius's solution to this dilemma proceeds in three steps, each dealing with a key term involved in the problem: knowledge, eternity, and necessity.[9] First, drawing from a principle from the Neo-Platonist philosopher Iamblichus, Boethius stipulates that knowledge is determined not merely by its object but by its subject: "Everything that is known is comprehended, not according to its own power, but rather according to the ability of the one knowing."[10] Unlike both animal

---

7. The alternating poetry and prose of *The Consolation*, drawing from earlier Menippean satire, contributes to the work's emotional complexity and urgency. On the genre of *The Consolation*, see Edmund Reiss, *Boethius*, Twayne's World Authors Series (Boston, MA: Twayne, 1982), 143–47.

8. Boethius, *De Consolatione Philosophiae* 5.1–3. All translations of Boethius are my own, from the critical edition of Claudio Moreschini, *De Consolatione Philosophiae, Opuscula Theologica*, Bibliotheca Teubneriana (Munich: K. G. Saur, 2000).

9. For a rigorous analysis of the logical structure of Boethius's argument, see John Marenbon, *Boethius*, Great Medieval Thinkers (Oxford, UK: Oxford University Press, 2003), 125–45.

10. Boethius, *De Consolatione Philosophiae* 5.4.25. Evans calls this the "Iamblichus principle." See Robert Sharples, "Fate, Prescience, and Free Will," in *The Cambridge Companion to Boethius*, ed. John Marenbon (Cambridge, UK: Cambridge University Press, 2009), 216.

and human knowledge, Boethius argues, divine knowledge is simple, taking in its object all at once rather than piece by piece. God's knowledge therefore embraces even uncertain future events—not as human knowledge would but as "the heights of knowledge without boundaries enclosed in simplicity."[11] Boethius will continue to refer to God's knowledge as "simple" through the book; that is, not composed of parts, but seeing the whole all at once in its present life.[12]

Both this step of the argument and the third step—his distinction between simple and conditional necessity[13]—draw from insights Boethius has already arrived at in chapter 9 of his commentary on Aristotle's *On Interpretation*. That text, however, is concerned with future truth more than future knowledge, and there is no discussion of divine eternality.[14] It is this appeal to divine eternality, the second step of the argument, that is the crucial move, and it is here that the complexity of his construal of the Creator/creation relationship becomes most visible. On the one hand, Boethius emphasizes the infinite abyss between Creator and creation and our consequent ignorance of God.[15] In fact, the whole reason that divine foreknowledge and human freedom is a problem at all involves the distinction between our knowledge and God's: "The cause of the darkness is that the operation of human reasoning cannot be moved towards the simplicity of the divine foreknowledge."[16]

On the other hand, Boethius's account of the Creator/creation relationship is more lively and incalculable than might be expected. For Boethius, precisely because the difference between God and everything that is not God is a thick one, it cannot be stated in terms of absolute negations. Thus, in distinguishing between everlastingness (perpetual duration in time) and eternality (the state outside time altogether), Boethius defines eternality in fundamentally positive terms as God's "whole, simultaneous, and perfect possession of unending life"

---

11. Boethius, *De Consolatione Philosophiae* 5.5.12.
12. E.g., C 5.6.15, C 5.6.41.
13. Boethius, *De Consolatione Philosophiae* 5.6.27. Here Boethius posits that God's foreknowledge entails the future conditionally but not simply or absolutely—just as present events are not absolutely necessary by being observed but only conditionally necessary.
14. Robert Sharples, "Fate, Prescience, and Free Will," in *Cambridge Companion to Boethius*, 208–14.
15. E.g., Boethius, *De Consolatione Philosophiae* 5.m.3.
16. Boethius, *De Consolatione Philosophiae* 5.4.2.

(*interminabilis vitae tota simul et perfecta possessio*).[17] Most modern philosophers tend to construe eternality in opposition to time; for Boethius, and most of the classical tradition that precedes him, eternity is more bound up with God's perfection and life.[18]

Because it is a function of God's unbounded life, eternity for Boethius involves not the negation of time but God's mastery over time. Boethius writes:

> It is one thing to be led through unending life . . . and another thing for the whole of unending life to be equally embraced in the present, which is apparent to be a property of the divine mind. For God should not be seen as older than created things in quantity of time, but in the property of his simple nature.[19]

Here Boethius explains the distinction between eternality and everlastingness, not merely in terms of God being outside of time but in terms of God embracing all other times within his own time, within his own "eternal present." In other words, Boethius does not say, "It is one thing to be led through time and another thing to be outside of time." Thus God is not simply *older* than the created world, and his relation to time is not simply quantitatively superior to that of created temporal beings. Rather, God has a qualitatively different relationship to time, such that all past, present, and future events in the created world are equally present to him. One might say that for Boethius, God is not merely beyond or outside time, but over it; not merely before the world, but around it. Implicit in this approach is the assumption that God and the created world simply cannot be compared on the same scale of being; God's eternal immediacy and our experience of the present do not have a univocal relationship. In other words, God and creation are not like two paintings next to each other on a wall that can be compared on equal terms by a viewer; rather, if creation were a painting, God would be like the world in which that painting exists.

---

17. Boethius, *De Consolatione Philosophiae* 5.6.4.
18. Brian Leftow, *Time and Eternity* (Ithaca, NY: Cornell University Press, 1991), 112–82, provides an interesting interpretation of Boethius's view of eternity as "atemporal duration," engaging with the thesis of Eleonore Stump and Norman Kretzmann.
19. Boethius, *De Consolatione Philosophiae* 5.6.10–11.

On the other hand—and this point is sometimes lost in contemporary philosophical discussion of Boethius's view of eternity—God's eternal present and our experience of the present moment do not have an equivocal relationship either. As soon as Boethius defines eternity, for instance, he immediately suggests that we can understand it better by comparing it to temporal things.[20] For Boethius, the constant changing of things in our time is a sort of imitation of the unchanging life of eternity. The present never ceases to be and in this sense imitates or represents eternity but continually fails to be equal to the simple and immobile divine present, falling into an infinite number of past and future moments instead.[21] Time and eternity, in other words, are not opposites but analogically correlated; time is the closest to eternity we can come. It is a faint "imitation" and "representation" of the immediacy of the divine eternal life.

Boethius's treatment of divine eternality is relatively well known. But in his *Opuscula Sacra*, Boethius explicated a similarly probing account of divine omnipresence, parallel to divine eternality. He begins by asserting, following Aristotle, that there are ten categories that can be universally predicated of created objects: substance, quality, quantity, relation (*ad aliquid*), place, time, condition, situation (*situm esse*), activity, and passivity.[22] But Boethius insists that when these categories are applied to God, they change their meaning entirely, because "substance in (God) is not really substantial but beyond substance (*ultra substantiam*)."[23] This phrase *ultra substantiam*, often translated "super-substantial," anticipates similar language in John of Damascus and Thomas Aquinas and is bound up with Boethius's doctrine of divine simplicity. For instance, because it is the same thing for God to be as it is for God to be just, the statement "God is just" does not denote an accidental quality in God, nor even a substantial quality in him, but a "super-substantial" quality. "For when we say God, we seem to signify a certain substance, but it is that which is beyond substance."[24]

20. Boethius, *De Consolatione Philosophiae* 5.6.4.
21. Boethius, *De Consolatione Philosophiae* 5.6.12.
22. Boethius, *Opuscula Sacra* 1, 4:173–77.
23. Boethius, *Opuscula Sacra* 1, 4:183–84.
24. Boethius, *Opuscula Sacra* 1, 4:187–88.

Then, following a long explication of divine simplicity as distinguishing God from all created reality, Boethius applies this rigorous
emphasis on divine transcendence both to divine omnipresence and
divine eternality:

> When "God is everywhere" is said, it does not mean that he is in
> every place (for he cannot be in any place at all), but that every
> place is present to him to be seized by him, though he himself is
> received by no place, and therefore is said to be nowhere in a place,
> since He is everywhere but in no place. Time is truly predicated
> in the same way, as when it is said concerning a man, "he came
> yesterday"; concerning God, "he is always." Here also something
> is said to be as if it were said concerning yesterday's coming, but is
> predicated to it according to the time he will come. What is truly
> said of God, "he is always," signifies a single thing, as though he
> would have been in all the past, is also in all the present in the way
> that he is, and will be in all the future.[25]

As Boethius defines divine eternality positively rather than negatively, he here defines divine omnipresence actively rather than pas-
sively, so that God is present in no place but rather all places are
present to him. Because God is "supersubstantial," the statements
"God is ever" and "man came yesterday" bear fundamentally different meanings, as do the statements "a man is here" and "God is
everywhere." And yet this does not entail that God is absolutely and
simply distant from space; rather, "all places are present to him." Thus
Boethius's account of divine omnipresence, as with his account of
divine eternality, involves both a strong disjunction as well as a fluid
correlation between Creator and creation. Creator and creation are
not basically similar to one another nor basically dissimilar. Instead,
their relationship is as unique as the Creator himself and cannot be
adequately compared to the relationship of any two things within
creation.

But for the purposes of stretching the human imagination, something of this blend of infinite distance and constant presence can be
compared to an author/story relation. An author is both utterly foreign

---

25. Boethius, *Opuscula Sacra* 1, 4:225–238.

and eerily familiar to his story: he is himself beyond the story, and yet everything in the story is contained within him; he is visible nowhere and yet revealed everywhere. Tolkien, for instance, is not present in any "place" in Middle-earth, and yet all the places of Middle-earth are present to him (omnipresence). He is not located at any "time" in Middle-earth, and yet all the times of the story are equally open to him (eternality). In one sense we may say that the characters of Middle-earth have never met him; in another sense they have never done anything but meet with him. They are *his* characters and as such belong to him, but they are his *characters* and as such do not know him.

With respect to divine eternity and foreknowledge, one might say, leaving room for qualification, that Tolkien's knowledge of Middle-earth is "simple" in the sense that the past and future events of that world are equally available to his present Oxford. As Boethius states that divine foreknowledge is not really foreknowledge but simply knowledge in the eternal present, we might say that Tolkien's knowledge of events in Middle-earth that are future with respect to Frodo or Saruman is not foreknowledge but simply knowledge in the Oxford present. Both God and Tolkien relate to their respective "creations" in a way that is better expressed by prepositions such as *beyond* or *outside* or *above* than the preposition *before*. Both are not simply older than the world they create but surround and penetrate that world in a unique relationship. Furthermore, just as Boethius's definition of divine eternality does not cut God off from time in a frozen, static relationship, so Tolkien's ability to see the entire story at once enables him to relate to it more freely, with a potentially infinite attentiveness to each moment in the story.

One might object that Tolkien's knowledge of Middle-earth is simple only once the book is complete, not during the process of writing it. When he is sitting at his desk in Oxford, ten pages in, one might say that the future of Middle-earth is as open to Tolkien as it is to Frodo and Saruman. To some extent, this is a weakness of the thought experiment, since Tolkien is himself a created being and God is not—but even within the metaphor, the objection might actually further our sensitivity to the ontological gulf between God and everything else. We might recall, for instance, Boethius's statement that eternity is not

God's timelessness but his mastery over time. In a similar way, while Tolkien doubtless experiences a kind of sequence and duration in the brainstorming and actual writing of the story, it is a *kind* of time that is totally different from that of the characters of the story—it might be compared, within the thought experiment, to the decrees of God from eternity past. One supposes that divine decrees are something like an act or event in the divine mind, but one really has no way of knowing.

In the same way, the characters of a story have no knowledge of the story as *being* written—only *as* written. Tolkien might speculate about the meaning of Tom Bombadil over tea with a friend and then alter his text as a result, but Tom Bombadil can know nothing of this (unless, of course, Tolkien decides to write about it). So Tolkien's knowledge of *The Lord of the Rings* is still "simple" insofar as its temporal duration is qualitatively distinct from that of Middle-earth, and even controlling over it. Tolkien can take as long as he wants to write it, and can rewrite it over and over again one thousand times if he wants, without this impinging upon the characters' knowledge in the slightest. Asking whether Tolkien knows the ending of the book before he writes it is like asking whether God knew about Satan's destruction before he decreed to create the world. The words "before he writes it" are as inaccessible to Frodo as God's eternal decrees are to us.

With respect to the challenge of human freedom, it should be clear that Tolkien's "foreknowledge" need not impinge upon the free will of his characters. One might say that all of the evil actions of Sauron have been "predestined" by Tolkien (although even this assertion is more complicated than it seems and can be disputed).[26] But there is no particular reason why, from Gandalf's point of view, the future

---

26. Sayers suggests that the analogy of procreation may be more illuminating than that of artistic creation with respect to free will, precisely out of concern that the characters invented by a writer are "helpless puppets" (*Mind of the Maker*, 63). But she also emphasizes that the deep human desire to create agents with free will can creep into artistic production, speculating that this may be one reason why many authors prefer writing for the stage to writing for publication (*Mind of the Maker*, 64). If the metaphor of writing a play is substituted for that of writing a story, greater complexity is introduced to the question of the characters' free will, since there is an element of spontaneity and choice in the actors' performance of the script. Other examples of creative production that allow for authorial noncontrol, beyond procreation and stage drama, can also be thought of (e.g., some kinds of video games or artificial intelligence). Furthermore, Sayers argues that in skilled writing, there is a kind of natural harmony between the will of the author and the will of the character (e.g., *Mind of the Maker*, 75), and it is a common testimony of writers that certain characters can take on a "life of their own" and act in ways that surprise even the author. So even in a novel, it is not clear that characters are best understood as "helpless puppets."

behavior of Sauron should be any less "necessary" than the past behavior. We might say, following Boethius again, that Sauron's evil is made conditionally necessary by Tolkien's "foreknowledge," but not absolutely necessary. So Gandalf might have his own "problem of evil" to puzzle over, wondering why Tolkien created Sauron in the first place. But this is not a problem with respect to foreknowledge (Boethius's concern), but sovereignty. And even here, in the classic dilemma of divine sovereignty/human responsibility, we might extend and leverage some Boethian principles to bring clarity to the challenge. After all, just as Boethius argues that divine knowledge is qualitatively different from human knowledge, might we not say that divine willing is qualitatively different from human willing? Little substance is added to Iamblichus's dictum if we tweak it to say, "Everything that is *willed* is willed, not according to its own power, but rather according to the ability of the one willing." Or put it in terms of the thought experiment: Does not an author's will over a story work itself out differently from the will of a character within that story? Just as Tolkien can see farther than Gandalf, so he can alter the story in ways Gandalf cannot, and in ways that would be unrighteous for Gandalf but are not unrighteous for him. For example, it would be unrighteous for Gandalf to will Sauron into existence. But it is really not Gandalf's place to say whether it is unrighteous for Tolkien to do so.

From the perspective of the thought experiment, exhaustive divine sovereignty over all things—for all the many conundrums it raises—is really the only way God could relate to the world, if he is really God, just as there is not a single leaf or blade of grass in all of Middle-earth that exists apart from the sovereign will of Tolkien. Where else would it come from?

Tolkien in Middle-earth: The *Extra Calvinisticum*[27]

Almost fifty years ago E. David Willis contributed a definitive account of the *extra Calvinisticum*.[28] Since that time the doctrine has received a

---

27. As a pejorative Lutheran label the term is doubly misleading, both by (1) conceiving the doctrine in essentially spatial categories (*extra*) and (2) identifying it specifically as Calvin's doctrine (*Calvinisticum*). Nevertheless, to avoid confusion I will bow to the popular terminology.

28. E. David Willis, *Calvin's Catholic Christology: The Function of the So-called Extra Calvinisticum in Calvin's Theology* (Leiden: E. J. Brill, 1966).

modest but increasing amount of scholarly attention, including several heavy-hitting monographs.[29] Nevertheless, the *extra* remains a cryptic notion for many. Andrew McGinnis refers to it as "the infield fly rule of Christology" because "like the obscure baseball rule, the extra is infrequently used and tends to be understood only among enthusiasts and specialists."[30] Here we attempt to approach the *extra Calvinisticum* from a relatively unique angle, using it to explore the nature of the Creator/creation relationship with reference to the categories of our thought experiment.

As a term, the *extra Calvinisticum* is the product of sixteenth- and seventeenth-century Lutheran versus Reformed disputes regarding the nature of Christ's presence during the Lord's Supper. But the doctrine itself—that the incarnate Son of God was not limited to his human flesh, but continued to uphold the universe even while incarnate— is much older, with wide attestation among patristic and medieval theologians. As Willis puts it, "The 'extra Calvinisticum,' because of its widespread and ancient usage could just as well be called the 'extra-Catholicum.'"[31]

Calvin was self-consciously operating within this ancient tradition of thought when he articulated what would come to be called the *extra Calvinisticum*. In his well-known affirmation of the extra in the *Institutes*, for instance, in which he excoriates the idea that "divinity left heaven to hide itself in the prison house of the body," Calvin explicitly refers to Lombard's *totus/totum* distinction.[32] Willis argues that Calvin's writings evidence awareness of the larger scholastic discus-

---

29. Andrew M. McGinnis, *The Son of God beyond the Flesh: A Historical and Theological Study of the Extra Calvinisticum*, T&T Clark Studies in Systematic Theology (New York: Bloomsbury, 2014), traces the *extra Calvinisticum* in the thought of Cyril of Alexandria, Thomas Aquinas, and Zacharias Ursinus. Daniel Y. K. Lee, *The Holy Spirit as Bond in Calvin's Thought: Its Functions in Connection with the Extra Calvinisticum* (New York: Peter Lang International Academic, 2011), explores the role of the Spirit in relation to the *extra Calvinisticum* in uniting believers to the ascended Christ. For a recent, thorough survey of scholarly treatment of the *extra Calvinisticum*, see McGinnis, *Son of God beyond the Flesh*, 3–4.

30. McGinnis, *Son of God beyond the Flesh*, 10.

31. Willis, *Calvin's Catholic Christology*, 153. In his chapter on this topic, still valuable despite being dated, Willis draws attention to explicit assertions of the doctrine in Thomas Aquinas, Gabriel Biel, Jacques LeFevre d'Estaples, John of Damascus, Augustine, Origen, Theodore of Mopsuestia, Athanasius, and Cyril of Alexandria. See Willis, *Calvin's Catholic Christology*, 34–60.

32. John Calvin, *Institutes of the Christian Religion*, ed. John T. McNeill, trans. Ford Lewis Battles, 2 vols. (Louisville, KY: Westminster John Knox, 2006), 4.17.30: "There is a commonplace distinction of the schools to which I am not ashamed to refer: although the whole Christ is present everywhere, still the whole of that which is in him is not present everywhere." This distinction is captured well by Charles Partee, *The Theology of John Calvin* (Louisville, KY:

sion of this point, and he also draws attention to Calvin's quotation of Augustine in the 1543 edition of the *Institutes* in connection to the *extra*.[33] Thus though here we engage with this doctrine as it finds particularly eloquent expression in Calvin's writings, we are at the same time bumping up against patterns of thought that have deep patristic and medieval moorings.

The two passages in the *Institutes* most famously associated with the *extra Calvinisticum* both appear fully only with the 1559 edition, but the second (4.17.30) is expanded from material already present in the 1536 edition—importantly, in a Eucharistic context. Calvin's Eucharistic concerns became obscured somewhat in the subsequent discussion. In their late sixteenth- and seventeenth-century Eucharistic disputes with the Reformed, the Lutherans claimed that the *extra Calvinisticum* was controlled by the philosophical principle embraced by the Reformed, *finitum non capax infiniti* (the finite cannot grasp the infinite).[34] This has been a consistent criticism of the *extra Calvinisticum* ever since. But it is noteworthy that originally, in Calvin's writings, this doctrine functioned as a safeguard against Eucharistic speculation—it was not first and foremost a constructive tool for solving "the two natures problem" but a device for delineating the manner of Christ's presence in the elements.[35] The Lutheran charge of speculation regarding the Supper is a bit ironic in light of their own preference for a strong *communicatio idiomatum* (communication of attributes) over the *extra*, where arguably there has been a tendency for the theological needs of the Eucharist to drive Christology, rather than the theological data of Christology to shape the Eucharist.

Because it has been hammered out in a Eucharistic context, the *extra Calvinisticum* has typically been conceived in spatial terms (hence the word *extra*). T. F. Torrance argues that this is the fundamental reason why the Lutherans (mistakenly) rejected the *extra*: because they operated with a "receptacle" view of space as "the place

Westminster John Knox, 2010), 151: "Christ is wholly God (*totus Deus*), but not the whole of God (*totum Deum*)."

33. Willis, *Calvin's Catholic Christology*, 30.

34. Early Reformed defenders of the *extra* such as Theodore Beza, Antoine de la Faye, Claude Auberry, Abraham Musculus, and Peter Hubner insisted, against the Lutherans, that humanity by definition is finite. See Willis, *Calvin's Catholic Christology*, 16–18.

35. Willis, *Calvin's Catholic Christology*, 27.

containing within its limits that which occupies it."[36] This spatial construal of the *extra Calvinisticum* has generated all kinds of misleading metaphors; for instance, Caspar Olevianus parodied the Lutheran account of Christ's location at "the right hand of God" with his "Antwerp and the ocean" syllogism, which is sometimes misconstrued as representing the *extra Calvinisticum* itself.[37]

Conceiving of the *extra* in spatial terms has been the unfortunate result, in part, of latching onto the two seminal passages concerning the *extra Calvinisticum* in the *Institutes* (especially 2.13.4) and neglecting Calvin's broader treatment of the dynamics of Christ's incarnate life in his sermons, commentaries, and other works. Calvin employs spatial language in those two passages in the *Institutes*, but in how the *extra Calvinisticum* actually functions in his exegesis and preaching, he far more frequently uses governmental, royal language. In discussing the incarnation in his commentary on the Lukan birth narrative, for instance, Calvin emphasizes the incarnate Christ's headship over the unfallen angels far more than his mere omnipresence.[38] Elsewhere Calvin stresses the incarnate Christ's continued mediatorship of sustenance (in distinction from his mediatorship of reconciliation) in which he continues in his fleshly life to "uphold the universe by the word of his power" (Heb. 1:3).[39] Or in a sermon on the Lukan birth narrative, Calvin emphasizes the *extra* as a matter of Christ's divine majesty and power, not mere omnipresence: "However much (Christ) was debased, it in no wise takes away from His Divine power. . . . He was not thus emptied without always retaining His Divine Majesty."[40] The reason Calvin often depicts the movement of the incarnation in political categories is that for him, it was not a matter of

---

36. Thomas F. Torrance, *Atonement: The Person and Work of Christ*, ed. Robert T. Walker (Downers Grove, IL: IVP Academic, 2009), 282. In contrast, Torrance (*Atonement*, 285) advocates a relational view of space and time in which they are viewed not as things in themselves but as inherently relational to bodies, forces, and events. This material is reprinted from his earlier *Space, Time, and Resurrection* (Grand Rapids, MI: Eerdmans, 1976).

37. See the discussion of this original dispute in McGinnis, *Son of God beyond the Flesh*, 88–89. Willis (*Calvin's Catholic Christology*, 19–20) discusses how this metaphor (and various others) were unhappily used by Calvinists to attempt to explain the *extra*.

38. John Calvin, *Commentary on a Harmony of the Evangelists: Matthew, Mark, and Luke*, vol. 1, trans. William Pringle (Grand Rapids, MI: Eerdmans, 1949), 25, calls Christ "the prince and Lord of angels." Cf. the discussion in Willis, *Calvin's Catholic Christology*, 76.

39. Willis, *Calvin's Catholic Christology*, 70, 76.

40. John Calvin, "The Nativity of Jesus Christ," in *The Deity of Christ and Other Sermons*, trans. Leroy Nixon (Grand Rapids, MI: Eerdmans, 1950), 38.

speculation but of soteriology; it concerned the extension of Christ's majesty, power, authority, and glory into the creaturely sphere. As Willis summarizes the significance of the *extra*: "The incarnation was not the Eternal Son's abdication of his universal empire but the reassertion of that empire over rebellious creation."[41]

Seventeenth-century Lutheran theologians who rejected "Calvin's *extra*" also wanted to affirm some kind of continued governance of the world by the incarnate Christ. For them, the *communicatio idiomatum* (communication of attributes) met this need—but different Lutheran theologians pressed this doctrine in different directions. The Tübingen party (following Johann Brenz) affirmed that Christ's use of divine attributes was merely hidden or concealed during Christ's human life (*krypsis*); the Giessen school (following Martin Chemnitz) affirmed a kind of renunciation of Christ's use of divine attributes during his human life (*kenosis*).[42] Eventually the Geissen emphasis held sway, resulting in the stronger notion of kenosis in which Christ's employment of divine powers is not merely hidden but actually abdicated or renounced in the incarnation. Barth is not alone in tracing nineteenth-century kenotic theory, in which the divine nature itself is in some sense discarded in the incarnation, as the logical outflow of this tradition of thought.[43]

Calvin and the later Reformed tradition had no trouble affirming a kind of *communicatio idiomatum*.[44] The real point of departure was with those tendencies of Lutheran thought that emphasized a communication directly between the human and divine natures of Christ (as opposed to one mediated through and controlled by his person), such that the human nature became clothed with divine attributes (as in the so-called *genus majestaticum*). The Calvinist tradition generally felt that in making this move, Lutheran Christologies have bordered dangerously close to monophysitism.[45]

41. Willis, *Calvin's Catholic Christology*, 99.
42. Darren O. Sumner, *Karl Barth and the Incarnation: Christology and the Humility of God*, T&T Clark Studies in Systematic Theology (New York: Bloomsbury, 2014), 49.
43. Karl Barth, *Church Dogmatics* 4.1, ed. Geoffrey Bromiley and T. F. Torrance, trans. Geoffrey Bromiley (1961; repr. New York: T&T Clark, 2009), 173–76. So also, e.g., G. C. Berkouwer, *The Work of Christ*, trans. Cornelius Lambregtse, Studies in Dogmatics (Grand Rapids, MI: Eerdmans, 1965), 240.
44. E.g., Calvin, *Institutes of the Christian Religion*, 2.14.1–2.
45. *The Calvin Handbook*, ed. Herman J. Selderhuis (Grand Rapids, MI: Eerdmans, 2009), 264.

Calvin found the Lutheran doctrine of the ubiquity of Christ "monstrous" precisely because it failed to preserve the twoness of Christ's two natures and instead resulted in "some sort of intermediate being which was neither God nor man."[46] Parsing this phrase in distinction from both Nestorius on the one hand and Eutyches on the other, Calvin asserted, "It is no more permissible to commingle the two natures in Christ than to pull them apart." This was Calvin's hallmark Christological emphasis—the distinctness of the two natures—and it helps explain why he regarded the Eutychean and Nestorian errors as *equally* dangerous. In his mind, blending the natures together destroys them as much as positing a "double Christ," because it detracts from his deity, which as divine is impassible and unchanging.[47] As he put it:

> From the Scripture we plainly infer that the one person of Christ so consists of two natures that each nevertheless retains unimpaired its own distinctive character. And they will be ashamed to deny that Eutyches was rightly condemned. It is a wonder they do not heed the cause of his condemnation; removing the distinction between the natures and urging the unity of the person, he made man out of God and God out of man. What sort of madness, then, is it to mingle heaven with earth rather than give up trying to drag Christ's body from the heavenly sanctuary?[48]

In so strongly emphasizing the distinctness of Christ's two natures, Calvin has often been charged with a Nestorian-like division of the unity of Christ's person. This is perhaps the most persistent criticism against the *extra Calvinisticum*, that it results in two Christs and thus two Gods, one hidden and one revealed. Even Wendel raises this concern,[49] and Barth also cannot affirm the *extra* without a solemn warning about the danger of speculating about a God other than the one we know through Jesus Christ.[50] This charge had already arisen in Calvin's own day, as he protests in the *Institutes*: "Servetus accuses us of making two Sons of God when we say that the eternal Word, before

---

46. Calvin, *Institutes of the Christian Religion* 4.17.30.
47. Calvin, *Institutes of the Christian Religion* 2.14.7.
48. Calvin, *Institutes of the Christian Religion* 4.17.30.
49. François Wendel, *Calvin: The Origins and Development of His Religious Thought*, trans. Philip Mairet (New York: Harper & Row, 1995), 225.
50. Barth, *Church Dogmatics* 4.1.

he was clothed with flesh, was already the Son of God."[51] The related concern is that Calvin has no room for a real and genuine human nature in Christ. For instance, Battenhouse charges that in Calvin's view, "Christ seems essentially a deity playing a stage part, putting on a mask of humanity as a temporary expedient."[52]

Reflecting on these criticisms gives us opportunity to draw out the Creator/creation relationship involved in the *extra Calvinisticum* discussion. The crucial move comes with the intuition, "local + omnipresent = two persons." The proper response is: *Why?* The instinct that one person cannot occupy two places at once assumes an essentially spatial conception of the Creator/creation relationship (as can be evidenced by probing the meaning of the word *places*). What happens if instead of construing the *extra Calvinisticum* in spatial terms, we draw it into the categories of our thought experiment?

So to return to Tolkien, suppose, just as Christ comes into his own creation at the incarnation, Tolkien had written himself into Middle-earth as a character of the story alongside Frodo and Merry and Pippin and the rest. Had Tolkien done so, he would not for that reason cease to exist in Oxford (in fact, his whole existence in Middle-earth depends on his continued writing). Nor has the unity of Tolkien's person been impaired, for one person can simultaneously be in Middle-earth and Oxford, because they are not two different "places" within one realm but two different realms altogether. In other words, it is one thing to be in Oxford and Cambridge at the same time, but another thing to be in the Shire and Oxford at the same time; and the relation of "heaven" and "earth," and with it the relation of Christ's divine and human natures, is more like the relationship between the Shire and Oxford. This is the value of the metaphor of story—the distinction between "author" and "story" is robust enough to retain two natures while fluid enough to retain one person. Middle-earth and Oxford may be *two* while Tolkien remains *one*.

The real determinative point of departure in the Lutheran-Calvinist dispute, then, is a different construal of the Creator/creation

51. Calvin, *Institutes of the Christian Religion* 2.14.5.
52. Roy W. Battenhouse, "The Doctrine of Man in Calvin and in Renaissance Platonism," *The Journal of the History of Ideas* 9 (October 1948): 460.

relationship. And to the extent that the story metaphor sheds light on this discussion, it would seem to further undermine the charge of Nestorianism against a Calvinist Christology while leaving as an open concern the Lutheran association with monophysitism (particularly in accounts that retain a *genus majestaticum*). After all, if God the Son has remained *extra* all throughout the incarnation, it is difficult to see what *need* there is for a *genus majestaticum*. Perhaps, one could argue, it is necessary in order to arrive at all the nuances of a specifically Lutheran account of "bodily presence" (as opposed to "real presence" more generally). But one already has the necessary tools for a strong doctrine of Christ's presence in the Eucharistic elements without positing any communication of divine properties onto the human nature of Christ, since the words "this is my body" are already spoken with reference to one person who has never been less than fully omnipresent. In this sense, it is as unnecessary to attribute ubiquity or omnipresence to the human flesh of Christ as it would be to require that the *incarnated* Tolkien be omnipresent throughout Middle-earth. Since Middle-earth and Oxford are separate realms, the notion of "omnipresence" derives its meaning from Tolkien's existence in Oxford, and the attempt to transmit this to the incarnated Tolkien would indeed seem to impinge upon Calvin's concern about "commingling." Any transposition, in fact, of the Oxford Tolkien's "properties" onto the Tolkien incarnated within Middle-earth would seem to confuse what should be kept distinct and is unnecessary for retaining the unity of his person in the first place.

Beyond clarifying the Lutheran-Reformed dialogue, comparing the incarnation to Tolkien writing himself into Middle-earth might additionally reinforce the danger of explicating the *extra Calvinisticum* in exclusively spatial categories in its contemporary articulation. It is not merely that Tolkien is not confined to the body of his incarnate character in Middle-earth; that is true, but that is just about the least significant thing one can say about him. Supposing the incarnated Tolkien is sitting in Frodo's home in the Shire for a meal; this does not in the least hinder the Tolkien in Oxford from going to sleep, or traveling to India, or putting the book down for twenty years. His incarnate existence in Middle-earth does not diminish him in the least or even distract him. He is not merely *extra* but completely and fully *extra*. In other words, it is not that he reduces himself to an incarnate life but leaves a tiny bit left over that is not exhausted by his incarnation; rather, that which is *extra* continues on without the slightest down-grade or even interruption during the incarnation. Hence Calvin's emphasis, for instance, on the incarnate Son's continued mediatorship over the angels and governance of the universe.

Finally, some classical Christological dilemmas may also come into greater view as a result of the thought experiment at this point. For instance, if Christ is God, and God is omniscient, how did he not know the hour of his coming (Mark 13:32)? The common response is that Christ is omniscient with respect to his divine nature but limited in knowledge with respect to his human nature. But what does this mean? Translating this answer into the metaphor of story can make it less abstract and more understandable, for it is not difficult to conceive that Tolkien may even know things in Oxford of which he is ignorant in Middle-earth. Why not? (Or as Einstein would ask, "What if?") The level of knowledge of the incarnate Tolkien would be entirely dependent on what the Tolkien writing in Oxford determines, and it would probably burden the story unnecessarily if they shared equal knowledge despite living in different worlds.

Or take the difficulty of understanding that Christ's suffering on the cross was only with respect to his human nature. How do we affirm a real suffering, and a real death, without detracting from the immortal-ity of Christ's divine nature or impairing the unity of his person? The classic response from theologians such as Cyril of Alexandria is that Christ suffered with respect to his human nature but not with respect to his divine nature. But again, what does this mean? If we consider that Tolkien's life in Oxford continues merrily uninterrupted even if his incarnated character in Middle-earth dies, we may have some category by which to conceive that the Word is still sustaining all things by his powerful word (Heb. 1:3) even while his cold body is wrapped in the linen strips, and that "in him all things hold together" (Col. 1:17) even while his body is decomposing in the dark on the eve of Easter. Fur-thermore, we are less surprised by what happens on the next morning, for it is unimaginable that the author of a story, who controls its every turn and twist, could be defeated or frustrated by anything that happens within it. In other words, the author/story metaphor also signals the logical fittingness of Christ's resurrection: it helps explain why it had to happen, why it is, in Narnian categories, "deeper magic from before the dawn of time." This leads to our final section.

Middle-earth Transported Back to Oxford: Torrance on the Ascension

Thomas Torrance's contributions to Christology are widely acknowledged, but in general the focus has been on his treatment of incarnation, atonement, and resurrection, while his view of the ascension has received relatively little attention.[53] Yet Torrance provides an illuminating account of the ascension, especially with respect to the Creator/creation distinction. Torrance's hallmark emphasis in his treatment of the ascension, consistent with his interest in the natural sciences, is how it relates to space-time reality. For Torrance, space-time is distinct from God and yet at the same time infused with his reality. Torrance opposes the common segregation of the spiritual and the material realms in modern thought, envisioning instead a multileveled and yet unified universe in which the spiritual realm is the ultimate animating cause of the material. He writes:

> The universe that is steadily being disclosed to our various sciences is found to be characterized throughout time and space by an ascending gradient of meaning in richer and higher forms of order. Instead of levels of existence and reality being explained reductionally from below in materialistic and mechanistic terms, the lower levels are found to be explained in terms of higher, invisible, intangible levels of reality.[54]

53. E.g., Paul D. Molnar, *Incarnation and Resurrection: Toward a Contemporary Understanding* (Grand Rapids, MI: Eerdmans, 2007), 81–119; Paul D. Molnar, *Thomas F. Torrance: Theologian of the Trinity* (Burlington, VT: Ashgate, 2009), 246–59; Elmer M. Colyer, *How to Read T. F. Torrance: Understanding His Trinitarian and Scientific Theology* (Downers Grove, IL: InterVarsity Press, 2001), 55–96; Elmer M. Colyer, "The Incarnate Saviour: T. F. Torrance on the Atonement," in *An Introduction to Torrance Theology: Discovering the Incarnate Saviour,* ed. Gerrit Scott Dawson (New York: T&T Clark, 2007), 33–54; Andrew Purves, "The Christology of Thomas F. Torrance," in *The Promise of Trinitarian Theology: Theologians in Dialogue with T. F. Torrance,* ed. Elmer M. Colyer (Lanham, MD: Rowman & Littlefield, 2001), 51–80.

54. Quoted in Alistair McGrath, *T. F. Torrance: An Intellectual Biography* (Edinburgh: T&T Clark, 1999), 232–33. For a fuller picture of Torrance's account of the relation of science and theology, see Thomas F. Torrance, *Theological Science* (Oxford, UK: Oxford University Press, 1969), 55–105, 281–352.

Against the backdrop of this conception of the universe, Torrance conceives of Christ's resurrection as a space-time event that simultaneously transcends space-time. As a result, there is a high level of mystery in his discussion of Christ's ascension. He acknowledges that we have no adequate language with which to describe it and that even the language we must use necessarily breaks down to point to a reality beyond language.[55]

Though Torrance will often speak about the ascension in close correlation with Christ's resurrection,[56] it is ultimately in relation to Christ's incarnation that it takes shape. Torrance portrays the ascension as "the reverse of the incarnation,"[57] calling it "the other pole of the question of the relation of the incarnation to space and time which . . . gave rise in the sixteenth century to the controversy of the so-called *extra Calvinisticum.*"[58] Einsteinian physics are a necessary ingredient in Torrance's correlation of Christ's incarnation and ascension. He emphasizes that space and time are not abstract entities—they do not exist independently of each other or of those active forces that move upon them. There is no such thing as "empty space"; there is only space for something.[59] Above all, Torrance objects to the Lutheran receptacle notion of space and time in favor of a "relational view of space and time differentially or variationally related to God and man."[60] Such a view of space-time is necessary, for Torrance, to avoid falsifying the incarnation.[61]

A presupposition of this account of space-time is a robust distinction between Creator and creation. Torrance writes, "When we say that God exists, we mean that God exists as God, in accordance with the nature of God, for divine existence is of an utterly unique and transcendent kind."[62] As a result, Torrance argues that when we think of the

---

55. Torrance, *Atonement*, 286.
56. Torrance can speak of "that fusion of resurrection with the ascension in one indivisible exaltation" (*Atonement*, 270) and reiterates this point several times, often drawing attention to their tight connection in the book of Hebrews (*Atonement*, 298). On other occasions he can emphasize the crucifixion, resurrection, and ascension altogether as the glorification of Jesus, even referring to the "unity of the crucifixion and ascension" (*Atonement*, 269).
57. Torrance, *Atonement*, 287.
58. Torrance, *Atonement*, 282, emphasis original.
59. Torrance, *Atonement*, 289.
60. Torrance, *Atonement*, 285.
61. Torrance, *Atonement*, 285.
62. Torrance, *Atonement*, 285.

incarnate Son as one person with two natures, we must think about one person who has two different relationships to space and time. Though Torrance denies that God is within space-time, he argues that God nevertheless has his own "time" (defined by his uncreated and creative life) and his own "place" (defined by his triune relations, and in particular their mutual indwelling [*perichoresis*]). The incarnate Christ is one who therefore exists in both "man's place" and "God's place."[63]

This view of the incarnation, in which a robust affirmation of the *extra Calvinisticum* is buttressed by an Einsteinian account of space-time, then lends Torrance a framework within which to interpret Christ's ascension. Specifically, Torrance conceives of the ascension as a sort of photographic negative to the *extra Calvinisticum*:

> As in the incarnation we have to think of God the Son becoming man without ceasing to be transcendent God, so in his ascension we have to think of Christ as ascending above all space and time without ceasing to be man or without any diminishment of his physical, historical existence.[64]

Thus for Torrance, the *extra Calvinisticum* establishes a kind of mode of thinking that must be maintained in considering the remainder of Christ's incarnate life. It can be summarized in a chiastic aphorism: at the incarnation the Word enters a body without leaving heaven; at the ascension the Word enters heaven without leaving a body. As the extra serves to preserve the full deity of Christ in his descending to us, the bodily and space-time nature of the ascension serves to preserve his full humanity in his ascending from us. God enters the world without ceasing to be God; God then leaves the world without ceasing to be man. In Torrance's account, these twin movements are the two poles of the work of Christ.

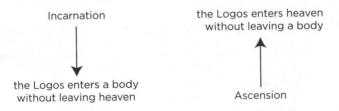

Incarnation

the Logos enters a body without leaving heaven

the Logos enters heaven without leaving a body

Ascension

---

63. Torrance, *Atonement*, 290.
64. Torrance, *Atonement*, 287.

Because it is correlated with the incarnation, the ascension has redemptive function in Torrance's theology, signaling the healing and restoration of space-time reality.[65] If the resurrection demonstrates God's care for material reality, the ascension represents its permanent confirmation in and for God.[66] Torrance interprets the ascension as representing the duality of two realms converging, fallen space-time and redeemed space-time.[67] He draws attention to Byzantine art in which the figure of Christ is depicted standing on a dais in which the lines are made to diverge rather than converge, as would be expected: "At one end of the icon or mosaic the figure of Christ stands in bounded space and time, but at the other end he transcends all such limitations." Consistent with such a depiction, Torrance claims that our statements about the ascension are both "closed at man's end" and "infinitely open at God's end."[68]

Because in Torrance's thought the ascension is a movement from "man's place" to "God's place," it is wrong to think of it purely in terms of departure or distance, as though it were a movement from one creaturely place to another creaturely place. Rather, Torrance claims, in his ascended life Christ is nearer to us: "In a real sense he comes again in the ascension."[69] This conception of the ascension assumes once again a strong distinction between Creator and creation, though not an equivocal one. Torrance stresses that Christ's continued presence among his people is specifically through the agency of the Spirit.[70]

According to Torrance, the ascension transforms our view of "God's place," or heaven: "The ascension of the incarnate, crucified, and risen Jesus Christ inevitably transforms 'heaven': something quite new has been effected in the heavenlies which must alter its material content in our understanding of what heaven is."[71] Specifically, because the ascension does not subtract or dilute any of God the Son's

---

65. Torrance, *Atonement*, 247.
66. Torrance, *Atonement*, 286.
67. Torrance, *Atonement*, 285–86.
68. Torrance, *Atonement*, 290–91.
69. Torrance, *Atonement*, 291.
70. Torrance, *Atonement*, 294: "Through the Spirit Christ is nearer to us than we are to ourselves."
71. Torrance, *Atonement*, 288. One might cite, as additional support to Torrance's notion that heaven can receive a physical body, the bodily translation of Enoch in Genesis 5:24 and Elijah in 2 Kings 2:11.

creaturely reality, it reveals heaven as the place of God that is friendly to creaturely existence as creaturely, for instance, bodily and spatiotemporal existence. Some theologians have expressed discomfort with the notion that heaven can accommodate a body, therefore interpreting the ascension as a kind of dematerialization of Jesus's body.[72] In contrast, Torrance insists that neither Christ's resurrection nor his ascension involves any diminishing of his physical, fleshly existence.[73] Torrance distinguishes this exaltation of the incarnate Christ from mysticism and pantheism, while insisting that because Christ is our forerunner (Heb. 6:20), we are exalted into the divine life with him.[74]

We might grasp something of the soteriological *function* of Torrance's account of Christ's ascension by translating it into our thought experiment. If the incarnation functions something like the author writing himself into his own story, the ascension would be like the author pulling the world of that story into his own world. If in the incarnation God penetrates the realm of creation, in the ascension God allows the realm of creation to penetrate back into himself. It would be like Tolkien transporting something of Middle-earth back into Oxford. Of course, at this point the story metaphor begins to break down a bit, since Tolkien has no power to do this, and since the Oxford Tolkien (unlike the preincarnate *Logos*) is already embodied, and thus the ascension of the incarnate Tolkien would conceivably result in two bodies for one person (unless one posited the two bodies somehow welding back together again; but this smacks too much of monophysitism). Nonetheless, if we give allowance for disanalogy on various points like this, even here the thought experiment may illumine some aspects of the ascension.

In particular, considering an incarnate and ascended Tolkien, writing from his desk in Oxford, underscores the redemptive significance of the ascension. The ascended body there in Oxford represents a kind

---

72. Thus Murray Harris, *From Grave to Glory: Resurrection in the New Testament* (Grand Rapids, MI: Zondervan, 1990), 142–43, affirms that while the resurrected body of Jesus was physical, at the ascension Jesus's body dematerialized and became "non-fleshly."

73. Torrance, *Atonement*, 299–300; cf. 294: "The staggering thing about this is that the exaltation of human nature into the life of God does not mean the disappearance of man or the swallowing up of human and creaturely being in the infinite ocean of the divine being, but rather that human nature, while remaining creaturely and human, is yet exalted in Christ to share in God's life and glory."

74. Torrance, *Atonement*, 294–95.

of transfer from one realm to another. The space-time of Middle-earth has been drawn into the space-time of Oxford. It is as though there has been a kind of "ontological upgrading" of the reality of Middle-earth: it has gone from a reality that exists in one realm to a reality that now exists in two. As Torrance speaks of the ascension as the "permanent confirmation" of material reality before God, so we might see an ascension of the incarnated Tolkien as a kind of cementing or binding of Middle-earth's status before Tolkien. And just as Torrance envisions that the ascension must transform our view of heaven as a place that is "friendly to embodied existence," we can conceive of Frodo and Gandalf more naturally hoping to make it to Oxford one day, since they have a "forerunner" (cf. Heb. 6:20) who has gone before them.

In a similar way, we might conceive of the incarnation, resurrection, and ascension of Christ as a sort of "ontological upgrading"—a transfer of created reality from one realm to another. But this transfer is not simply from an imaginary world to a real world but from creaturely, contingent existence into the eternal, divine life. This may explain why Torrance emphasizes the harmony of natural law and miracle, since it is ultimately the miracles of Christ's incarnation and ascension that bring creation to its designed completion. One might say that for Torrance, the resurrection and ascension of Christ are therefore not best cast as infractions of "natural laws" but rather their deepest fulfillment, meaning, and *telos*. The distinction between nature and miracle, in other words, and at the widest angle between nature and resurrection, is not basically a chaotic one, but one like two puzzle pieces fitting together. Nature was born to be reborn; creation was designed with a view to resurrection.

In every good story there are climactic turning points that reorient or reveal the meaning of the whole plot. If creation is compared to a story, then in Torrance's thought the incarnation and ascension of Christ are the two poles of that climactic, pivotal event on which everything else hangs. Specifically, the incarnate work of Christ fundamentally restructures the Creator/creation relationship and signals the redemption of creation into the divine life. Therefore, in one sense, the incarnation and ascension of Christ are more than mere miracles, since they involve a greater kind of contact between Creator and creation than other miracles do, and exert a qualitatively greater significance over their relation. One might say that incarnation/ascension is to miracle what miracle is to nature—that is, as miracles fundamentally redetermine nature, so incarnation/ascension fundamentally redetermines everything else, *including* other miracles. They are meta-miracles; they are the deepest and truest events, the "turning points of the plot" that illumine everything else in the story.

Conclusion

The three doctrines surveyed in this chapter all evidence a complex understanding of the Creator/creation distinction. On the one hand, the chasm between Creator and creation is as rich and potent as can be imagined. Creator and creation are different realms, different worlds, different realities; the one is so real that in relation to it the other is as if it were not. At the same time, the Creator/creation distinction visible in these doctrines is not static and frozen. God and the world turn out to be something other than mere opposites; for opposition implies mutual standing within the same scale of comparison. Precisely because God is realer than the world, he may be present to the world; precisely because God is different from the world, he can relate freely to it. This way of construing Creator/creation is richer and more nuanced than many strands of contemporary theology, not only more revisionist progressive theologies but also some staler conservative trajectories of thought.[75]

Our thought experiment, as we have traced it through three test cases in church history, offers to the imagination a kind of heuristic device for envisioning something of the simultaneous vastness and flexibility that is involved in the Creator/creation distinction. For some, the story metaphor could be taken to imply that creation, and God's involvement in it, is not real. But even here the metaphor prompts probing into the deeper question: What, exactly, does it mean to be

---

75. E.g., Wayne Grudem, *Systematic Theology: An Introduction to Biblical Theology* (Grand Rapids, MI: Zondervan, 1995), 617–18, responding to other evangelical theologians claiming that heaven is not a "place," asserts that heaven is an unseen place within the space-time universe, even suggesting that "we are justified in thinking of heaven as somewhere 'above' the earth"; though he qualifies that because the earth is round and rotates, we are unable to say more precisely where heaven is. Grudem seems to assume that if heaven is a place, it must be a place within our space-time universe and apparently does not consider that it might exist as a different realm altogether.

"real?" Viewed from within, all stories are real; the characters know no other reality. Is Oxford more real to Tolkien than the Shire is real to Frodo? Someone may object that Middle-earth is not an actual place; it exists only in people's minds and imaginations. But what does it mean to say that our world is an actual place except that it is sustained in the mind and imagination of God? "In him we live and move and have our being" (Acts 17:28). Are we not as "less real" to God as Middle-earth is to us? Does not our finitude and contingency make us infinitely more similar to Frodo than either of us is to God?

The story metaphor thus highlights God's qualitative ontological priority over creation. It is not as though God is simply more real or more important than the world—rather, reality is fully God's possession, and our contact with it is wholly derivative. God is the great truth, the great Fact that simply is—and we are his story.

5

God Is Not a Thing

Divine Simplicity in Patristic and Medieval Perspective

No one, not of men only, but even of supramundane powers, and the Cherubim, I say, and Seraphim themselves, has ever known God, save he to whom He revealed Himself.

—John of Damascus

✝

Since the publication of Alvin Plantinga's *Does God Have a Nature?* in 1980,[1] the doctrine of divine simplicity has received a significant increase of attention from a number of philosophers and theologians. Much of the recent treatment of divine simplicity has been critical. A wide variety of arguments has been raised against divine simplicity, including: (1) abstract properties cannot be identified with a concrete, personal God;[2] (2) if God is identical to his properties, his properties

---

1. Alvin Plantinga, *Does God Have a Nature?* (1980; repr. Milwaukee, WI: Marquette University Press, 2007).
2. John S. Feinberg, *No One Like Him: The Doctrine of God* (Wheaton, IL: Crossway, 2001), 330–35; Christopher Stead, *Divine Substance* (Oxford, UK: Clarendon Press, 1977), 180–89.

are all identical to each other;[3] (3) a simple God must either have only
one property or be a property or both;[4] (4) it is impossible to predicate
diverse attributes of a simple God;[5] (5) divine simplicity makes God
unknowable;[6] (6) divine simplicity denies God's freedom;[7] (7) divine
simplicity is unbiblical;[8] (8) divine simplicity creates problems for the
incarnation;[9] (9) divine simplicity is at odds with the doctrine of the
Trinity;[10] and many others. This body of literature has given occasion for a number of defenses of divine simplicity, perhaps the most
significant of which is the work of James Dolezal.[11]

   While much of the developing discussion concerning divine simplicity is philosophical, this chapter seeks to approach divine simplicity from a historical route in an effort at theological retrieval. It will
explore how divine simplicity has been formulated in patristic and
medieval theology, particularly with a view to the problem of how
divine simplicity relates to the doctrine of the Trinity, and with special attention to some treatments of divine simplicity in the church's
history that have hitherto received less attention, such as those of Anselm of Canterbury and John of Damascus.[12] It will be suggested that

---

3. Richard M. Gale, *On the Nature and Existence of God* (Cambridge, UK: Cambridge University Press, 1991), 24.
   4. Plantinga, *Does God Have a Nature?*, 47.
   5. Thomas Morris, *Our Idea of God: An Introduction to Philosophical Theology* (Notre
Dame, IN: University of Notre Dame Press, 1991), 117.
   6. Ronald H. Nash, *The Concept of God: An Exploration of Contemporary Difficulties with
the Attributes of God* (Grand Rapids, MI: Zondervan, 1983), 85.
   7. The discussion of Eleonore Stump, *Aquinas* (New York: Routledge, 2003), 100–127, is
particularly helpful on this point.
   8. J. P. Moreland and William Lane Craig, *Philosophical Foundations for a Christian World-
view* (Downers Grove, IL: InterVarsity Press, 2003), 524.
   9. R. T. Mullins, "Simply Impossible: A Case Against Divine Simplicity," *Journal of Reformed
Theology* 7 (2013): 200–201.
   10. Christopher Hughes, *On a Complex Theory of a Simple God: An Investigation in Aquinas'
Philosophical Theology* (Ithaca, NY: Cornell University Press, 1989), 153–86, provides a good
overview and response to this argument.
   11. James E. Dolezal, *God without Parts: Divine Simplicity and the Metaphysics of God's
Absoluteness* (Eugene, OR: Pickwick, 2011), provides a defense of the classic doctrine of divine
simplicity; James E. Dolezal, "Trinity, Simplicity, and the Status of God's Personal Relations,"
International Journal of Systematic Theology 16 (2014): 79–98, sought to demonstrate the compatibility of divine simplicity with the doctrine of the Trinity; James E. Dolezal, *All That Is in
God: Evangelical Theology and the Challenge of Classic Theism* (Grand Rapids, MI: Reformation Heritage, 2017), offers a critique of the "theistic mutualism" Dolezal sees as at the root of
evangelical rejections of divine simplicity. Another insightful account of divine simplicity, more
constructively oriented though still in dialogue with the challenges, is Steven J. Duby, *Divine
Simplicity: A Dogmatic Account*, T&T Clark Studies in Systematic Theology 30 (New York:
Bloomsbury T&T Clark, 2015).
   12. We have reflected in chapter 3 on the neglect of John's theology in the East. In the West,
Augustinian and Thomistic versions of divine simplicity have tended to eclipse Anselm's. Yet
Anselm and John both make unique contributions to the church's reflection on divine simplicity;

approaching divine simplicity from a historical angle may enrich the contemporary discussion and supplement some of Dolezal's claims.

In particular, four theses will be set forth. First, throughout the Christian tradition theologians have worked with significantly different understandings of divine simplicity, though most contemporary philosophers focus on the version of divine simplicity formulated by Thomas Aquinas.[13] Second, in classical theology, divine simplicity was not an awkward philosophical appendage to the doctrine of God but integrally related to the witness and worship of the church, to be approached with humility and prayer. Third, many of the different leanings in contemporary versus classical treatments of divine simplicity are related to deeper, ontological differences in which the Creator/creation relationship is understood differently. Fourth, for the ancients, the doctrine of divine simplicity was a means of both illuminating the meaning of the Trinity as well as grounding it firmly within monotheism. Stemming from this claim, it will be suggested in conclusion that divine simplicity may provide a more consistent and robust means of safeguarding divine unity amidst Trinitarianism than the doctrine of *perichoresis*, which is often used today for a similar purpose.

The Complexity of Simplicity

It is frequently noted that the doctrine of divine simplicity has been a recurrent feature of the church's theology throughout patristic, medieval, and post-Reformation traditions.[14] The diversity of expressions of divine simplicity throughout these different eras, however, has been less frequently appreciated. It is a doctrine both enduring and elastic—standard and yet slippery. What unites all versions of divine simplicity is the negative claim that God lacks any composition or parts. When it comes to an affirmation of what divine simplicity positively entails, differences emerge. The differences could be categorized into two

---

Anselm's doctrine of divine simplicity is not identical with that of Augustine or Aquinas, nor is John's merely a recapitulation of earlier Eastern thought. On Anselm's version of divine simplicity, see F. G. Immink, *Divine Simplicity* (Kampen: J. H. Kok, 1987), 97–122.

13. Plantinga, e.g., seems exclusively focused on the Thomistic version of divine simplicity in his rebuttal, *Does God Have a Nature?*, 28–61. So also Hughes, *On a Complex Theory of a Simple God*; Barry Miller, *A Most Unlikely God: A Philosophical Enquiry into the Nature of God* (Notre Dame, IN: University of Notre Dame Press, 1996), and many others.

14. E.g., Richard Muller, *Post-Reformation Reformed Dogmatics: The Rise and Development of Reformed Orthodoxy, ca. 1520. to ca. 1725*, vol. 3 (Grand Rapids, MI: Baker, 2003), 39.

broad camps.[15] First, there is a stronger version of divine simplicity commonly called the "identity thesis" or the "identity account." This version, in addition to denying any composition in God, affirms that God's essence is identical with his existence and attributes. Thus, it is claimed, all that is in God *is* God,[16] and God *is* what he *has*.[17] Second, there are a number of weaker versions of divine simplicity that can be lumped together by the fact that they reject the notion that God is identical with attributes. Some claim that God merely instantiates his properties rather than that God is identical with them;[18] others claim that what divine simplicity entails is that the divine attributes exist in harmony with divine unity rather than identify with the divine essence;[19] yet others claim that divine simplicity simply affirms the lack of spatial and temporal parts in God.[20]

Examples of the weaker version of divine simplicity are not merely present in contemporary literature as accommodations to the criticisms of Plantinga and others. Andrew Radde-Gallwitz has demonstrated, for example, that Gregory of Nyssa and Basil of Caesarea went to great lengths to oppose the identity thesis, even while upholding a softer version of divine simplicity.[21] For them, divine simplicity required that God's attributes are not parts of God and that they do not contradict one another—but not that they are identical with God's nature.[22] Their version of divine simplicity took on different proportions because it *functioned* differently in their theology. For them, divine simplicity was less concerned with upholding divine aseity and absoluteness; it was a more basic exegetical concern in their struggle

---

15. Thomas H. McCall, "Trinity Doctrine, Plain and Simple," in *Advancing Trinitarian Theology: Explorations in Constructive Dogmatics*, ed. Oliver D. Crisp and Fred Sanders (Grand Rapids, MI: Zondervan, 2014), 54–55, also emphasizes the diversity of divine simplicity throughout the tradition, though he breaks the doctrine down into three broad categories: "strict simplicity," "formal simplicity," and "generic simplicity." This ways of categorizing variations of divine simplicity is more nuanced than, but not incompatible with, my twofold distinction.

16. Dolezal, *God without Parts*, 125.

17. William F. Vallicella, "Divine Simplicity," *The Stanford Encyclopedia of Philosophy* (Spring 2015), ed. Edward N. Zalta, accessed February 19, 2019, https://plato.stanford.edu/entries/divine-simplicity/.

18. So William Mann, "Divine Simplicity," *Religious Studies* 18 (1982): 451–71.

19. So John Frame, *The Doctrine of God: A Theology of Lordship* (Phillipsburg, NJ: P&R, 2002), 229, as discussed in Dolezal, *God without Parts*, 141.

20. So Joshua Hoffman and Gary S. Rosenkrantz, *The Divine Attributes* (Oxford, UK: Blackwell, 2002), 59–68.

21. Andrew Radde-Gallwitz, *Basil of Caesarea, Gregory of Nyssa, and the Transformation of Divine Simplicity* (Oxford, UK: Oxford University Press, 2009).

22. Radde-Gallwitz, *Basil of Caesarea*, 5–7.

for orthodox Trinitarianism *contra* Eunomius and in their opposition to the negative theology of Clement of Alexandria.[23] For Gregory and Basil, divine simplicity served as part of their effort to establish the full deity of the Son and the Holy Spirit, while also grounding orthodox Trinitarianism as firmly monotheistic. It did not entail that God was identical with his properties, and both theologians rejected this idea.

In affirming a weaker version of divine simplicity, these Cappadocian Fathers were not breaking with earlier Eastern thought but developing and extending it. Lewis Ayres has demonstrated that divine simplicity was utilized consistently and yet in diverse ways in the struggle for Nicene orthodoxy.[24] Pro-Nicene theologians such as Gregory of Nyssa, Didymus the Blind, Hilary, and Ambrose routinely used divine simplicity to ground Trinitarian doctrine as monotheistic but refrained from making further specifications concerning the implications of the doctrine, as later Western medieval theologians would.[25] Similarly, Gregory of Nazianzus, in his orations blasting away at the neo-Arianism of Eunomius and his followers, would routinely reference God's nature as noncomposite and undivided, without further explication of what this meant.[26] Unlike the later Western tradition, which put divine simplicity to use for more ambitious, constructive purposes concerning the nature of theology itself,[27] Eastern theologians tended to utilize divine simplicity in a more negative, apophatic way to set conditions for discussion of the nature of personal distinctions in the one divine essence.[28]

In the seventh century, John of Damascus represents the maturing of this Eastern strand of thought concerning divine simplicity. John's

---

23. Although the Cappadocians are often portrayed as proponents of negative theology, theirs was a relative apophaticism, and they opposed the radical apophaticism of Clement. See Radde-Gallwitz, *Basil of Caesarea*, 38–66.

24. Lewis Ayres, *Nicaea and Its Legacy: An Approach to Fourth-Century Trinitarian Theology* (Oxford, UK: Oxford University Press, 2004), 281, 287.

25. Ayres, *Nicaea and Its Legacy*, 286–88.

26. Gregory of Nazianzus, *On God and Christ: The Five Theological Orations and Two Letters to Cleodinus*, Popular Patristics 23 (Crestwood, NY: St. Vladimir's Seminary Press, 2002), 42, 70, 78, 86, 127.

27. Thomas Aquinas, e.g., put divine simplicity at the front end of his *Summa Theologica*, using it to set the conditions for everything else he says about God's attributes. Thomas Aquinas, *Summa Theologica* I, Q. 3, 14–20.

28. Ayres, *Nicaea and Its Legacy*, 287. In its earliest articulations, divine simplicity was often invoked even more basically, apart from Trinitarian discussion, as a necessary component of the Creator/creation distinction (e.g., by Irenaeus *contra* his Gnostic opponents). Cf. Duby, *Divine Simplicity*, 7–8.

theology is often interpreted as a synthesis of the earlier Eastern tradition, especially the Cappadocian Fathers. Yet John also makes some unique contributions. For example, while the Cappadocian Fathers used the term *perichoresis* to refer to the relation of the two natures of Christ, John applied it to the relations between the three divine persons.[29] His treatment of divine simplicity also contains some unique contributions. Near the beginning of his *On the Orthodox Faith*, John divided all reality into two classes: the created (mutable) and the uncreated (immutable).[30] Divine simplicity was utilized in this context in order to distinguish God from creation and demonstrate the necessity of his existence as the source of creation. In this context, divine simplicity was emphasized primarily in terms of a lack of *spatial* composition. He claims, for example, that God is "infinite, and boundless, and formless, and intangible, and invisible, in short, simple and uncompound."[31] John also appeals to negative theology and to Exodus 3:14 in order to explain the doctrine of divine simplicity, calling God's self-identification in this passage "the most proper of all the names given to God."[32] If there is anything at the core of what divine simplicity means throughout *On the Orthodox Faith*, it is this emphasis on God's lack of spatial parts and formlessness: "The Deity is indivisible, being everywhere wholly in His entirety and not divided up part by part like that which has a body, but wholly in everything and wholly above everything."[33]

In his later chapter devoted to divine simplicity, *On the Orthodox Faith* 1.9, John responds to the difficulties raised by predicating diverse attributes of a simple God by appealing to the Cappadocians' distinction between the essence and energies of God. John affirms that each of God's attributes is itself simple—thus, his omnipresence (what he refers to as God being "uncircumscribed") is simple,[34] as is

---

29. John of Damascus, *On the Orthodox Faith*, *Nicene and Post-Nicene Fathers*, Second Series: *Hilary of Poitiers, John of Damascus*, 14 vols., ed. Philip Schaff and Henry Wace (1899; repr. Peabody, MA: Hendrickson, 2012), 1.8, 11, claims that the Father, Son, and Spirit are "made one not so as to commingle, but so as to cleave (Greek *perichoresin*) to each other, and they have their being in each other without any coalescence or commingling."

30. John of Damascus, *On the Orthodox Faith* 1.9, 12.

31. John of Damascus, *On the Orthodox Faith* 1.3, 2–3.

32. John of Damascus, *On the Orthodox Faith* 1.4, 3.

33. John of Damascus, *On the Orthodox Faith* 1.13, 15.

34. John of Damascus, *On the Orthodox Faith* 1.13, 15.

God's knowledge.[35] But John denies that God's diverse attributes are identical with his simple essence, instead linking God's attributes with his *energies*.[36] Thus, for John, divine simplicity is ultimately swallowed up into divine incomprehensibility and hiddenness, for it concerns his unknown, hidden essence. This version of divine simplicity stands in stark contrast to that which developed in the West, which strongly emphasized the identity of God's essence and attributes.[37]

Divine Simplicity in the Life of the Church

In the contemporary literature divine simplicity is often regarded as a philosophical consequence within the doctrine of God, disconnected from church life. Christians of earlier eras, however, consistently regarded divine simplicity as a living part of their witness and worship. In the late second century Athenagoras appealed to the doctrine of divine simplicity as part of his apology for the Christian faith to the emperors Aurelius and Commodus. For him, to accept an uncreated, impassible, indivisible God without parts or composition was part and parcel of rejecting the polytheism of his day.[38] Later, Boethius would use divine simplicity to establish that the divine essence was "beautiful and stable."[39] To consider divine simplicity as an aspect of divine beauty, or to utilize it in the context of theistic apologetics, is to step into a larger domain of concerns than is typically present in contemporary treatments of the doctrine.

While Thomas Aquinas's treatment of divine simplicity is the most influential and perhaps the most sophisticated in the church's history, it is not the sum total of what the church has had to say about divine simplicity, and when studies of divine simplicity limit their focus to Thomistic versions of the doctrine, its context in the life and worship

---

35. John of Damascus, *On the Orthodox Faith* 1.14, 17.

36. John of Damascus, *On the Orthodox Faith* 1.9, 12.

37. As an example, consider the particularly strong statement of William Ockham: "Divine wisdom is the same as the divine essence in every way in which the divine essence is the same as itself. Similarly, for divine goodness and justice. Nor is there any distinction at all, or even any nonidentity there in the nature of the thing." Quoted in Marilyn McCord Adams, *William Ockham*, 2 vols. (Notre Dame, IN: University of Notre Dame Press, 1987), 2:942.

38. Athenagoras, *A Plea for the Christians, Ante-Nicene Fathers: Hermas, Tatian, Athenagoras, Theophilus, Clement of Alexandra*, 10 vols., ed. Alexander Roberts and James Donaldson (1885; repr. Peabody, MA: Hendrickson, 2012), 2:132.

39. Boethius, *De Trinitate* II, in *The Selected Works of Boethius*, trans. W. V. Cooper (1905; repr. Oxford, UK: Benediction Classics, 2010), 14.

of the church can be obscured. For instance, in Bonaventure's *The Journey of the Mind to God*, divine simplicity is invoked in the context of describing the soul's contemplation of God as the "most pure Being" who, in addition to being primal and eternal and pure actuality, has no defect and is most perfect.[40] Bonaventure proceeds to associate divine simplicity with divine power: "Since it is utterly simple in essence, it is greatest in power, because the more a power is concentrated in one, the more it is infinite."[41] Having drawn divine power as a consequence of divine simplicity, Bonaventure then employs these doctrines to determine the divine relation to all other things: "Because it is the most simple and the greatest, it is wholly within all things and wholly outside them; hence it is 'the intelligible sphere, whose center is everywhere and whose circumference is nowhere.'"[42] Whereas modern theology tends to conceive divine simplicity as a limiting notion, slicing God off from contact with composite reality, for Bonaventure it is, along with divine truth and goodness, the very basis for the Creator/creation relationship: "Through its supremely simple unity, its most serene truth, and its most sincere goodness, it contains in itself all power, all exemplarity, and all communicability."[43]

An even more prayerful, meditative employment of divine simplicity comes in Anselm's *Proslogion*. Anselm's articulation of divine simplicity is interwoven throughout his exploration of God as that than which nothing greater can be conceived, rather than (as with Thomas) placed at the front end of a systematic walk-through of divine attributes. In *Proslogion* 18, for example, Anselm laments the loss of the vision of God that occurred at the human fall, petitions God to strengthen and cleanse his soul so that he might see more of the divine, and then unpacks divine simplicity as a response to his question, "What are you, Lord, what are you? What shall my heart understand you to be?"[44] At

---

40. Bonaventure, *The Journey of the Mind to God*, ed. Stephen F. Brown, trans. Philotheus Boehner (Indianapolis: Hackett, 1993), 30.

41. Bonaventure, *Journey of the Mind to God*, 31.

42. Bonaventure, *Journey of the Mind to God*, 31. The quotation here is from Alan of Lille's *Theological Rules*.

43. Bonaventure, *Journey of the Mind to God*, 32.

44. Anselm, *Proslogion* 23, in *Anselm: Basic Writings*, ed. and trans. Thomas Williams (Indianapolis: Hacket, 2007), 94. For my purposes in this book I use Williams's translations, in consultation with *S. Anselmi Cantuariensus Archiepiscopi Opera Omnia*, ed. F. S. Schmitt, 6 vols. (Edinburgh: Thomas Nelson & Sons, 1946–1961). All subsequent references to Anselm draw from the page numbers of Williams's collection of Anselm's writings.

the climax of Anselm's discussion of divine simplicity in *Proslogion* 23 (which will be explored below), Anselm quotes Jesus's assertion to Martha in Luke 10:42 that "one thing is necessary."[45] Upon first consideration, this might seem like an unlikely verse to correlate with divine simplicity, but Anselm claims that what has been established by divine simplicity is "that one necessary which is all good—or rather, which is itself the complete, one, total, and unique good." For Anselm, divine simplicity establishes God as the aim of the human soul, the supreme good which captures every human longing. Anselm's treatment of divine simplicity differs from Aquinas's in its worshipful tone and its theological purpose; if for Thomas divine simplicity is a placeholder by which to organize divine attributes, for Anselm it is a ladder by which to see more of the divine beauty.

One reason classical theologians approached divine simplicity in a devotional frame was that many of them believed it was related to God's redeeming of fallen creation. It was for them not confined to the realm of theology proper but had soteriological implications. Pseudo-Dionysius, whose writings on divine simplicity had great significance for medieval thought, called God "the principle of simplicity for those turning toward simplicity, point of unity for those made one."[46] To begin his discussion of divine names, he claims that the Bible treats God as "a monad or henad, because of its supernatural simplicity and indivisible unity, by which unifying power we are led to unity. We, in the diversity of what we are, are drawn together by it and led into a godlike oneness, into a unity reflecting God."[47] Thus in Pseudo-Dionysius's thought, redemption consists of being transformed in some sense from creational complexity into divine simplicity. He even wrote of the incarnation as a movement bridging this chasm and thus making this redemption possible: "The simplicity of Jesus became something complex, the timeless took on the duration of the temporal."[48] So also John of Damascus could write of God as the "simplicity of those who love simplicity."[49] For him, a simple God was not

---

45. Anselm, *Proslogion* 23, 94.
46. Pseudo-Dionysius, *The Complete Works*, trans. Colin Luibheid (New York: Paulist Press, 1987), 51.
47. Pseudo-Dionysius, *Complete Works*, 51.
48. Pseudo-Dionysius, *Complete Works*, 52.
49. John of Damascus, *On the Orthodox Faith* 1.12, 13.

cut off from composite creation by virtue of its simplicity but rather had a dynamic relationship with creation, grounding its own diversity and ultimately converting divided creation into its own simplicity:

> The divine effulgence and energy, being one and simple and indivisible, assuming many varied forms in its own goodness among what is divisible and allotting to each the component parts of its own nature, still remains simple and is multiplied without division among the divided, and gathers and converts the divided into its own simplicity.[50]

For John, as for Pseudo-Dionysius, the redemption of fallen creatures involved some kind of translation into divine simplicity, making this doctrine a part of the church's salvation as well as her theology.

Just as contemporary philosophical treatments of divine simplicity should recognize diversity in how divine simplicity has been defined through church history, not considering a refutation of Aquinas as tantamount to a refutation of divine simplicity wholesale, so also contemporary treatments of divine simplicity may be strengthened by considering this liturgical, aesthetic dimension to divine simplicity and the way it has been so naturally correlated with other Christian doctrines. Sensitivity to divine simplicity's setting in the life of the church over the centuries may, for instance, raise questions and concerns about the *implications* of its acceptance or rejection that do not otherwise come into view. Even if it ultimately needs to be removed, a doctrine so embedded in the church's life and worship throughout the centuries probably requires something more like a surgical procedure than a swift amputation.

"The Supraessential Essence": Simplicity and Ontology

One of the theses undergirding Dolezal's defense of divine simplicity is his claim that the common thread throughout the various criticisms of divine simplicity is the assumption of a univocal relationship between God and creation rather than an analogical relationship.[51] Similarly, Nicholas Wolterstorff (not himself a defender of divine simplicity)

---

50. John of Damascus, *On the Orthodox Faith* 1.14, 17.
51. Dolezal, *God without Parts*, xvii–xviii, 29–30.

has suggested that medieval and contemporary thinkers have such different instincts concerning divine simplicity because of differing ontologies.[52] A brief foray into the church's historical reflection on this topic provides a greater vantage point for considering the strength of these claims, especially Dolezal's.

The writings of Plotinus, which exerted great influence on the church's formulation of divine simplicity, particularly reveal the close relationship between divine simplicity and how one construes the Creator/creation relationship. Plotinus differed from earlier Platonists by claiming that "the One" or "the Unity" existed prior to the divine intellect, because the divine intellect is composite. He wrote:

> Generative of all, the Unity is none of all; neither thing nor quantity nor quality nor intellect nor soul; not in motion, not at rest, not in place, not in time: it is the self-defined, unique in form or, better, formless, existing before Form was, or Movement or Rest, all of which are attachments of Being and make Being the manifold it is.[53]

Because he viewed the One/Unity as prior to being itself, Plotinus regarded it as belonging to an entirely different ontological framework than the rest of reality and as such not subject to the language and logic that govern all other reality.

The writings of Pseudo-Dionysius also exerted a great influence on the church's understanding of divine simplicity, at least up until the time of the Reformation. Following Plotinus's language about the One, Pseudo-Dionysius conceived of God as the cause of all unity and distinction, which itself transcends the very categories of unity and distinction. He called God a "supra-existent Being" and "mind beyond mind, word beyond speech." He wrote: "Cause of all existence, and therefore itself transcending existence, it alone could give

---

52. Nicholas Wolterstorff, "Divine Simplicity," in *Inquiring about God: Selected Essays*, vol. 1, ed. Terence Cuneo (Cambridge, UK: Cambridge University Press, 2010), 100–101. According to Wolterstorff, the ancients operated with a "constituent ontology," whereas contemporary thinkers operate with a "relation ontology." In a constituent ontology, an entity does not relate to its nature and properties as external components but as ontological constituents. In other words, entities do not have a nature; they are their nature. In a relation ontology, an entity is related to its nature by necessarily exemplifying it.

53. Plotinus, *6th Ennead*, "On the One and the Good," trans. Stephen Mackenna and B. S. Page (Boston: Hale, Cushman, & Flint, 1930), 241.

an authoritative account of what it really is."[54] Repeatedly, Pseudo-Dionysius drew a connection between God's transcendence over unity/diversity and his ability to ground and define unity/diversity within creation. He wrote: "The One cause of all things is not one of the many things in the world but actually precedes oneness and multiplicity and indeed defines oneness and multiplicity."[55] And elsewhere he claimed that God "transcends the unity which is in beings. He is indivisible multiplicity, the unfilled overfullness which produces, perfects, and preserves all unity and all multiplicity."[56] In a more lengthy statement to this effect, he applied this notion to God's unity and triune life:

> The fact that the transcendent Godhead is one and triune must not be understood in any of our own typical senses. . . . We use the names Trinity and Unity for that which is in fact beyond every name, calling it the transcendent being above every being. But no unity or trinity, no number or oneness, no fruitfulness, indeed, nothing that is or is known can proclaim the hiddenness beyond every mind and reason of the transcendent Godhead which transcends every being.[57]

For a thinker like Pseudo-Dionysius, the relation of divine simplicity and Trinity is not a problem to be explained in creational categories, since both terms apply to that which is "beyond every name." He uses divine simplicity and Trinity to explain unity and diversity in creation; he apparently does not consider that they need explanation themselves.

Though the writings of Pseudo-Dionysius are hardly representative of catholic Christian thought, it is noteworthy how many other theologians have followed in his steps in rejecting a univocal Creator/creation relation, with the frequent implication drawn that God is above the very categories of being and distinction. Aquinas, for instance, was quite swift in his rejection of univocal language for God and creation; in the *Summa Theologica* it is asserted as axiomatic, as a premise in the establishment of other disputed points, not as itself requiring

---

54. Pseudo-Dionysius, *Complete Works*, 50.
55. Pseudo-Dionysius, *Complete Works*, 128.
56. Pseudo-Dionysius, *Complete Works*, 66–67.
57. Pseudo-Dionysius, *Complete Works*, 129.

establishment.[58] Referencing "Dionysius," he claimed that while creatures are like God in some ways, God is like them in no ways, "for, we
also say that a statue is like a man, but not conversely."[59] Like Pseudo-
Dionysius, Aquinas held that God and creatures have different kinds
of being, since God is the author of all being: "God is not related to
creatures as though belonging to a different *genus*, but as transcending every *genus*, and as the principle of all *genera*."[60] He therefore
claimed, "God is more distant from creatures than any creatures are
from each other."[61]

Because of her emphasis on God's transcendence over creation,
the church has often exhibited great caution in drawing conclusions
about God on the basis of creational forms of thought and logic. Augustine's caution in his *De Trinitate* reflects this restraint: "Whatever
is said of a nature, unchangeable, invisible and having life absolutely
and sufficient to itself, must not be measured after the custom of
things visible, and changeable, and mortal, or not self-sufficient."[62]
So also, Anselm repeatedly insisted upon the uniqueness of God's
existence in *Monologion* 16 and *Proslogion* 18–22, claiming that
because God is simple, he exists in a different way from all other existing things. In both books, Anselm moves from God's simplicity to
his eternity: because God is *wholly* whatever he is (*Monologion* 17;
Proslogion 18), he must necessarily be *everywhere* and *at all times*
whatever he is (*Monologion* 18; *Proslogion* 19–21). The significance
of divine simplicity for Anselm, in part, is that it points to God's
being above all other things and possessing his own self-derived,
necessary existence. As he puts it in *Proslogion* 19, "You, although
nothing exists with you, do not exist in a place or a time; rather, all
things exist in you. For nothing contains you, but you contain all
things."[63] This last assertion bears resemblance to a similar statement
by John of Damascus: "[God] is not one of the things that are, but

58. E.g., ST I, Q. 3, Art. 8, ad. 1, 19. Cf. Aquinas's fuller case for an analogical view of theological language, over and against an equivocal and univocal view, in ST 1, Q. 13, Art. 5, 63–64.
59. ST I, Q. 4, Art. 3, ad. 4, 23.
60. ST I, Q. 4, Art. 3, ad. 2, 23.
61. ST I, Q. 13, Art. 5, 64.
62. Augustine, *On the Holy Trinity, Nicene and Post-Nicene Fathers*, First Series: *Augustine:
On the Holy Trinity, Doctrinal Treatises, Moral Treatises*, 14 vols., ed. Philip Schaff (1887; repr.
Peabody, MA: Hendrickson, 2012), 3:87.
63. Anselm, *Proslogion* 19, 92.

over all things."[64] John claimed that while we can truly know God in accordance with his gracious revelation, ultimately the divine essence remains incomprehensible. Thus, when discussing the divine essence, he at times uses the word *supraessential*, since God is above all essence and being, sovereignty and rank, word and thought, as the fountain of all these things.[65] He also called God "the super-essential essence, the Godhead that is more than God, the beginning that is above beginning."[66]

This approach to the relation of God and creation among classical theologians differs from that implicit in many contemporary treatments of divine simplicity. One might summarize the matter by suggesting that much of the discussion of divine simplicity in contemporary philosophy tends to approach God within a larger structure of reality, while its discussion in classical theology tended to approach reality itself as subsisting within the being of God. In classical theology, God was not an existing thing as much as he was above existence as the ground of existing things; it was not a question of whether his simplicity was logically coherent as much as a question of how to ground logical coherence itself. Classical theologians did not approach God and creation as two different items within the same genus or rank, or even two different kinds of genus or rank, for the very potential for distinction between different kinds of reality was itself grounded in the being of God. For classical theology, God was the basis for being itself and therefore cannot be subjected to a scale of being. He was the ground of every spectrum and therefore could not be placed on any spectrum.

If someone objects, "The idea that God is beyond the very distinction between unity and diversity is irrational," it may be questioned

---

64. John of Damascus, *On the Orthodox Faith* 1.12, 14.

65. John of Damascus, *On the Orthodox Faith* 1.8, 6.

66. John of Damascus, *On the Orthodox Faith* 1.12, 14. John apparently did not sense a danger here in separating God in himself from God in his revelation or feel a need to reconcile his positive theological claims with the notion of God's incomprehensibility. Part of the explanation for such emphasis on divine hiddenness may be that John, along with many other classical theologians, was reacting to the extreme apophaticism of much Jewish and Muslim thought. Maimonides, e.g., explicitly affirmed an equivocal view of the Creator/creation relation and argued that God has no relation to that which is non-God. See Maimonides, *The Guide for the Perplexed*, trans. Shlomo Pines (Chicago: University of Chicago Press, 1963), 130–31. He therefore claimed that the closest one can come to intellectually cognizing God is picturing whiteness (163). The intellectual tilt of the entire medieval world, and not just the church, seems to have been, at least with respect to the knowability of God, in the opposite direction of much contemporary thought.

whether there is a certain relationship between God and creation being assumed in which both are subsumed within the same ontological framework, subject to the same laws and expectations. It would be irrationalism to claim that God simply *defies* logic, but it is not obviously irrationalism to claim that God *defines* logic, for the claim here is not that God is an exception to the rules but that he is the ground of all rules and rule itself, and as such is utterly unique. It is not difficult to see, therefore, how the ancients' differing ontological starting point and priorities did indeed pertain, in their minds, to issues touching upon the integrity of divine absoluteness and aseity. To put it in Anselm's language, if God does not contain all things, then he would seem to be contained by something. To put it in John's language, if God is not over all things, then he does seem to be one of the things that is, rather than the supraessential essence.

1+1+1=1? Simplicity and Trinity

Many contemporary defenses of divine simplicity attempt to reconcile it with theism *simpliciter* rather than the Trinitarian God of the Christian faith. William Mann, for example, takes this route in his influential 1982 article.[67] In this approach, the Trinity is seen as a subsequent topic to be reconciled with divine simplicity once its meaning has been already established. Classical theologians, however, apparently believed that the Trinity can and should be seen as a *resource* to be utilized with respect to the meaning of divine simplicity, not a problem to be overcome once the meaning of divine simplicity has been established.[68]

In this connection, it is worth noting that non-Trinitarian theists have generally formulated a different kind of divine simplicity than that of the Christian tradition. For medieval Jewish and Muslim theologians, for example, the doctrine of the Trinity was fundamentally at odds with divine simplicity. In his well-known treatment of divine simplicity in *The Guide for the Perplexed*, Moses Maimonides opened his treatment of the nature of God with a strong emphasis on divine

---

67. Mann, "Divine Simplicity," 451.
68. As Muller, *Post-Reformation Reformed Dogmatics*, vol. 3, 276, notes, "From the time of the fathers onward, divine simplicity was understood as a support of the doctrine of the Trinity."

simplicity. Maimonides claimed that God has no essential attributes, associating the alternative to this view with polytheism and the doctrine of the Trinity.[69] For Maimonides, God's actions may be diverse as the outworking of his simple essence on creation, but the idea that there are essential attributes in God is, like Trinitarianism, one with polytheism.[70] A slightly weaker version of divine simplicity is affirmed by the Muslim theologian Avicenna, who taught that attributes may be ascribed to God but only negatively, as "privations." In Avicenna's thought, we may say that God has existence, but all his other characteristics should be described in negation, by their difference from the characteristics of all other beings.[71] This emphasis on the strict unity of God was at the heart of the medieval Islamic faith, and divine simplicity was wielded in order to exclude any notion of diversity in God, including personal distinctions. Hence divine simplicity was stressed in the strongest possible terms. Al-Kindi referred to God as "pure and simply unity, [having] nothing other than unity,"[72] and Al-Farabi claimed God's unity *was* his essence.[73]

In light of these versions of divine simplicity outside of the church, it is all the more striking that, in general, classical theologians have spent little time seeking to reconcile divine simplicity and the Trinity. The greater interest of most classical theologians has been to *use* divine simplicity to ground the Trinity as firmly monotheistic. Basil the Great, for example, compared the relation of God the Father and God the Son to that of an emperor and his image on a coin: "How does one and one not equal two Gods? Because we speak of the emperor, and the emperor's image—but not two emperors." We could restate Basil's question here in Trinitarian terms: How does 1+1+1 not add up to 3? Basil then appealed to divine simplicity to explain the metaphor: "Since the divine nature is not composed of parts, union of the persons is accomplished by partaking of the whole."[74] This sentence serves

69. Maimonides, *Guide for the Perplexed*, 111.
70. Maimonides, *Guide for the Perplexed*, 145.
71. Ian Richard Netton, *Allah Transcendent: Studies in the Structure and Semiotics of Islamic Philosophy, Theology, and Cosmology* (New York: Routledge, 1989), 154.
72. As quoted in Netton, *Allah Transcendent*, 48.
73. See Netton, *Allah Transcendent*, 105.
74. Basil the Great, *On the Holy Spirit* 18.23, trans. David Anderson (Yonkers, NY: St. Vladimir's Press, 1980), 72.

as a good sample of the kind of reasoning one finds with surprising regularity throughout the Christian tradition, both East and West. 1+1+1=1 because the sum total of the equation is "not composed of parts."

Aquinas, drawing from Boethius, related divine simplicity and the Trinity by claiming that divine simplicity excluded a plurality of "absolute things" in God but not a plurality of relations. He claimed: "The supreme unity and simplicity of God exclude every kind of plurality of absolute things, but not plurality of relations. Because relations are predicated relatively, and thus the relations do not import composition in that of which they are predicated."[75] In a lengthy discussion of what terms and grammatical genders may be used to signify the unity and diversity of the Godhead, drawing from Augustine, Hilary, John of Damascus, Jerome, and Ambrose, Aquinas repeatedly grounded the Trinity in the divine essence by means of divine simplicity.[76] So also, Augustine sought to ground divine unity amidst the Trinity by means of divine simplicity. He claimed, for example, that God's attributes belonged to his one essence, not his three persons, because of divine simplicity. Specifically, he claimed that God has one greatness, not three greatnesses, because God *is* his own greatness, and so with his goodness, eternity, omnipotence, and indeed whatever may be predicated of him.[77] Later, Augustine used divine simplicity to deny that the Father and the Son are two separate gods:

> But in God to be is the same as to be strong, or to be just, or to be wise, or whatever is said of that simple multiplicity, or multifold simplicity, whereby to signify His substance. Wherefore, whether we say God of God in such way that this name belongs to each, yet not so that both together are two Gods, but one God; for they are in such way united with each other.[78]

He also correlated divine simplicity to the entire Trinity, arguing that if God were not simple, each individual person in the Godhead would be less than the entire Godhead all at once:

---

75. ST I, Q. 30, Art. 1, 160.
76. ST I, Q. 31, Arts. 1–2, 164–66.
77. Augustine, *De Trinitate* 5.10, 92–93.
78. Augustine, *De Trinitate* 6.4, 100.

His greatness is the same as His wisdom . . . and His goodness
is the same as His wisdom and greatness, and his truth the same
as all those things; and in Him it is not one thing to be blessed,
and another to be great, or wise, or true, or good, or in a word
to be Himself. Neither, since He is a Trinity, is He therefore to be
thought triple (triplex), otherwise the Father alone, or the Son
alone, will be less than the Father and Son together.[79]

For Augustine, then, the very same movement that required God's
attributes to be identical with each other equally required the divine
persons to be bound together as one God.

John of Damascus likewise grounded the Trinity in the one divine
essence by means of divine simplicity. In distinguishing between the
relation of God and God's Spirit to a human being and his or her
spirit, he claimed:

But in the case of the divine nature, which is simple and uncompound, we must confess in all piety that there exists a Spirit of
God, for the Word is not more imperfect than our own word. Now
we cannot, in piety, consider the Spirit to be something foreign
that gains admission into God from without, as is the case with
compound natures like us.[80]

Later he wrote: "When I combine and reckon the three [subsis-
tences] together, I know one perfect God. For the Godhead is not
compound but in three perfect subsistences, one perfect indivisible
and uncompound God."[81] A similar argument had been made earlier
by the Cappadocian Fathers.[82] In fact, Lewis Ayres has argued that the
primary concern in early Eastern formulations of divine simplicity was
the protection of the unity of the Godhead amidst affirmations of the
three divine persons.[83]

One of the clearest examples of seeking to ground the Trinity as
monotheistic by means of divine simplicity is Anselm's *Proslogion*

---

79. Augustine, *De Trinitate* 6.7, 101. Cf. his later summary of this argument in 8.1, 115, where
he claims that the three divine persons are not three gods because they belong to the same essence
in which to be is the same as to be great, good, wise, and whatever else God is.
80. John of Damascus, *On the Orthodox Faith* 1.7, 5.
81. John of Damascus, *On the Orthodox Faith* 1.12, 14.
82. See the discussion in Dolezal, *God without Parts*, 4.
83. Ayres, *Nicaea and Its Legacy*, 286–88.

23. Already in *Proslogion* 5 Anselm had stipulated divine aseity as a foundational implication of the divine name, and divine simplicity has repeatedly been affirmed as a necessary consequence of aseity throughout the book. Anselm's version of divine simplicity is solidly in the camp of the identity thesis of Augustine and Aquinas. In *Proslogion* 18, for example, he prays, "You are in fact unity itself. . . . Life and wisdom and the rest are not parts of you; they are all one. Each of them is all of what you are, and each is what the rest are."[84] In *Proslogion* 23, Anselm seeks to demonstrate that the one supreme good whose existence and nature he has been establishing in the preceding chapters is equally the Father, the Son, and the Spirit. First, he establishes the unity of the Father and the Son on the basis of divine simplicity: "You are so simple that nothing can be born of you that is other than what you are."[85] Then he draws the Spirit into this unity in the same way: "Moreover, the one who is equal to both you and him is not other than you and him, nothing can proceed from the supreme simplicity that is other than from which it proceeds."[86] Using his characteristic chiastic literary device, Anselm concludes:

> Thus, whatever each of you is individually, that is what the whole Trinity is together, Father, Son, and Holy Spirit; for each of you individually is nothing other than the supremely simple unity and the supremely united simplicity which cannot be multiplied or different from itself.[87]

For Anselm, divine simplicity does not rule out personal distinctions in the Godhead, but it does require that each person of the Godhead contains the entirety of the Godhead. There are thus three persons via begottenness and procession, but these comprise one unity via divine simplicity, the "supremely simple unity" and "supremely united simplicity."

It is beyond the scope of this chapter to *apply* these historical findings to all of the various contemporary concerns about divine simplicity and Trinity. But it may be useful in passing to draw attention

---

84. Anselm, *Proslogion* 18, 92. Anselm makes the same declaration in *Monologion* 17.
85. Anselm, *Proslogion* 23, 94.
86. Anselm, *Proslogion* 23, 94.
87. Anselm, *Proslogion* 23, 94.

once again to the ontological issues that are *underneath* the different approaches of, say, an Alvin Plantinga and a Thomas Aquinas on this issue. Why is it that the concerns that spring up so frequently and so urgently in the contemporary literature often do not even come into view in classical treatments? How is it that classical theologians tended to approach divine simplicity as a solution to, rather than aggravation of, the seeming numerical contradiction in the formula 1+1+1=1? In an important passage in his *On the Holy Spirit*, Basil demonstrated awareness of this challenge. His response is revealing:

> When the Lord taught us the doctrine of Father, Son, and Holy Spirit, he did not make arithmetic a part of this gift. . . . The Unapproachable One is beyond numbers, wisest sirs; imitate the reverence shown by the Hebrews of old to the unutterable name of God.[88]

By distinguishing between the Trinity and arithmetic and calling God the "Unapproachable One . . . beyond numbers," Basil situates the difficulty of the Trinity and simplicity within the larger framework of the Creator/creation distinction. For him, and for most classical theologians, God and creatures were not correlatives within the same order of being, and thus it was assumed that the laws of logic and differentiation that apply in the creational realm do not apply in the same way to the Creator. In other words, God was held to be not irrational or anumerical but uniquely related to logic and differentiation as their source.

Contemporary treatments of divine simplicity may arrive at a deeper understanding of this doctrine by examining it in relation to the ontological framework evident in much of its historical articulation. Even those who follow the modern instinct in rejecting divine simplicity as utterly arcane or incoherent (in Barry Smith's terminology, "a piece of scholastic arcanity"[89]) may, by giving greater attention to these underlying ontological issues, be better positioned to understand

---

88. Basil the Great, *On the Holy Spirit* 18.44, 71. Gregory of Nazianzus, *On God and Christ*, 107, would likewise claim that "our starting-point must be the fact that God cannot be named," commending the Hebrew practice of using special symbols to venerate the divine name.

89. As quoted in D. Stephen Long, *The Perfectly Simple God: Aquinas and His Legacy* (Minneapolis, MN: Fortress, 2016), *xxvi*.

why it has been so prevalent throughout the history of the church and why it seemed important and sensible to those who held it.

Divine Simplicity and Perichoresis

I close with an observation, stemming from examination of patristic and medieval thought. In recent years it has become common to rely upon the notion of *perichoresis* to ground Trinitarianism within monotheism. Jürgen Moltmann's social Trinitarianism, for instance, places great stress on perichoresis. He claims that the doctrine of perichoresis provides a means of maintaining both God's unity and his triunity: "The unity of the triunity lies in the eternal perichoresis of the Trinitarian persons. Interpreted perichoretically, the Trinitarian persons form their own unity by themselves in the circulation of the divine life."[90] Throughout church history, as well, perichoresis has been utilized in the service of a Trinitarian monotheism. The term was first used with reference to the two natures of Christ by Gregory of Nazianzus,[91] and began to be used with reference to the Trinity after John of Damascus.[92] But perichoresis was always used in conjunction with divine simplicity, which was the more recurrent and consistent basis for divine unity throughout church history. Today, by contrast, it has become common to seek to establish the Trinity as one through perichoresis *instead* of divine simplicity. In fact, some social Trinitarians utilize their model explicitly to downplay or discard divine simplicity.[93]

I want to suggest that divine simplicity (or better, some combination of divine simplicity and perichoresis) may provide a more solid grounding for a monotheistic Trinity than perichoresis alone.[94] The

90. Jürgen Moltmann, *The Trinity and the Kingdom* (1981; repr. Minneapolis: Fortress, 1993), 175.
91. Cf. Verna Harrison, "Perichoresis in the Greek Fathers," *St. Vladimir's Theological Quarterly* 35 (1991): 55. I am grateful to Timothy Kleiser for directing me to this article.
92. Andrew Louth, *St John Damascene: Tradition and Originality in Byzantine Theology* (Oxford, UK: Oxford University Press, 2002), 112–13.
93. E.g., Cornelius Plantinga Jr., "Social Trinity and Tritheism," in *Trinity, Incarnation, and Atonement: Philosophical and Theological Essays* (Notre Dame, IN: University of Notre Dame Press, 1990), 39, draws the following as a consequence to his social Trinitarianism: "Simplicity theory of the Augustinian, Lateran, and Thomistic sort cannot claim much by way of biblical support. . . . Simplicity doctrine finds its way into Christian theology via Neoplatonism, and ought therefore to be viewed with the same cool and dispassionate eye as any other potentially helpful or harmful philosophical contribution to theological elaborations of biblical truth."
94. Paul R. Hinlicky, *Divine Simplicity: Christ the Crisis of Metaphysics* (Grand Rapids, MI: Baker Academic, 2016), 112, responding to an earlier version of this chapter in the *International*

reason is that divine simplicity is able to bind the three persons not merely into *each other* but into the one divine essence. Strictly on the grounds of interpenetration, we are left further to explain why the interpenetration of the Father, the Son, and the Spirit does not entail three interpenetrating gods. Why should the interpenetration of three persons yield one undivided unity and not some complex aggregate? What is needed is not simply a mechanism by which to bring the divine persons into proximity with each other in the "circulation of the divine life," but a mechanism by which to unite the divine persons as *one*. Where perichoresis may make oneness among the three persons possible, divine simplicity makes it necessary.

This certainly does not entail that the notion of perichoresis should not be applied to the divine persons; it does not even entail that it has no explanatory power for how Trinitarianism is monotheistic (as we have seen, John of Damascus apparently felt the need to utilize *both* perichoresis and divine simplicity to explain the relation of God's threeness and oneness). It means that *in and of itself*, perichoresis does not seem sufficiently able to ground Trinitarianism in monotheism.[95]

Conclusion

This chapter has been concerned with how historical theology may stabilize, broaden, and/or resource current reflection on divine simplicity. In closing, it is appropriate to reiterate a consideration that has been implicit throughout, especially the third and fourth points above, namely, that the church's reflection may particularly serve as a caution against the dangers associated with free-floating speculation concerning the divine nature. Something of this way of thinking can

---

Journal of Systematic Theology (not, as incorrectly cited, *Modern Theology*), argues that perichoresis is never "alone" because it is not an abstract metaphysical postulate competing with divine simplicity in the service of safeguarding divine unity. This may be a valid qualification for how perichoresis has functioned historically and in relation to its biblical foundations, but I submit that perichoresis has come to play a more ambitious function in modern theology; e.g., as we have noted, it is often set over and against divine simplicity as an alternative means for grounding divine unity.

95. This criticism is more applicable to modern articulations of perichoresis such as that of Moltmann than to those more nuanced articulations of perichoresis in the tradition. E.g., Harrison, "Perichoresis in the Greek Fathers," 53–54, argues that the earliest usage of perichoresis involved the notion of "alternation" or "repetition," drawing from the Stoic conception of "mixture." This way of understanding perichoresis could, perhaps, have more utility with respect to divine unity.

be summarized, in a general but vivid way, by referencing a passage in C. S. Lewis's *Till We Have Faces*. In this scene, the priest of Ungit is narrating to King Trom and his courtiers of the existence of a Shadow-brute who demands a human sacrifice. One of the king's advisors, "the Fox," endeavors to point out contradictions in the priest's description in order to question the priest's account. The priest responds with these chilling words:

> We are hearing much Greek wisdom this morning, King. And I have heard most of it before. I did not need a slave to teach it to me. . . . They demand to see such things clearly, as if the gods were no more than letters written in a book. I, King, have dealt with the gods for three generations of men, and I know they dazzle our eyes and flow in and out of one another like eddies on a river, and nothing that is said clearly can be said truly about them. Holy places are dark places. It is life and strength, not knowledge and words, that we get in them. Holy wisdom is not clear and thin like water, but thick and dark like blood. Why should the Accursed not be both the best and worst?[96]

Although the content of the priest's theology in this passage is obviously troubling, his willingness to accommodate counterintuitive notions when dealing with divine things captures something of the caution that premodern theology may commend to contemporary theology, as both reminder and warning. Divine simplicity is a difficult doctrine, to be sure. But then would we not expect at the outset difficulties of its kind? Why should God not be different than we expect and other than we can fathom? It would be strange indeed if God were not strange.

---

96. C. S. Lewis, *Till We Have Faces: A Myth Retold* (1956; repr. Orlando, FL: Harcourt, 1984), 50.

6

Substitution as Both Satisfaction and Recapitulation

Atonement Themes in Convergence in Irenaeus, Anselm, and Athanasius

There can be another explanation, besides the one I offered [in *Cur Deus Homo*], for how God took a sinless human being out of the sinful mass of the human race. . . . After all, nothing prohibits there being a plurality of reasons for one and the same thing, any one of which can be sufficient in itself.

—Anselm

It is not only within the doctrine of God, of course, that evangelical theology tends to reflect certain oddities of its age and context. Evangelical treatment of the atonement, as well, has taken new shape and direction in the modern era. In particular, evangelical reflection on the atonement generally takes place in a more polarized context than classical, catholic Christian thought. A common trend in atonement theology in recent years has been toward what Oliver Crisp and Fred Sanders have called an "egalitarian approach to atonement doctrine"—that is, a view of the atonement in which no single model subsumes or explains the others (in contrast to historical models that generally sought to develop one model or account of the atonement).[1] In particular, so-called objective models of the atonement have been increasingly displaced from their once central status, especially those involving the notion of penal substitution.[2] In response to these developments, treatment of the atonement in evangelical contexts is frequently organized around either the renunciation or reaffirmation of this doctrine.[3]

On the one hand, critics of penal substitution have been criticized for relying on caricature[4] and false dichotomy,[5] for failing to appreci-

---

1. Oliver D. Crisp and Fred Sanders, eds., *Locating Atonement: Explorations in Constructive Dogmatics* (Grand Rapids, MI: Zondervan, 2015), 13–14.

2. A critical early text was Gustav Aulén, *Christus Victor: An Historical Sketch of the Three Main Types of the Idea of Atonement*, trans. A. G. Hebert (1931; repr. Eugene, OR: Wipf & Stock, 2003), which popularized the now commonplace threefold taxonomy of major atonement theories as objective (Anselmian), subjective (Abelardian), and classical (*Christus victor*). Aulén's portrayal of the *Christus victor* model as the classical one, and particularly his attribution of this view to Luther, has been subjected to serious critique. E.g., see Timothy George, "The Atonement in Martin Luther's Theology," in *The Glory of the Atonement: Biblical, Theological, and Practical Perspectives*, ed. Charles A. James and Frank E. Hill III (Grand Rapids, MI: IVP Academic, 2004), 272–75.

3. Debate about penal substitution exploded among evangelicals in the UK in the early twenty-first century, e.g., following the publication of Stephen Chalke and Alan Mann, *The Lost Message of Jesus* (Grand Rapids, MI: Zondervan, 2003), which led to the 2005 London Symposium on the Theology of the Atonement, and the follow-up publication, *The Atonement Debate*, ed. Derek Tidball, David Hilborn, and Justin Thacker (Grand Rapids, MI: Zondervan, 2008).

4. E.g., Mark D. Baker and Joel B. Green, *Recovering the Scandal of the Cross: Atonement in New Testament and Contemporary Contexts*, 2nd ed. (Downers Grove, IL: IVP Academic, 2011), target a somewhat reductionistic and unsophisticated *version* of penal substitution as their object of critique rather than the best expressions of this doctrine. In response to charges of caricature, the authors state that their concern is with popular-level articulations of penal substitution (e.g., 46); in a follow-up volume, Mark Baker reiterates this, stating his appreciation for two more nuanced expressions of penal substitution, those of Hans Boersma and Kevin Vanhoozer, *Proclaiming the Scandal of the Cross: Contemporary Images of the Atonement*, ed. Mark Baker (Grand Rapids, MI: Baker Academic, 2006), 29–30. Nonetheless, both books' overarching purpose seems to be pushing against penal substitution itself rather than reformulating it alongside other images for the atonement (see how *Recovering the Scandal of the Cross* presents its aims on 14–15). In my judgment, while the authors rightly emphasize the importance of interpreting texts and events within their cultural narrative, they downplay the extent to which every cultural narrative is connected to a larger *human* narrative. The authors at times set Western notions of guilt and justice at odds with other features of the atonement, referencing the "huge populations of the world for whom guilt is a non-issue" (45). But if all human beings are fallen, it is difficult to see how guilt is a nonissue for any human culture. Furthermore, while it is true that there are a variety of images and metaphors used to convey the meaning of the atonement in the New Testament, this does not entail that the various images cannot be organized under a broader heading or rubric.

5. E.g., even N. T. Wright, who has been critical of many expressions of penal substitution, recognizes the frequency with which the doctrine is caricatured and advocates affirming the proper expression of it over and against caricature rather than simply discarding it altogether. See his

ate the Trinitarian structure of penal substitutionary models,[6] and for ultimately failing to deal adequately with many relevant biblical texts (e.g., the Day of Atonement ritual in Leviticus 16, or the description of the suffering servant in Isaiah 52:12–53:13, or the meaning of *hilasterion* in Romans 3:25).[7] In the other direction, defenses of penal substitution have been criticized as vulgar and crude (especially at the popular level),[8] as promoting violence,[9] and as reductionistic.[10]

In my view, the problems of vulgarity and violence, however much they might impinge in popular presentations of the atonement, are difficult to pin upon the ablest articulations of penal substitution.[11] The

---

"The Cross and Its Caricatures," accessed December 2, 2016, http://www.virtueonline.org/cross -and-caricatures-tom-wright. For an account of Wright's own view of Jesus's death as taking on meaning in relation to the story of Israel, see his *Jesus and the Victory of God*, Christian Origins and the Question of God 2 (Minneapolis: Fortress, 1996), 477–611; more recently, see his *The Day the Revolution Began: Reconsidering the Meaning of Jesus' Crucifixion* (New York: HarperOne, 2016), where Wright occasionally seems to lapse into his own stated danger of false dichotomy between the penal element of the cross and other aspects of its meaning.

6. This is especially the case with respect to the now common charge of "cosmic child abuse," leveled, e.g., by Chalke and Mann, *The Lost Message of Jesus*, 182. I have engaged this critique in Gavin Ortlund, "On the Throwing of Rocks: An Objection to Hasty and Un-careful Criticisms of Anselm's Doctrine of the Atonement," *The Saint Anselm Journal* 8.2 (Spring 2013): 16, where I argue that the child abuse charge overlooks (1) the unity of God the Father and God the Son in their common divinity; (2) Christ's willingness and initiative to suffer; and (3) the redemptive consequence of his suffering. No victims of abuse can speak of their suffering as Jesus did: "No one takes it from me, but I lay it down of my own accord. I have authority to lay it down, and I have authority to take it up again. This charge I have received from my Father" (John 10:18). And no victims of abuse endure their suffering for the joy that comes through it (Heb. 12:2). For further critique of the child abuse/violence charge, see Donald Macleod, *Christ Crucified: Understanding the Atonement* (Downers Grove, IL: IVP Academic, 2014), 63–64, 95–100.

7. E.g., see Leon Morris's classic treatment of ἱλαστήριον, responding to C. H. Dodd, in *The Apostolic Preaching of the Cross*, 3rd ed. (London: Tyndale, 1965), 144–213. More recently, see D. A. Carson, "Atonement in Romans 3:21–26," in *Glory of the Atonement*, 129–35.

8. This was a frequent criticism among twentieth-century liberal Protestant theologians as well as in more progressive circles today. Harry Emerson Fosdick, e.g., was fond of calling traditional atonement theology "slaughterhouse religion"; in his famous 1922 sermon "Shall the Fundamentalists Win?" he ridiculed the notion that Jesus's death "placates an alienated deity" as a kind of "pre-civilized barbarity." See the discussion in Richard Mouw, "Why *Christus Victor* Is Not Enough," *Christianity Today* (May 2012), 30.

9. This critique is especially common from feminist and liberation theologies and from pacifists. E.g., J. Denny Weaver, *The Nonviolent Atonement*, 2nd ed. (Grand Rapids, MI: Eerdmans, 2011) charges the satisfaction view of Anselm with supporting violence and passive submission to victimization; S. Mark Heim, *Saved from Sacrifice: A Theology of the Cross* (Grand Rapids, MI: Eerdmans, 2006), 27–29, all but charges penal substitution with sanctioning physical abuse.

10. E.g., Aulén, *Christus Victor*, 87–88; Baker and Green, *Recovering the Scandal of the Cross*, 49.

11. A classic (and masterful) defense of penal substitution is offered in J. I. Packer, "What Did the Cross Achieve? The Logic of Penal Substitution," in J. I. Packer and Mark Dever, *In My Place Condemned He Stood: Celebrating the Glory of the Atonement* (Wheaton, IL: Crossway, 2007), 53–100. More recently, a compelling treatment of the atonement is offered in Kevin J. Vanhoozer, "Atonement," in *Mapping Modern Theology: A Thematic and Historical Introduction*, ed. Bruce L. McCormack and Kelly M. Kapic (Grand Rapids, MI: Baker Academic, 2012), who affirms penal substitution but situates it in a broader covenantal context in relation to various other atonement motifs.

charge of reductionism, however, is more difficult to dodge entirely. In many penal substitutionary models, salvation is reduced to atonement, and atonement is reduced to guilt-bearing. As a result, the crucifixion of Christ is emphasized to the neglect of the broader narrative arc of Christ's incarnate and ascended work so that all the focus falls upon the cross, with little role for the empty tomb, the manger, or the final trumpet. Thus, even in the best accounts of penal substitution, one can find statements to the effect that Calvary is salvation; Bethlehem is mere preparation; Easter is mere confirmation.[12]

In recent years greater attention has been paid to the soteriological significance of Christ's resurrection while the incarnation has continued to be neglected, particularly in evangelical circles.[13] As Chris Armstrong describes the evangelical instinct: "We tend to hurry over the incarnation, seeing it as a necessary step to get Jesus to the cross."[14] In numerous publications Thomas F. Torrance has emphasized the soteriological significance of Christ's incarnation, drawing upon the *anhypostatic-enhypostatic* distinction to affirm Christ's "vicarious humanity."[15] But Torrance's proposal is often resisted by evangelicals on account of his affirmation that Christ assumed a *fallen* human nature and for allegedly drawing too close to the Eastern Orthodox notion of *theosis*.[16] While contextual theologians have given the incarnation more focus,[17] evangelical theology tends to regard Christ's incarnation as instrumentally salvific (in leading to his death and resurrection), not as intrinsically salvific (in doing much of anything

---

12. John Stott, *The Cross of Christ* (Downers Grove, IL: InterVarsity, 1986), 233: "The resurrection was essential to confirm the efficacy of his death, as the incarnation had been to prepare for its possibility." Cf. his strictures on the saving significance of the resurrection throughout 232–34.

13. A key text is Richard Gaffin, *Resurrection and Redemption: A Study in Paul's Soteriology* (Phillipsburg, NJ: P&R, 1987); more recently, see Richard Gaffin, "The Work of Christ Applied," in *Christian Dogmatics: Reformed Theology for the Church Catholic*, ed. Michael Allen and Scott R. Swain (Grand Rapids, MI: Baker Academic, 2016), 268–90. I explore the relation of Christ's resurrection to the execution of his messianic office in Gavin Ortlund, "Resurrected as Messiah: The Risen Christ as Prophet, Priest, and King," *Journal of the Evangelical Theological Society* 54.4 (2011): 749–66. Christ's ascension has also received greater attention as a saving event, e.g., Michael Horton, "Atonement and Ascension," in *Locating Atonement*, 226–50.

14. Chris R. Armstrong, *Medieval Wisdom for Modern Christians: Finding Authentic Faith in a Forgotten Age with C. S. Lewis*, 187. Armstrong rightly regards C. S. Lewis as an exception to this tendency (see esp. 196–99).

15. See especially Thomas F. Torrance, *Incarnation: The Person and Life of Christ*, ed. Robert T. Walker (Downers Grove, IL: IVP Academic, 2009); and Thomas F. Torrance, *Atonement: The Person and Work of Christ*, ed. Robert T. Walker (Downers Grove, IL: IVP Academic, 2009).

16. See, e.g., Macleod, *Christ Crucified*, 211–19.

17. E.g., Kenneth Leech, *We Preach Christ Crucified* (New York: Church, 1994).

itself). Thus, while helpfully emphasizing the soteriological significance to the resurrection, Robert Peterson argues that the incarnation
does not contribute to salvation in itself; it is only saving insofar as
it is a "prerequisite" and "precondition" to Christ's death and resurrection.[18] A slightly more nuanced view is offered by Robert Letham,
who stipulates that Christ's incarnation "by itself does not accomplish
salvation" and "is not by itself redemptive,"[19] while nonetheless regarding it as more than a *sine qua non* for salvation. Following Calvin's language that Christ's union with us in incarnation is a "weak
union," Letham argues that the incarnation is "central to redemption"
in that it is the *basis* for our union with Christ, which has intrinsic
soteriological weight.[20]

This chapter, building on other recent efforts,[21] seeks to move toward the proper emphasis and proportion assigned to each aspect of
Christ's saving work, affirming a central role for Christ's substitutionary death but also exploring how it coheres with the more peripheral
elements of his saving work (including the incarnation) that combine
to make a more complex, multiform whole. Against revisionist theologies of atonement it affirms a central significance and objective meaning to the cross, involving though not reducible to the notion of penal
substitution. Against reductionistic theologies of atonement it affirms
a broader narrative compass to the doctrine such that there is more to
atonement than penal substitution, more to salvation than atonement,
and more to both salvation and atonement than the cross. We will
thus attempt to situate the cross in relation to the broader sweep of

---

18. Robert A. Peterson, *Salvation Accomplished by the Son: The Work of Christ* (Wheaton, IL: Crossway, 2012), 16, 28, 39. He also affirms later that Christ's sinless life does not contribute to salvation (60). For Peterson's helpful treatment of the soteriological significance of Christ's resurrection, see 139–50.

19. Robert Letham, *Union with Christ: In Scripture, History, and Theology* (Phillipsburg, NJ: P&R, 2011), 40–41.

20. Letham, *Union with Christ*, 41.

21. Fleming Rutledge, *The Crucifixion: Understanding the Death of Jesus Christ* (Grand Rapids, MI: Eerdmans, 2016), develops the meaning of Christ's crucifixion in relation to the narrative context of Christ's incarnate work, remains careful not to overreact against substitutionary themes, and emphasizes the compatibility of the recapitulative and representative aspects of Christ's work. Hans Boersma, *Violence, Hospitality, and the Cross: Reappropriating the Atonement Tradition* (Grand Rapids, MI: Baker Academic, 2006), combines the Irenaean notion of recapitulation with the other traditional "models," including penal substitution (though he faults the "juridicizing, individualizing, and de-historicizing" tendencies that have often marred this doctrine). We will draw upon both Rutledge's and Boersma's insights in what follows despite differing with them both on a few points.

the incarnation but without flattening out the narrative so that Christ's crucifixion loses its central, dramatic significance. All that Christ does for us is important, but it is not all *equally* important—we remember the gospel on Easter and Christmas as well as Good Friday, but there is nonetheless something pivotal and decisive about the darkness, the torn curtain, and the cry of dereliction.[22]

To this end, this chapter retrieves some of the key motifs in three of the most significant treatments of the atonement in church history, in an effort at resourcing the current discussion. Approaching atonement from a *historical* angle may be helpful in two ways: (1) it may help us to approach the atonement without the rejection or defense of penal substitution controlling the discussion or steering it from the outset; (2) it may offer perspective on how to parse out the varying soteriological contributions of Christ's various incarnate accomplishments, seeking to find the balance of *emphasizing* what is central while still *affirming* what is peripheral. We will observe how those very themes and emphases that are often set at odds in contemporary atonement discussion were seen, in different historical contexts, as harmonious and mutually reinforcing. More specifically, we will suggest that tracing out points of convergence between Irenaeus, Athanasius, and Anselm (particularly between the *recapitulation* motif of Irenaeus and Athanasius and the *satisfaction* motif of Anselm) will help us conceptualize an atonement theology in which the various pieces can all be integrated under the broader rubric of *substitution*. Drawing from this historical study, an intrinsic (as opposed to merely instrumental) soteriological significance to the incarnation will be suggested, with reference to Christ's transfiguration, an often neglected episode in his incarnate life. Finally, a series of synthesizing conclusions will be offered, involving an excursus on the nature of atonement in C. S. Lewis's *The Lion, The Witch, and the Wardrobe*.

Recapitulation in Irenaeus

Recapitulation is a key term throughout *Adversus Haereses*, and it is often regarded as the centerpiece or key to Irenaeus's theology as

---

22. The cry of dereliction refers to Jesus's quotation of Psalm 22 in Mark 15:34 and the Synoptic parallels.

a whole.[23] In Latin (*recapitulato*) and Greek (ἀνακεφαλαιώσασθαι, *anakephalaiosasthai*), as in modern English, the term broadly refers to an act of *summarizing* or *repeating*—although it has more technical biological and musical meanings. (We reference both Latin and Greek because much of Irenaeus's *Adversus Haereses* is reconstructed from a Latin translation from the original Greek, combined with an Armenian translation of books 4 and 5, and Syriac fragments).[24] John O'Keefe and R. R. Reno suggest that Irenaeus borrows his notion of recapitulation from ancient rhetoric, where the term refers to the end of a speech, when a speech climaxes with a summary of its argumentation. Thus, it is not merely that Christ "repeats" the history of humanity generally or Israel specifically but that he is the final and summative speech of God the Father.[25]

But recapitulation in Irenaeus's thought is a notoriously complicated concept, and it would also be wrong to reduce its meaning to lexical considerations. Eric Osborn lists eleven distinct ideas involved in different permutations of the concept (unification, repetition, redemption, perfection, inauguration and consummation, totality, the triumph of *Christus Victor*, ontology, epistemology, and ethics [or being, truth, and goodness]), while ultimately summing up the idea by saying that the work of Christ corrects and perfects humanity, and the person of Christ is the new Adam who consummates and inaugurates a new humanity.[26] Recapitulation is indeed a comprehensive concept for Irenaeus, involving not merely Christ's headship over humanity but his uniting and summing up all things, which includes the entire

---

23. As noted by Thomas Holsinger-Friesen, *Irenaeus and Genesis: A Study of Competition in Early Christian Hermeneutics*, Journal of Theological Interpretation Supplement 1 (Winona Lake, IN: Eisenbrauns, 2009), 3–26, who approaches recapitulation in the context of Irenaeus's biblical hermeneutics, arguing that its typical interpretation has been distorted by von Harnack's early treatment of it as a systematic and speculative concept—a trend which was then continued through Brunner and Aulén and up into present-day Irenaean scholarship.

24. Here I use the translations of A. Cleveland Cox in *Ante-Nicene Fathers: The Apostolic Fathers, Justin Martyr, Irenaeus*, ed. Alexander Roberts and James Donaldson, 10 vols. (1885; repr. Peabody, MA: Hendrickson, 2012), 1:315–567, though I engage at points with the critical edition of William Wigan Harvey's Latin and Greek texts in *Sancti Irenaei, episcopi Lugdunensis, Libros quinque adversus haereses* (1857), American Theological Library Association Historical Monographs Collection: Series 1, EBSCOhost; and I have also consulted with the translation of key passages provided in Robert M. Grant, *Irenaeus of Lyons*, The Early Church Fathers (New York: Routledge, 1997).

25. John O'Keefe and R. R. Reno, *Sanctified Vision: An Introduction to Early Christian Interpretation of the Bible* (Baltimore, MD: Johns Hopkins University Press, 2005), 38–39.

26. E. F. Osborn, *Irenaeus of Lyons* (Cambridge, UK: Cambridge University Press, 2001), 97–98.

cosmos, in himself.[27] For our purposes here our focus will be broad, focused on the overall effect of recapitulation in Irenaeus's thinking. By *recapitulation* Irenaeus means the restoration of human nature by Christ's obedient, triumphant, incarnate life, reversing the effects of Adam's fall and spreading divine incorruptibility and immortality to humanity.[28]

At the core of this understanding of recapitulation is the notion that at the incarnation, divine nature and human nature were joined such that human nature is fundamentally reconstituted and renewed. In *Adversus Haereses* he refers to Christ's redemption as "attaching man to God by His own incarnation, and bestowing upon us at His coming immortality durably and truly."[29] Elsewhere he writes that Christ "caused human nature to cleave to and to become one with God."[30] Irenaeus's account of atonement is thus characterized by a divine-human movement leading to a human-divine movement, descent leading to glorification, incarnation leading to *theosis*. Hence, Irenaeus frequently speaks of recapitulation as the divine becoming human so that the human can become divine, as famously quoted: "The Word of God, our Lord Jesus Christ did through His transcendent love, become what we are, that He might bring us to be even what He is Himself."[31] It is because of this "divine-human movement of humiliation" involved in Irenaeus's account of the atonement that McDonald suggests, "Irenaeus' position may be conceived as an extended exposition of Paul's classical passage in Philippians 2:1–11."[32]

Irenaeus emphasizes the logical necessity of recapitulation. In his mind, this is not merely the way God has happened to open up the possibility of salvation, but the only possible way that salvation could have come to fallen humanity. Thus he writes:

27. Cf. Osborn, *Irenaeus of Lyons*, 115; so also W. Brian Shelton, "Irenaeus," in *Shapers of Christian Orthodoxy: Engaging with Early and Medieval Theologians*, ed. Bradley G. Green (Downers Grove, IL: IVP Academic, 2010), 22.

28. Cf. Bryan Litfin's complementary definition, who calls recapitulation the idea of "Jesus undoing the sin of Adam so that humans can be elevated into God's life by being joined to the perfect and victorious God-Man." Bryan M. Litfin, *Getting to Know the Church Fathers: An Evangelical Introduction*, 2nd ed. (Grand Rapids, MI: Baker Academic, 2016), 76.

29. Irenaeus, *Against Heresies* 5.1.1.

30. Irenaeus, *Against Heresies* 3.18.7.

31. Irenaeus, *Against Heresies* 5.preface.

32. H. D. McDonald, *The Atonement of the Death of the Christ: In Faith, Revelation, and History* (Grand Rapids, MI: Baker, 1985), 128.

For it was for this end that the Word of God was made man, and He who was the Son of God became the Son of man, that man, having been taken into the Word, and receiving the adoption, might become the son of God. For by no other means could we have attained to incorruptibility and immortality, unless we had been united to incorruptibility and immortality. But how could we be joined to incorruptibility and immortality, unless, first, incorruptibility and immortality had become that which we also are, so that the corruptible might be swallowed up by incorruptibility, and the mortal by immortality, that we might receive the adoption of sons?[33]

In this passage Irenaeus stipulates two distinct reasons why the incarnation was necessary for our salvation: first, the only way to attain incorruptibility and immortality is by being united (Latin *adunatus*) to it; second, the only way to be united to it is if it first became what we are. These reasons are stipulated against the broader backdrop of the divine-human exchange involved in recapitulation, here articulated not generically but in terms of our adoption as the children of God (itself an often underexplored aspect of Irenaeus's soteriology).[34]

For Irenaeus, the immortality that results from this divine-human union is not some arbitrary addition to human nature that otherwise could not have been conceived. Rather, it is precisely what would have come about had humanity not sinned; it is the end of being made in God's "likeness." Irenaeus held that "Adam was not created perfect, but rather created in the image of God and intended to come to be in the likeness of God at the end of a process of development."[35] It was the fall that interrupted this process, and thus Irenaeus casts recapitulation as the reversal of the original effects of the fall, particularly the death produced by sin: "God recapitulated in Himself the ancient formation of man, that he might kill sin, deprive death of its power,

---

33. Irenaeus, *Against Heresies* 3.19.1. Grant, *Irenaeus of Lyons*, 137, translates "mingled with" instead of "taken into" for *commistus* here.

34. Donald Fairbairn, "Patristic Soteriology: Three Trajectories," *Journal of the Evangelical Theological Society* 50.2 (2007): 294–97, argues that where other Greek fathers (Origen, Gregory of Nyssa) explicated participation with God in terms of sharing in the divine energies or attributes, Irenaeus explicated it in terms of the doctrine of adoption.

35. Denis Minns, *Irenaeus: An Introduction* (New York: T&T Clark, 2010), 75, describes this as "Irenaeus' most characteristic understanding of Gen. 1:26," though he points out that at times Irenaeus will also say that Adam was created in the image and likeness of God.

and vivify man."[36] Repeatedly Irenaeus will clarify that the goal of Christ's incarnate saving work is that we would arrive at our goal of bearing God's image and likeness, that which in his mind was interrupted by Adam's fall into sin: "When He became incarnate, and was made man, he recapitulated in himself the long line of human beings, and furnished us, in a brief comprehensive manner, with salvation, so that what we had lost in Adam—namely, to be according to the image and likeness of God—that we might recover in Christ Jesus."[37] And elsewhere, in responding to the objection that God should have made humanity immortal and perfected from the beginning, Irenaeus will argue that "it was necessary, at first, that nature should be exhibited; then, after that, that what was mortal should be conquered and swallowed up by immortality, and the corruptible by incorruptibility, *and that man should be made after the image and likeness of God*, having received the knowledge of good and evil."[38]

Thus it almost goes without saying that for Irenaeus, the doctrine of atonement is closely linked with the doctrine of creation—and not just in general terms, but specifically with his teleological, developmental vision of humanity (and with humanity, the entire created order).[39] Specifically, Irenaeus develops the notion of recapitulation from a strong Adam-Christ typology, buttressed by occasional references to a corollary Eve-Mary typology (thus, just as Christ triumphed where Adam failed, so Mary triumphed where Eve fell).[40] This typology is born out in terms of both the opposite behavior of Adam and Christ and the opposite consequences that result from their behavior. Christ's obedience brings life to others, just as Adam's disobedience brought death to others: "For as by one man's disobedience sin entered, and death obtained a place through sin; so also by the obedience of one

---

36. Irenaeus, *Against Heresies* 3.18.7.
37. Irenaeus, *Against Heresies* 3.18.1.
38. Irenaeus, *Against Heresies* 4.38.4; emphasis added.
39. Cf. M. C. Steenberg, *Irenaeus on Creation: The Cosmic Christ and the Sage of Redemption* (Leiden: Brill, 2008), 6: "When Irenaeus speaks of creation, he does so through the lens of human growth and salvation that he sees as its aim. Cosmology is bound up in soteriology, and as soteriology is intrinsically bound up in the life of the human person, so does the whole thrust of creation become, in a word, anthropocentric."
40. E.g., on the Eve-Mary contrast, see Irenaeus, *Against Heresies* 3.22.4. The Eve-Mary typology is important to Irenaeus, at least in part because of his desire to hold both the Old and New Testaments together as one story of redemptive history. Cf. Mary Ann Donovan, *One Right Reading? A Guide to Irenaeus* (Collegeville, MN: Liturgical Press, 1997), 88.

man, righteousness having been introduced, shall cause life to fructify in those persons who in times past were dead."[41] Irenaeus even draws a connection between Christ's virgin birth from Mary and Adam's creation from the "virgin soil" (since it was yet untilled according to Genesis 2:5), associating Adam and Christ for their mutual lack of ordinary human parentage: "If the former was taken from the dust, and God was his Maker, it was incumbent that the latter also, making a recapitulation in himself, should be formed as man by God, to have an analogy with the former as respects His origin."[42] As Boersma points out, he even argues that Christ had to die on the sixth day of the week since Adam and Eve had also sinned and thus died on the sixth day of the week.[43]

In expounding our corporate solidarity with both the sin/death of Adam and the righteousness/life of Christ, Irenaeus frequently employs military imagery that resembles some expositions of a *Christus Victor* atonement motif: "For (Christ) fought and conquered; for He was man contending for the fathers, and through obedience doing away with disobedience completely; for He bound the strong man, and set free the weak, and endowed his own handiwork with salvation, by destroying sin."[44] Drawing from Genesis 3:15, Irenaeus argues that the victory Christ accomplished over Satan was that which Adam should have accomplished, involving here the Eve-Mary contrast as well:

> For indeed the enemy would not have been fairly vanquished, unless it had been a man [born] of a woman who conquered him. For it was by means of a woman that he got the advantage over man at first, setting himself up as man's opponent. And therefore does the Lord profess Himself to be the Son of man, comprising (*recapitulans*) in Himself that original man out of whom the woman was fashioned in order that, as our species went down to death through a vanquished man, so we may ascend to life again through a victorious one; and as through a man death received the

---

41. Irenaeus, *Against Heresies* 3.21.10.
42. Irenaeus, *Against Heresies* 3.21.10; cf. the same argument in 3.18.7, where an allusion to the logic of Romans 5 is even clearer.
43. Boersma, *Violence, Hospitality, and the Cross*, 125.
44. Irenaeus, *Against Heresies* 3.18.6.

palm [of victory] against us, so again by a man we may receive the palm against death.[45]

This passage demonstrates how far Irenaeus is willing to press the Adam-Christ typology, which in turn sheds light on an important and somewhat distinctive aspect of his doctrine of recapitulation: his insistence that Christ recapitulated every *stage* of human existence. Thus, Irenaeus claims that in order to save those of all different ages, Christ

> passed through every age, becoming an infant for infants, thus sanctifying infants; a child for children, thus sanctifying those who are of this age, being at the same time made to them an example of piety, righteousness, and submission; a youth to youths, becoming an example to youths, and thus sanctifying them for the Lord. So, likewise, he was an old man for old men, that He might be a perfect Master for all, not merely as respects the setting forth of the truth, but also as regards age, sanctifying at the same time the aged also.[46]

Irenaeus's language here ("infant for infants," "youth to youths," etc.) indicates that he does not conceive of recapitulation as an alternative rubric to substitution (as it is sometimes portrayed in the contemporary literature), but rather as involving it. Precisely because his aim is to sum up human nature, Christ must stand in the place of every kind of human being. This is arguably why Irenaeus adopts the peculiar position that Christ lived to an old age and also emphasizes the soteriological significance of Christ's passing through the stage of human infancy, so that he might have solidarity with all of humanity.[47] Later, for instance, he emphasizes that in order for us to partake in the adoption of sons, Christ "passed through every stage of life, restoring all to communion with God."[48] For Irenaeus, salvation involves solidarity with all and hence requires substitution for all.

---

45. Irenaeus, *Against Heresies* 5.21.1. Grant, *Irenaeus of Lyons*, 173, sensibly translates *recapitulans* "recapitulating" rather than "comprising" here.
46. Irenaeus, *Against Heresies* 2.22.4.
47. Irenaeus, *Against Heresies* 4.38.2.
48. Irenaeus, *Against Heresies* 3.18.7.

Irenaeus is sometimes regarded as possessing a weaker doctrine of sin than later theologians such as Tertullian or Augustine,[49] and consequently a weaker view of the cross. Rashdall, for example, claims that for Irenaeus, recapitulation "was affected primarily by the incarnation, and the theory is not brought into any very close connection with the death of Christ, except, in so far as the death was necessary to the resurrection."[50] It is true that the *emphasis* of *Adversus Haereses* is on Christ's entire recapitulatory life. To this extent, Rutledge is right to note that Irenaeus fails to emphasize the hideousness and gruesomeness of crucifixion as the way in which Christ died.[51] However, it is also true that within the larger schema of recapitulation, Christ's death—and particularly Christ's death *as substitionary*—plays a critical role for Irenaeus. For instance, in the context of correlating Eden's tree of the knowledge of good and evil with Christ's cross, Irenaeus declares, "The Lord thus has redeemed us through His own blood, giving His soul for our souls, and His flesh for our flesh, and has also poured out the Spirit of the Father for the union and communion of God and man."[52] Here Irenaeus conceives of Christ's work of redemption (and related, his pouring out of the Spirit) as deriving from his *substitutionary* death on our behalf, giving his soul and his flesh for ours. It would appear that Irenaeus does not set the recapitulatory and substitutionary aspects of the atonement at odds. They are complementary or, better stated, substitution is an entailment and aspect of recapitulation, for only one who stands in our place can sum up and restore our nature.

Appropriation of Irenaeus's theology is often too narrowly focused on *Adversus Haereses*, which is a polemically occasioned writing, written to refute Gnostic heresies. It is this struggle that dominates Irenaeus's *Adversus Haereses* and thus gives the account of recapitulation there its distinctive flavor. The charge that recapitulation has little

49. Cf., e.g., Adolf von Harnack, *History of Dogma*, trans. Neil Buchanan, 7 vols. (London: Williams & Norgate, 1894–1899), 2:271, who discusses how for Irenaeus the fall was "conducive to man's development" and thus a necessary step toward the perfection for which humanity was created.
50. Hastings Rashdall, *The Idea of Atonement in Christian Theology* (London: Macmillan, 1919), 238.
51. Rutledge, *The Crucifixion*, 549, 563.
52. Irenaeus, *Against Heresies* 5.1.1.

use for Jesus's crucifixion arguably draws its strength from a failure to read Irenaeus's doctrines of sin and salvation in their own distinctive context, that is, his struggle with Gnostic heresies.[53] When one looks at Irenaeus's other major work, the shorter, catechetical *On the Apostolic Teaching*, the important place of Christ's substitutionary death on the cross in Irenaeus's understanding of recapitulation becomes even clearer.[54] This book was written as a "summary memorandum" to help the individual named Marcianus come to know the basic truths of the gospel. It is not only, as Iain MacKenzie puts it, "the very distillation of Irenaean thought,"[55] but also, according to John Behr, "the earliest summary of Christian teaching, presented in a non-polemical or apologetic manner, that we now have."[56] The book is structured as an account of how Christ's incarnate life, death, and resurrection sum up all of God's redemptive work in prior history. Strikingly, Irenaeus does not draw from the apostolic writings to establish this account of Christian teaching but rather (particularly in the lengthy second part of the book) expounds Christ's incarnate work as the fulfillment of various Old Testament Scriptures.[57] He is concerned to establish not just what the orthodox faith affirms about the incarnation of the Son of God but how this affirmation represents the fulfillment and "summing up" of all prior redemptive history.

Irenaeus unpacks the same recapitulation theme in *On the Apostolic Preaching*. He quotes the reference to Christ "recapitulating all things" in Ephesians 1:10, draws out the same Adam-Christ typology, and affirms that at the incarnation Christ "united man with God . . . that we might, in all ways, obtain a participation in incorruptibility."[58]

---

53. As noted by McDonald, *Atonement of the Death of the Christ*, 127.

54. This work was discovered in the early twentieth century in Armenian translation. I use here the translation of John Behr in St. Irenaeus of Lyons, *On the Apostolic Preaching*, trans. John Behr, Popular Patristics 17 (Crestwood, NY: St. Vladimir's Seminary Press, 1997).

55. Iain M. MacKenzie, *Irenaeus' Demonstration of the Apostolic Preaching: A Theological Commentary and Translation* (Burlington, VT: Ashgate, 2002), 31, characterizes it as the ideal entryway into Irenaeus's thought because it is written after *Adversus Haereses* in order to summarize it—he calls it "an *encheiridion*, a pocket dogmatics" (31).

56. As cited in Irenaeus, *On the Apostolic Preaching*, 7.

57. The book is structured in two parts. The first concerns the apostolic preaching, which he recounts after establishing the rule of faith—starting with God the Father and then moving through the topics of angels, the creation of Adam, the garden of Eden, Cain and Abel, Noah, and so forth—all the way through the Old Testament up to Christ. The second part concerns the demonstration of the prophets and seeks to establish how orthodox doctrine about God and Christ is the fulfillment of Old Testament Scripture.

58. Irenaeus, *On the Apostolic Preaching* 1.3.30–31.

Much of the same language and imagery used, including the comparison between Adam's creation from untilled ground (Gen. 2:5) and the virgin birth of Christ,[59] as well as the Eve-Mary typology: "for it was necessary for Adam to be recapitulated in Christ . . . and Eve in Mary, that a virgin, become an advocate for a virgin, might undo and destroy the virginal disobedience by virginal obedience."[60] Nonetheless, in this work, with the Gnostic threat less pressing than it was in *Adversus Haereses*, Christ's birth is expounded more clearly in the context of his entire incarnate life, and Christ's death and resurrection as the fulfillment of Old Testament Scripture (particularly the Abrahamic and Davidic covenants) are accented. From an extended quotation of Isaiah 53, combined with a few other Scriptures, Irenaeus emphasizes the necessity of Christ's scourges and physical tortures for his accomplishment of our salvation.[61] Reflecting specifically on Isaiah 53:8, Irenaeus affirms that Christ's death on the cross was vicarious for believers even while it signals the final condemnation of unbelievers: "The judgment has been taken from the believers in Him, and they are no longer under it."[62] But this very judgment, he intimates, will come in the form of fire on unbelievers at the end of this world.[63] From Isaiah 57:1–2, he affirms that Christ's death brought about reconciliation between believers;[64] from a quotation of Jeremias acquired through Justin, that Christ descended into hell for the salvation of the deceased;[65] from Psalms 68 and 23, that Christ ascended into heaven to overthrow the rule of the fallen angels.[66]

From these quotations it is evident that Irenaeus has a conception of the saving significance of Christ's accomplishments throughout his incarnate life and that when it comes to Christ's death specifically, he affirms Christ's vicarious taking away of our judgment, in line with Isaiah 53:8. While the theme of Christ's entire life as recapitulative predominates, the substitutionary death of Christ plays an important

---

59. Irenaeus, *On the Apostolic Preaching* 1.3.32.
60. Irenaeus, *On the Apostolic Preaching* 1.3.33.
61. Irenaeus, *On the Apostolic Preaching* 2.3.68.
62. Irenaeus, *On the Apostolic Preaching* 2.3.69.
63. Irenaeus, *On the Apostolic Preaching* 2.3.69.
64. Irenaeus, *On the Apostolic Preaching* 2.3.72.
65. Irenaeus, *On the Apostolic Preaching* 2.3.78; for a discussion of this apocryphal quote, which Justin claimed had been erased by the Jews, see Behr, *On the Apostolic Preaching*, 116.
66. Irenaeus, *On the Apostolic Preaching* 2.3.83–84.

role within this theme.[67] Boersma notes that there are even suggestions of a doctrine of propitiation in Irenaeus's treatment of Old Testament sacrifices, though he acknowledges this is a marginal aspect of his thought.[68] MacKenzie divides Christ's obedience in Irenaeus's thought into active and passive dimensions, calling the latter at this point in the commentary Christ's "submission to the righteous judgment of the righteous Father on the fallen and disobedient flesh and nature which He assumed at the incarnation, standing in our place for our sake, bearing that judgment and bearing it away."[69]

Irenaeus's inclusion of Christ's ascension in his recapitulatory work, mentioned briefly above, corresponds to a theme throughout the later parts of *Against Heresies* concerning the redemption of physical creation. Irenaeus argues that if Christ has not become real flesh and blood, he could not truly redeem us; but because his body was real, just like ours, his incarnation and ascension into heaven must include a resurrection of physical creation to immortality.[70] Elsewhere he specifies that it is specifically as a result of Christ's resurrected glory that this new, redeemed human nature emerged, speaking of Christ not only descending to us but also ascending "to the height above, offering and commending to His Father that human nature which had been found, making in His own person the firstfruits of the resurrection of man."[71] Thus Christ's ascension functions as a kind of *presentation* to God the Father of perfected humanity.

Toward the end of the *Adversus Haereses*, Irenaeus returns to this depiction of Christ's recapitulation as effecting final redemption by employing the imagery of a ladder. Specifically, he speaks of Christ's incarnation as his descending a ladder and of human salvation as the corollary climbing up that ladder into divinity, passing through the Trinity from Spirit to Son to Father. Referring to "the gradation and arrangement of those who are saved," he claims that "they ascend through the Spirit to the Son, and through the Son to the Father,

---

67. E.g., when summarizing the apostolic message of Christ's work of salvation at the end of this section, he states that Christ endured his passion "for the destruction of death and the vivification of the flesh." Irenaeus, *On the Apostolic Preaching* 2.4.86.
68. Boersma, *Violence, Hospitality, and the Cross*, 161–62.
69. MacKenzie, *Irenaeus' Demonstration of the Apostolic Preaching*, 199.
70. Irenaeus, *Against Heresies* 5.14.2.
71. Irenaeus, *Against Heresies* 3.19.3.

and that in due time the Son will yield up His work to the Father."[72] Irenaeus then proceeds to identify the Son's handing over of his work to the Father as the fulfillment of 1 Corinthians 15:25–28, indicating that he does not envision this work to be completed until Christ's final appearance and the final resurrection.[73] Thus, for Irenaeus, Christ's recapitulation of humanity works along the entire arc of not only his incarnate earthly life but his risen and ascended life, such that Easter is only the "firstfruits" of what is begun in Bethlehem; the ultimate goal is realized only at the final trumpet.

Anselm's Doctrine of Satisfaction

How might an Irenaean account of Christ's entire incarnate work as recapitulation cohere with an Anselmian view of Christ's death as satisfaction?[74] Contemporary atonement theology, as we have seen, tends to pit Anselmian and Irenaean themes against one another—and to be sure, there are important points of discontinuity between Anselm and Irenaeus on the atonement. For example, Anselm does not stress Christ's recapitulating each stage of human life as Irenaeus does, nor does he hold to a hierarchical view of salvation up into *theosis*. Nevertheless, contrary to its frequent caricatures as guilt-obsessed, individualistic, and narrowly juridical,[75] Anselm's *Cur Deus Homo* has in fact an account of the recapitulatory role of Christ's incarnate birth that is strikingly resonant to what is found in Irenaeus's *Adversus Haereses*. Specifically, though he spends the greater bulk of space in *Cur Deus Homo* exploring the mechanics of Christ's death, he also repeatedly situates Christ's atoning death within a larger framework of Christ's

---

72. Irenaeus, *Against Heresies* 5.36.2.

73. Irenaeus, *Against Heresies* 5.36.2. Cf. the discussion in Shelton, "Irenaeus," 48. For discussion of Irenaeus's conceptions of *theosis* and the *visio Dei* as the goal of redemption, see Boersma, *Violence, Hospitality, and the Cross*, 257–61.

74. The term *satisfaction* in the context of atonement theology generally refers to the view that Christ's death restored to God the honor that sin had stolen, thus satisfying the claims of divine justice.

75. Anselm's doctrine of atonement is a frequent target of caricature. So notes John McIntyre, *St. Anselm and His Critics: A Re-interpretation of the* Cur Deus Homo (Edinburgh: Oliver & Boyd, 1954), 2: "No major Christian thinker has suffered quite so much as St. Anselm from the hit-and-run tactics of historians of theism and soteriology." For an instance of such caricature, see von Harnack, *History of Dogma*, 6:76, who objects to "the worst thing in Anselm's theory" as "the mythological conception of God as the mighty private man, who is incensed at the injury done to His honor and does not forego His wrath till He has received an at least adequately great equivalent." More recently, see Weaver, *Nonviolent Atonement*, 219–320.

entire incarnate life as restoring human nature to its original blessed immortality, lost by Adam at the fall. Here for the sake of space I will simply summarize some of the features of Anselm's view of the atonement that I've drawn out at greater length elsewhere.[76]

In his summary of the argument of *Cur Deus Homo* in the preface, Anselm claims that what is established in Book 2 of *Cur Deus Homo* is that "human nature was established in order that the whole being, both body and soul, should at some time enjoy blessed immortality" and that in order for it to achieve this creational intent, "it was necessary that everything we believe about Christ should take place."[77] And then in chapter 1, Anselm sets up the question on which the whole book hangs: "By what reason or necessity did God become a human being and, as we believe and profess, restore life to the world by his own death?"[78] Later Boso hones the question more specifically with reference to human nature: "Given that God is omnipotent, by what necessity and reason did he assume the lowliness and weakness of human nature, in order to restore human nature?"[79] What is striking about these important summary statements early on in the book is not only the absence of guilt and recompense themes but also this repeated emphasis on the restoration of human nature and Christ's entire incarnate work. One must, in fact, get well into the bulk of *Cur Deus Homo* until one is able to locate a systematic explanation of why Christ's *death* was the fitting mechanism for human redemption (one must wait until 2.11; even 2.6, which I take to be the climax of the argument, does not focus specifically on Christ's death).[80]

In the earlier sections of *Cur Deus Homo*, Anselm's focus is much broader and bears much resemblance to the Ireneaen theme of recapitulation, in which God's very assumption of human nature at the incarnation unites it with divinity and incorruptibility. With Irenaeus, Anselm declares that the union between divine and human forged at the

76. Gavin Ortlund, "On the Throwing of Rocks," 4–7. Some of the material here I have drawn loosely from this article, and there I situate my exposition of Anselm more rigorously in relation to the larger Anselm scholarship.

77. Anselm, *Cur Deus Homo praefatio.*

78. Anselm, *Cur Deus Homo* 1.1.

79. Anselm, *Cur Deus Homo* 1.1.

80. Rutledge, *The Crucifixion,* 157–58, also emphasizes the centrality of 2.6 to the logic of *Cur Deus Homo.*

incarnation fundamentally altered human nature: "There was [not] any degradation of God in his Incarnation; rather, we believe that human nature was exalted."[81] Later, toward the end of the book, Anselm argues that when Christ assumed a sinless human being from the sinful mass at the incarnation, "God restored human nature more wonderfully than he first established it."[82] Moreover, like Irenaeus, Anselm defines this restoration of human nature in terms of an Adam-Christ typology, such that Christ's obedient life brought about the immortality that was originally lost through Adam's disobedience: "It was fitting that just as death entered the human race through the disobedience of a human being, so too life should be restored by the obedience of a human being."[83] One cannot help but think of Irenaeus's similar assertions, for instance: "As our species went down to death through a vanquished man, so we may ascend to life again through a victorious one; and as through a man death received the palm of victory against us, so again by a man we may receive the palm against death."[84]

Anselm expounds the doctrine of the atonement in close relation to the doctrine of creation in a remarkably similar manner to Irenaeus. Specifically, Anselm's understanding of the incarnation is tied to his understanding of the purpose of human nature as attaining what he calls "blessed immortality." Like Irenaeus, he claims that if Adam and Eve had not sinned, they would have been "transformed into incorruptibility," but they lost this because of the fall. The incarnation occurred because "God will complete what he began in human nature, or else he made so sublime a nature for so great a good in vain."[85] So for Anselm, as for Irenaeus, the incarnation accomplished what would have happened if Adam and Eve had not sinned, namely, the completion and transformation of human nature into incorruptibility—and it is in *this* context that satisfaction themes are introduced. He asserts, thus, that a "perfect recompense for sin" was required not to satisfy some arbitrary legal demand, but rather in order that God "complete what he began in human nature."[86] Here and elsewhere, recompense

---

81. Anselm, *Cur Deus Homo* 1.8.
82. Anselm, *Cur Deus Homo* 2.16.
83. Anselm, *Cur Deus Homo* 1.3.
84. Irenaeus, *Against Heresies* 5.21.1.
85. Anselm, *Cur Deus Homo* 2.4.
86. Anselm, *Cur Deus Homo* 2.4.

for sin complements the larger theme of the restoration of human nature to the blessed immortality for which it was originally designed. Thus, for Anselm, satisfaction serves recapitulation; forgiveness serves flourishing. As he puts it, "Remission of sins is necessary for human beings if they are to attain happiness."[87]

And this is true as a general observation of the argument of *Cur Deus Homo*: the satisfaction theme (focused primarily on Christ's death) operates within a larger restoration theme (focused on Christ's incarnation and obedience, *including* his death). David Bentley Hart, for instance, an Eastern Orthodox theologian who has drawn attention to points of continuity between the atonement theology of Anselm and the church fathers, has pointed out that Anselm's emphasis on God's honor functions logically as an outgrowth of his understanding of God's goodness in maintaining the harmony and beauty of his creation.[88]

From these passages in *Cur Deus Homo* it is evident that however much Anselm's modern interpreters might have cast his atonement theology in exclusively legal categories, Anselm himself saw the satisfaction of divine justice and the restoration of human nature as complementary, not contradictory, themes. Indeed, the resonance between Anselm and Irenaeus on Christ's birth is remarkable. Kevin McMahon puts it well: "It is undeniable that Irenaeus' organic idiom lends his teaching a richness that is missing in Anselm; yet one may fairly describe Anselm as drawing out a continuous line of thought, already present in Irenaeus, according to which our salvation proceeds as an incorporation into the action of Christ."[89] Or as Hart puts it, going even further: "In the end Anselm merely restates the oldest patristic model of atonement of all: recapitulation."[90]

We are left, then, with this startling fact: arguably the most influential exposition of the satisfaction motif of the atonement in church history also affirms repeatedly, in remarkably similar terms to those

---

87. Anselm, *Cur Deus Homo* 1.10.
88. David Bentley Hart, *The Beauty of the Infinite: The Aesthetics of Christian Truth* (Grand Rapids, MI: Eerdmans, 2003), 360–72, esp. 369–70.
89. Kevin A. McMahon, "The Cross and the Pearl: Anselm's Patristic Doctrine of the Atonement," in *Saint Anselm: His Origins and Influence*, ed. John R. Fortin, Texts and Studies in Religion 91 (Lewiston, NY: Edwin Mellen, 2001), 62.
90. Hart, *Beauty of the Infinite*, 371.

of Irenaeus himself, a recapitulation motif. In fact, more than that, it casts satisfaction as serving the larger end of recapitulation, for the whole purpose of Christ's repayment to divine honor is to restore human nature to the blessed immortality it lost at the fall. Moreover, for Anselm, as for Irenaeus, both recapitulation and satisfaction are thematically integrated under the larger motif of substitution, since both Christ's restoration of human nature and payment of human debt come through his standing in our place as both *Deus* and *homo*.

Recapitulation and Satisfaction in Athanasius

A brief look at Athanasius's *De Incarnatione*, another classic text on the atonement, will press these points of continuity still further.[91] The significance of Athanasius's theology is often reduced to, or overly focused on, his defense of the deity of Christ against the threat of Arianism.[92] But Athansius's theology contains many constructive insights of its own, and his doctrine of redemption—particularly as expressed in *De Incarnatione*—provides a good window into broader patterns of patristic thought as a whole. Thus, Litfin describes *De Incarnatione* as a text that "lays out the patristic doctrine of salvation in very clear terms."[93] In particular, there are strong continuities between the thought of Irenaeus and that of Athanasius, particularly with respect to the doctrine of the atonement.[94] Brunner goes so far

---

91. All quotations are from St. Athanasius, *On the Incarnation*, trans. a religious of C.S.M.V., Popular Patristics 3 (Crestwood, NY: St. Vladimir's Seminary Press, 1977), 3–10, in consultation with the Greek text found in Robert Pierce Casey, *The* De Incarnatione *of Athanasius: The Short Recension*, ed. Kirsopp Lake and Carsten Höeg (Philadelphia: University of Pennsylvania Press, 1946). I will mostly limit myself to this work of Athanasius—which was originally published along with *Against the Heathen* soon after the Council of Nicaea—for the sake of space and because it is a good representation of his thought on this matter (though at a few key points we quote his *Against the Arians* as well).

92. As Khaled Anatolios, *Athanasius: The Coherence of His Thought*, Routledge Early Church Monographs (NY: Routledge, 1998), points out that Athanasius's theology is often engaged piecemeal or selectively and thus the inner logic of his thought is often not appreciated. He analyzes Athanasius's theology through the lens of the Creator/creation relationship, particularly God's simultaneous distance from and closeness to the world. For another recent more expansive overview of Athanasius's thought, see Peter Leithart, *Athanasius*, Foundations of Theological Exegesis and Christian Spirituality (Grand Rapids, MI: Baker Academic, 2011).

93. Litfin, *Getting to Know the Church Fathers*, 157.

94. Anatolios, *Athanasius: The Coherence of His Thought*, claims that there are "strong grounds for considering Athanasius as continuing a distinctly Irenaean tradition" (23) and draws attention to textual parallels that "strongly raise the possibility of Athanasius having direct access to the writings of Irenaeus" (214). Specifically, he suggests that Athanasius works with the same complex Creator/creation relationship as Irenaeus (one that stresses both divine transcendence and immanence) and thus shares the same broad anthropology in which humanity is "fundamentally

as to claim that "the fundamental structure of his thought, the meaning of the Logos, of the Incarnation, and its necessary union with the
doctrine of the cross, the meaning of the knowledge of faith and of
the Church is exactly the same in all essential points in Athanasius as
it is in Irenaeus."[95]

Though we also will emphasize points of continuity between
Irenaeus and Athanasius, Brunner's statement should probably be
qualified. While Athanasius certainly affirms that the incarnation
accomplished the restoration of human nature from corruption to
incorruptibility, he does not affirm, so far as I can see, that Christ
reconstituted the various stages of human life (infancy, childhood,
etc.), and his emphasis seems to be on Christ's resurrection more than
his birth per se, as the mechanism for the transformation of human
nature. Nevertheless, his overall emphasis is that Christ abolished the
law of death to which humanity was subject and thus transformed
human nature to incorruptibility and immortality. Moreover, he
speaks of this change as the driving purpose of the incarnation (triggered specifically at the resurrection), and so he does appear to share
many of the same general features of Irenaeus's account of recapitulation. Furthermore, many broader features of his theology, such as the
doctrines of creation and sin that undergird his view of atonement,
bear distinct similarities to Irenaeus's theology.[96]

Athanasius's understanding of salvation is often summarized with
reference to his famous assertion toward the end of *De Incarnatione*
that the Word "assumed humanity that we might become God."[97] In
connection with this emphasis, it is often claimed that Athanasius has
little purpose with Christ's death and no doctrine of substitution what-
soever. Thus one reads claims that Athanasius's "whole presentation
of the matter shows that he regards the incarnate Logos as achieving

receptive to the divine," as well as the same broad soteriology in which redemption consists of
"repairing human receptivity and re-instituting the union of divine and human" (24).

95. Emil Brunner, *The Mediator: A Study of the Central Doctrine of the Christian Faith*, trans.
Olive Wyon (Philadelphia: Westminster Press, 1947), 263. Brunner acknowledges some differences
between the two but limits them to individual formulae that can mostly be explained from differences of historical environment.

96. For an overview of Athanasius's view of creation and sin, particularly his emphasis on
humanity as created in the image of the Word, see Thomas Gerard Weinandy, *Athanasius: A
Theological Introduction*, Great Theologians Series (Burlington, VT: Ashgate, 2007), 11–26.

97. Athanasius, *On the Incarnation* 8.54.

all his work of redemption as the representative, not as the substitute, of man";[98] or even that Athanasius's account of the incarnation "almost does away with a doctrine of the Atonement."[99]

But a close reading of *De Incarnatione* reveals a more nuanced and multifaceted understanding of salvation in Athanasius's thinking than is sometimes grasped—indeed, immediately after his famous assertion that God became man so that man may become God, he affirms, in a lesser-known but equally significant assertion, "such and so many are the Saviour's achievements that follow from His Incarnation, that to try to number them is like gazing at the open sea and trying to count the waves."[100] Thus we must be sensitive at the outset to the danger of pitting one atonement motif against another. Indeed, as we shall see, for Athanasius even more so than for Irenaeus, the recapitulation motif does not work in isolation but in coordination with an emphasis on Christ's death as paying the debt that all humanity owed because of our fall into sin and death.

In the early chapters of *De Incarnatione* Athanasius situates Christ's redeeming work in relation to the doctrine of creation and stipulates several reasons for the incarnation, including its ultimate result of refuting idols and demons and the spread of the knowledge of God. As with Irenaeus, the *imago Dei* comprises an important part of recapitulation. Because Christ himself is the image of God, after which humanity is fashioned, it is Christ's incarnation that effects the renewal of that image in *all* men. In a striking metaphor, Athanasius compares Christ's recapitulation of human nature to a worn-out portrait being repainted:

> You know what happens when a portrait that has been painted on a panel becomes obliterated through external stains. The artist does not throw away the panel, but the subject of the portrait has to sit for it again, and then the likeness is re-drawn on the same material. Even so was it with the All-holy Son of God. He, the

---

98. J. F. Bethune-Baker, *Introduction to the Early History of Christian Doctrine to the Time of the Council of Chalcedon* (1903; repr. London: Methuen & Co., 1958), 346.

99. R. P. C. Hanson, *The Search for the Christian Doctrine of God: The Arian Controversy 318–381* (Edinburgh: T&T Clark, 1998), 450. Hanson acknowledges that Athanaius believes in Christ's death as saving but states that he cannot explain why Christ must die. Cf. the critique of this view by Anatolios, *Athanasius: The Coherence of His Thought*, 75–76.

100. Athanasius, *On the Incarnation* 8.54.

Image of the Father, came and dwelt in our midst, in order that He might renew mankind made after Himself.[101]

These final words, "made after Himself," signal a theme that is drawn out particularly in chapter 1 of *De Incarnatione*, namely, that Christ is the image of the Father after whose likeness humanity was created, and thus our redemption consists of being restored to that original status (like a painting being redrawn).[102] Athanasius claims that before the fall, human nature was subject to corruption, but nevertheless human beings would have been preserved from the natural law if they had remained in a state of innocence because of "the grace of their union with the Word."[103] Thus for Athanasius humanity is united to Christ in some sense already *before* the incarnation, because we are made in his likeness.

The doctrines of creation and anthropology reflected in chapter 1 of *De Incarnatione* help explain the strong emphasis in chapters 2 and 3 on the notion of recapitulation, in which Christ's incarnation spreads incorruption to the human race through its union of the divine and human natures. Thus, he claims, "through this union of the immortal Son of God with our human nature, all men were clothed with incorruption in the promise of the resurrection."[104] This language of Christ's resurrection as the "promise" of the incarnation makes clear that the transformation of human nature that is entailed in the incarnation is not actually effected until the resurrection, a point Athanasius will make elsewhere as well. Athanasius declares that it is in light of the corporate solidarity of the human race that this transformation of human nature in the incarnation is possible, "for the solidarity of mankind is such that, by virtue of the Word's indwelling a single human body, the corruption which goes with death has lost its power over all."[105] To explain how the Word's incarnation in one

---

101. Athanasius, *On the Incarnation* 3.14.
102. Later, e.g., he asserts that "only the Image of the Father could re-create the likeness of the Image in men." Athanasius, *On the Incarnation*, 4.20. Anatolios, *Athanasius: The Coherence of His Thought*, 56–57, 68–69, stresses that the logic involved in this assertion draws from Athanasius's participatory ontology in which humanity stands in desperate dependence upon God's sustaining involvement.
103. Athanasius, *On the Incarnation* 1.5.
104. Athanasius, *On the Incarnation* 2.9.
105. Athanasius, *On the Incarnation* 2.9.

body can spread immortality to all of humanity, Athanasius employs an analogy:

> You know how it is when some great king enters a large city and dwells in one of its houses; because of his dwelling in that single house, the whole city is honored, and enemies and robbers cease to molest it. Even so it is with the King of all; He has come into our country and dwelt in one body amidst the many, and in consequence the designs of the enemy against mankind have been foiled, and the corruption of death, which formerly held them in its power, has simply ceased to be.[106]

Thus, for Athanasius, God's entering into and dwelling in one human body is like a royal visitation; it "honors" the entire human race by both foiling Satan's purposes against us and ending the corruption of death. The notion that God's union with one particular human body is the mechanism by which human nature is itself transformed into incorruptibility is a fundamentally similar doctrine of recapitulation to that of Irenaeus. The metaphor of royal visitation corresponds to the metaphor in Irenaeus of an antidote spreading throughout an entire system and reversing a pervasive sickness. It also corresponds to the imagery used in some contemporary accounts of Athanasius's thought of the incarnation as a "blood transfusion," as though through the incarnation an ailing human race "appropriates—at the most intimate, particular, and undeniably material level—an animating substance that enhances his or her liveliness."[107]

Nonetheless Leithart is right to caution that it is not the incarnation in isolation that works this change but rather the incarnation in connection to the whole complex of events it initiates, ultimately leading to Christ's vicarious glorification on behalf of humanity through his resurrection.[108] While this emphasis in Irenaeus's account of Christ's incarnate work falls on the incarnation itself, the emphasis for Athanasius falls upon Christ's resurrection. He even claims, "The

---

106. Athanasius, *On the Incarnation* 2.9.

107. Virginia Burrus, *Begotten, Not Made: Conceiving Manhood in Late Antiquity* (Stanford, CA: Stanford University Press, 2000), 42, qualifies this imagery from Hanson, *The Search for the Christian Doctrine of God*, 451, warning against the suggestion of human passivity inherent in the metaphor.

108. Leithart, *Athanasius*, 154–55.

supreme object of His coming was to bring about the resurrection of the body."[109]

At the same time, it would also be a mistake to think that for Athanasius, the incarnation is *merely* instrumental, i.e., that it contributes nothing to salvation in itself. Athanasius develops his conception of recapitulation in chapters 2 and 3 of *De Incarnatione*, and here—before his treatment of Christ's death in chapter 4—he emphasizes the saving significance of the event of Christ's incarnation *itself* in spreading immortality to human nature. Significantly, this theme is bound up with some components of a satisfaction theme, without any perceived tension between them. So, for example, he argues that mere repentance by human beings would not restore human nature, because it would make God's threat of death upon disobedience untrue.[110] He then writes, intermingling both restoration and satisfaction themes:

> His part it was, and His alone, both to bring again the corruptible to incorruption and to maintain for the Father His consistency of character before all. For He alone, being Word of the Father and above all, was in consequence both able to recreate all, and worthy to suffer on behalf of all and to be ambassador for all with the Father.[111]

Here Athanasius seems to weave together recapitulatory and substitutionary language, emphasizing that Christ was able to "bring the corruptible to incorruption" and "recreate all" but also stipulating the importance of the consistency of God's character and affirming Christ's vicarious suffering and serving as an ambassador (πρεσβευσαι) for his people (a reference to Christ's intercession and mediatorship between God and his people).

While the earlier chapters of *De Incarnatione* show striking resemblance to Irenaeus, continuities with Anselm emerge most clearly in chapter 4 of *De Incarnatione*, where Athanasius turns to focus more specifically on the death of Christ. At the beginning of this chapter,

---

109. Athanasius, *On the Incarnation* 4.22.
110. Athanasius, *On the Incarnation* 2.7.
111. Athanasius, *On the Incarnation* 2.7.

he summarizes his argument in the previous chapters that humanity had been made in the image of God and yet subject to the corruption of death through sin (chapter 1), that only the incarnation of the one who had created them from nothing could restore that image and spread incorruptibility to humanity (chapter 2), and that the incarnation was further necessary to reveal the knowledge of the one true God (chapter 3).[112] Having grounded the incarnation in the context of the doctrine of creation and provided two reasons why it was necessary, Athanasius then expands on the purpose of the incarnation with an additional reason for its necessity, this time with a more explicit focus on Christ's death:

> But beyond all this, there was a debt owing which needs be paid; for, as I said before, all men were due to die. Here, then, is the second reason why the Word dwelt among us, namely that having proved His Godhead by His works, He might offer the sacrifice (θυσιαν) on behalf of all, surrendering his own temple to death in place of all, to settle man's account with death and free him from the primal transgression (αρχαιας παραβασεως).[113]

The substitutionary language used there with reference to Christ's death ("on behalf of all" and "in place of all") combined with the legal language and imagery used to interpret that act of substitution ("debt owing which needs be paid" and "to settle man's account") suggest that Athanasisus has a conception, like Anselm, of Christ's crucifixion as constituting the satisfaction of our debt to God as sinful human beings. For Athanasius, in other words, the incarnation does not merely serve to restore humanity to incorruption and immortality through Christ's incarnate life; it also serves to pay humanity's debt to spiritual death on account of our

---

112. For Athanasius, the incarnation occurs not strictly to bring about atonement. It also serves a revelatory purpose, to teach humanity how to know God, and it is in connection with this point that Athanasius emphasizes Christ as the *imago Dei*. After lamenting human ignorance of God because of idolatry, he writes: "What else could (God) possibly do, being God, but renew His image in mankind, so that through it men might once more come to know Him? And how could this be done save by the coming of the very Image Himself, our savior Jesus Christ? . . . The Word of God came in His own person, because it was He alone, the Image of the Father, who could recreate man after the image." Athanasius, *On the Incarnation* 3.13.

113. Athanasius, *On the Incarnation* 4.20. Cf. Casey, *The De Incarnatione of Athanasius*, 30.

"primal transgression" through Christ's substitutionary death.[114] Thus, the mechanism of atonement in Athanasius's theology is not merely the union of human and divine natures, but that in this union the human nature was destroyed and then resurrected. Interestingly, in his *Against the Arians* Athanasius affirms the purpose of the incarnation in terms of intercession and mediatorship between the human and the divine, affirming that the stages of Christ's human suffering (his hunger, tears, and weariness during his life, as well as the cry of dereliction on the cross) represent real human affections, and that Christ "receives these from us and offers them up to the Father, and He intercedes for us that our human woes and weaknesses may be remedied and redressed."[115] Here Athanasius situates Christ's atoning death ("offers them up") in relation to his substitutionary life ("receives them for us") as both serving the comprehensive salvation of humanity ("that our human woes and weaknesses may be remedied and redressed"). Statements like this give the impression of a harmonious relationship between satisfaction and recapitulation motifs in Athanasius's thought and suggest points of continuity with Irenaeus and Anselm.

At the same time, it would appear that Athanasius, on the whole, has a more thoroughgoing emphasis than Irenaeus on Christ's death, which Athanasius refers to as "the very centre of our faith."[116] The reason that death plays such a central role for Athanasius is that he regards death as the *penalty* for sin and transgression, drawing from Genesis 2:16.[117] It would be accurate therefore to affirm the presence of a species of so-called *penal substitution* in Athanasius's view of the atonement, though his focus tends to be on the incarnation's

---

114. The need for both recapitulation and satisfaction stems from the multifaceted nature of our sinful need. For Athanasius, sin is understood as *both* a transgression and a sickness and thus atonement consists of *both* payment of debt and spreading of life. On this point, see the argumentation against Derek Flood in Garry L. Williams, "Penal Substitutionary Atonement in the Church Fathers," *Evangelical Quarterly* 83.3 (2011): 203–10.

115. Athanasius, *Against the Arians* 4.6 (London: Griffith Farran, 1912), 268–69. εξαφανισθη is often translated as "satisfied" here; "remedied and redressed" is rather elaborate and unwarranted. It is worth pointing out that later in this same context, Athanasius once again weaves together the motif of recapitulation, claiming soon after that "it was necessary, therefore, that God and man should be personally united, in order that human nature might be invested with power and exalted to glory. The Divine exalted the human nature, which it had taken into itself; and the human nature, being assumed into the Divine, received from that its glory and power" (269).

116. Athanasius, *On the Incarnation* 4.19.

117. Athanasius, *On the Incarnation* 2.10.

broader significance, and when he speaks of penal substitution his emphasis falls on the penalty of *death* and less on Christ bearing specifically the penalties of guilt and/or punishment.[118] Nonetheless, Athanasius uses sacrificial and substitutionary language throughout *De Incarnatione* to refer to the act of Christ's crucifixion—he calls it an "offering" and "sacrifice" to the Father, as well as a "substitute" and an "exchange" and an "equivalent" (i.e., of the death of his "brethren"),[119] such that "in His death all might die."[120] Later, affirming from Galatians 3:13 that Christ had to "become a curse for us," he calls Christ's death our "ransom."[121] Athanasius can also speak of Christ's crucifixion as the purpose of the incarnation, since, as he puts it (sounding very Anselmian), only the human is able to die, and only the divine can offer a death that is a sufficient substitute for others:

> The Word perceived that corruption could not be got rid of otherwise than through death; yet He Himself, as the Word, being immortal and the Father's Son, was such as He could not die. For this reason, therefore, He assumed a body capable of death, in order that it, through belonging to the Word who is above all, might become in dying a sufficient exchange for all, and, itself remaining incorruptible through his indwelling, might thereafter put an end to corruption for others as well, by the grace of the resurrection.[122]

Here again Athanasius incorporates the broader recapitulation motif alongside Christ's substitutionary death: Christ not only died

---

118. Steve Jeffrey, Michael Ovey, and Andrew Sach, *Pierced for Our Transgressions: Rediscovering the Glory of the Atonement* (Wheaton, IL: Crossway, 2007), perhaps go too far from the evidence they marshal in concluding that "penal substitution is thus *central* to Athanasius' thought" (173, emphasis added). Nonetheless, they are right to affirm its presence in his writings; in addition to their engagement with *De Incarnatione*, e.g., they cite his comment from John 3:17 in his *Against the Arians*: "Formerly the world, as guilty, was under the judgment from the Law; but now the Word has taken on Himself the judgment, and having suffered in the body for all, has bestowed salvation to all" (169). The authors could have added many other quotes from this work: "Christ endured death for us" (*Against the Arians* 1.41); "The death of the incarnate Logos is a ransom for the sins of men" (*Against the Arians* 1.45); "The Lord offered for our sakes the one death" (*Against the Arians* 4.25). Cf. the helpful commentary on these quotes and this discussion by McDonald, *The Atonement of the Death of Christ*, 133–34 (his translations used here).
119. Athanasius, *On the Incarnation* 2.9.
120. Athanasius, *On the Incarnation* 2.8. The Greek text at this point is rich with terminology from the biblical sacrificial system, such as θυμα and ιερειον. Cf. Casey, *The De Incarnatione of Athanasius*, 13.
121. Athanasius, *On the Incarnation* 4.25.
122. Athanasius, *On the Incarnation* 2.9.

as an "exchange for all"; he did so while "remaining incorruptible through his indwelling" and rising again to "put an end to corruption for others as well." For Athanasius, therefore, Christ's death constitutes a satisfaction of our debt to God, while Christ's birth and resurrection constitute the recapitulation of human nature. As with Anselm and Irenaeus, the notion of *substitution* would appear as a common link between these two themes.[123]

Christ's Transfiguration in Relation to the Atonement

Thus far we've seen that Irenaeus, while emphasizing Christ's recapitulatory work throughout his incarnate and ascended life, also affirmed his suffering on the cross to take away judgment. Similarly, Anselm, in the midst of his argument in *Cur Deus Homo* for a satisfaction view of Christ's death on the cross, also claims that Christ's incarnation restores human nature to its creational goal of incorruptibility and "blessed immortality." Finally, we've seen satisfaction and recapitulation themes blended harmoniously in another classic text on the atonement, Athanasius's *De Incarnatione*.

Having explored these points of convergence between these three historical accounts of atonement, we may be better positioned to envision how both satisfaction and recapitulation themes might be integrated in constructing a doctrine of atonement today. Such a dual emphasis would be well represented by our hymnody and liturgy and would accord well with the nature of the incarnation event as a unique and ontologically pivotal event, effecting the second basic change to reality after creation. Creation and incarnation are the two fundamental turning points for reality: at creation, something other than God emerges (thus there are now two things); at the incarnation, God now unites himself to this second thing (thus those things become one). One might already wonder at the outset if God has indeed united the human nature to the divine nature, bringing the two fundamental kinds of reality (Creator and creation) into unity—how could such a pivotal event *not* fundamentally alter human nature and all created reality with it?

---

123. For a discussion of the challenging issue of Christ's body as an "instrument," see Anatolios, *Athanasius: The Coherence of His Thought*, 70–84.

Some would object, perhaps placing Athanasius's emphasis against that of Irenaeus, that the change to human nature comes at Christ's resurrection rather than at his incarnation. But considering the different emphases of these three theologians may help us appreciate that the truth is more complex on this point. Doubtless, the crucial change to human nature was specifically manifested and triggered at Christ's resurrection, as (for instance) the apostle Paul emphasizes in 1 Corinthians 15. But we should not regard the change accomplished at Easter as an entirely new development imposed on a normal human body. It is the God-man who is resurrected; his resurrection is not an arbitrary event but related to his person—it is what must happen when the one who is life itself is put to death. The one who claims, "I have authority to take [my life] up again" (John 10:18) also claims, "I am the resurrection and the life" (John 11:25). The glory Christ inherited at his resurrection was not a generic glory but a revelation and declaration of his divine identity ("declared to be the Son of God in power . . . by his resurrection from the dead" [Rom. 1:4]). As T. F. Torrance has written, "*What Jesus Christ is in his resurrection, he is in himself.* The resurrection was not just an event that happened to Christ, for it corresponded to the kind of person he was in his own being."[124] What happened on Easter, in other words, is best understood as a fuller outworking of, rather than an arbitrary addition to, what had already happened at Bethlehem—it was, we might say, the organic *completion* of the incarnation.

The suggestion of a close correlation between Christ's incarnate birth and resurrection may derive further plausibility from a consideration of his transfiguration. This event is typically not given much weight in Protestant theology, but it was highly significant for the church fathers and in modern Roman Catholic theology.[125] For instance, when the Catechism of the Catholic Church correlates Christ's transfiguration and his baptism, noting the divine voice of approval

---

124. Torrance, *Atonement*, 221, emphasis original.
125. John Anthony McGuckin, *The Transfiguration of Christ in Scripture and Tradition* (Lewiston, NY: Edwin Mellen, 1986), explores themes in the patristic interpretation of the transfiguration. Hans Boersma, *Seeing God: The Beatific Vision in Christian Tradition* (Grand Rapids, MI: Eerdmans, 2018), 129–62, explores the transfiguration in the thought of Gregory Palamas and Thomas Aquinas.

at both events and their respective placement at the beginning of his public ministry and passion,[126] it is drawing from Thomas Aquinas's treatment of the transfiguration, who himself was drawing from Jerome, John of Damascus, Chrysostom, Gregory, and others.[127] What should evangelicals make of this significant episode, as it pertains to our understanding of the nature of Christ's incarnate life? Mark's version reads as follows:

> And after six days Jesus took with him Peter and James and John, and led them up a high mountain by themselves. And he was transfigured before them, and his clothes became radiant, intensely white, as no one on earth could bleach them. And there appeared to them Elijah with Moses, and they were talking with Jesus. And Peter said to Jesus, "Rabbi, it is good that we are here. Let us make three tents, one for you and one for Moses and one for Elijah." For he did not know what to say, for they were terrified. And a cloud overshadowed them, and a voice came out of the cloud, "This is my beloved Son; listen to him." And suddenly, looking around, they no longer saw anyone with them but Jesus only.[128]

Now, if we say that Christ's transformation of human nature began exclusively at his resurrection, we have to provide some kind of explanation of this unique and significant event in his incarnate life. How does Christ have resurrection glory before he is actually resurrected? One way to read the story is as a kind of proleptic anticipation of what will happen at Easter—at the transfiguration, God supernaturally bestows the glory that Christ will one day have when he is risen from the dead (hence his charge in Mark 9:10 that the disciples tell no one about this event "until the Son of Man had risen from the dead"). More basically, the transfiguration can be interpreted simply as God the Father's bestowal of approval upon Jesus, indicating his favor and blessing upon Jesus and his ministry. Finally, we could interpret the glory of the transfiguration in connection to Jesus's divine nature—it is

---

126. Catechism of the Catholic Church 556, 2nd ed. (Vatican: Libreria Editrice Vaticana, 2012).

127. See the discussion in Thomas Aquinas, *Summa Theologica*, Q. 45.

128. Mark 9:2–8.

a *revelation* of Jesus's own glory and divinity as the eternal Son of God in human form.

Both of the first two options—the transfiguration as a *prediction* or as a *communication*—see the transfiguration as fundamentally the bestowal upon Jesus of something from outside him. By contrast, in the third view—the transfiguration as a *revelation*—the white clothes and blinding light represent the manifestation of Jesus's real identity. It is not a falling from the sky of some new gift but rather a pulling back of the curtain to see what has always been there. This interpretation of the transfiguration would accord well with the *divine* interpretation offered at the climax of the narrative: "This is my beloved Son" (v. 7)—as well as other features of the story, such as biblical-theological connotations of the appearance of Moses and Elijah, suggesting that this episode represents a theophany.[129]

Understanding the transfiguration as ultimately a revelation of Jesus's true identity need not preclude the first two interpretations—doubtless the transfiguration *also* anticipates the resurrection and communicates God's favor. Thus Peter can refer to this event with the words "when he received honor and glory from God the Father" (2 Pet. 1:17); the emphasis, from this angle, is "this is *my* Son." But Jesus himself is also fully divine, the Father's glory is his glory as well, for "he is the radiance of the glory of God" (Heb. 1:3); thus Peter can also say, "We were eyewitnesses of *his* majesty" (2 Pet. 1:16; "his" here refers to "the Lord Jesus Christ"). From this angle, the emphasis is revelatory: "*This* is my Son." In this sense, the white clothes are best understood not as a gift to, but as a revelation of, Jesus; the voice from heaven is not merely an approval from, but also identification with, the Father.

Typically, the transfiguration is interpreted as a unique, unusual moment in the life of Christ. But if we regard it as a *revelatory* event, then there is a sense in which the transfiguration is where we find God incarnate most truly; it is all the *other* moments between the manger and the empty tomb that are cryptic and disguised. This

---

129. The event seems to recall comparable theophanies with Moses at Sinai (Exodus 33) and Elijah at Horeb (1 Kings 19; Horeb is the same mountain). Note the appearance of a cloud, the location on a mountain, etc.

accords with the long tradition of thinking about Christ's preresurrection incarnate life as "hidden" and as a "mystery." Thomas, for instance, distinguishes the glory of the transfiguration from Jesus's *possession* of a glorified body, attained at resurrection. But he nonetheless insists, citing John of Damascus, that "the clarity of Christ's body in His transfiguration was derived from His Godhead . . . and from the glory of His soul."[130] But this, of course, raises the question of why Christ's glory was not *always* manifest. Thomas continues:

> That the glory of His soul did not overflow into His body from the first moment of Christ's conception was due to a certain Divine dispensation, that . . . He might fulfil the mysteries of our redemption in a passible body. This did not, however, deprive Christ of His power of outpouring the glory of His soul into his body.[131]

While Thomas proceeds to argue that Christ's transfiguring himself was miraculous, like his walking on water, it is clear that he nonetheless regards it as an activity and revelation of Christ himself.

Now, we are not given much detail in Scripture to help us navigate our precise understanding of the transfiguration, and so we should be cautious about placing too much weight on this event or speculating too much about the details. Nonetheless, if we are right in seeing the transfiguration as, in some sense, revelatory, then it offers us a hint that the resurrection is not an unanticipated event—there was something *unique* about Christ's earthly body, even prior to his resurrection. The glory and immortality into which it burst forth on Easter morning was not an arbitrary addition to, but rather the organic outworking of, what the God-man already was.

Synthesizing Reflections

Our survey of the atonement theologies of Irenaeus, Anselm, and Athanasius, together with our reference to the event of the transfiguration, provides the opportunity to draw out a number of general conclusions with respect to the meaning of the atonement in contemporary theological discussion.

---

130. Aquinas, *Summa Theologica*, 3a, Q. 45, Art. 2.
131. Aquinas, *Summa Theologica*, 3a, Q. 45, Art. 2.

1. Holding Together Recapitulation with Satisfaction/Penal Substitution

Our survey of these theologians brings into greater visibility the possibility of a doctrine of atonement that can hold together an affirmation
of Christ's entire incarnate life as recapitulating human nature with
an affirmation of Christ's death as satisfying divine honor/wrath.[132] At
the outset, one is not surprised to find that the meaning of the atonement is multifaceted (as Sinclair Ferguson puts it, "multidimensional,
polyvalent"[133]), since the reconciliation of God and fallen human beings that it achieves requires the overcoming of several related but
distinct forces: sin, guilt, death, and demonic and structural powers. Complex problems rarely have simple solutions. Moreover, there
is no obvious conceptual incompatibility with emphasizing Christ's
incarnation as saving in one sense and his crucifixion as saving in
another sense. In fact, it is plausible to conceive of recapitulation and
satisfaction as not just compatible but mutually explanatory so that
the incarnation helps explain the nature of atonement, and atonement
helps explain the nature of incarnation. This is certainly Anselm's
procedure; in *Cur Deus Homo* 2.7 he sets forth his book as, most
basically, a commentary on Chalcedon (hence the word *Cur* in the
title *Cur Deus Homo?*). By exploring the meaning of Christ's satisfying death we gain greater insight into the necessity that our redeemer
be a God-man.

In the other direction, as can be seen in some contemporary accounts of atonement, a doctrine of recapitulation can shed further
light on the nature of Christ's vicarious death. For Hans Boersma,
for example, recapitulation is a formal concept, while the traditional
atonement models (including penal substitution) are material concepts—recapitulation tells the broader aim of Christ's atonement, but
not how he actually brings it about.[134] Boersma thus combines recapitulation with all three of the primary traditional atonement models
and links them with Christ's messianic office, arguing that Christ's

---

132. Of course, there are a host of issues concerning the *relation* of penal substitution and
satisfaction (which are not identical) that need to be explored further; my interest here is, more
broadly, affirming an objective atonement generally as compatible with recapitulation.
133. Sinclair Ferguson, "Preaching the Atonement," in *Glory of the Atonement*, 436.
134. Boersma, *Violence, Hospitality, and the Cross*, 112.

"recapitulation has a prophetic element (moral influence), a priestly element (representative punishment), and a royal element (Christus victor)."[135] Specifically with respect to Christ's death, he draws from the biblical theological insights of N. T. Wright to affirm a penal substitutionary view of Christ's death as a recapitulation of the banishment of failed Adam and fallen Israel from God's presence (in the garden and temple, respectively).[136]

Beyond noting their mutually explanatory power, we might further describe the logical relation between recapitulation and satisfaction by drawing attention to the notion of *substitution*, which (as we have seen) is intrinsic to them both and can be seen to hold them together: Christ both bears divine judgment on the cross and restores humanity in his life via the mechanism of self-substitution. One way of encapsulating the harmony of recapitulation with satisfaction under the broader rubric of substitution is with the simple formula often referenced in popular presentations of the gospel (e.g., in Tim Keller's sermons): *Christ lived the life we should have lived; Christ died the death we should have died.* These are two different kinds of substitution, to be sure. One is an inclusive substitution; the other, a strict substitution. One is representation ("in him"); the other is replacement ("for us").[137] One is a positive fulfilling; the other is a negative absorbing. But both are fundamentally and irreducibly *substitutionary*; the statement hangs together.

From this vantage point, there is indeed a sense in which Christ's very humanity, as well as his death, is vicarious; indeed, his death is the climactic expression of a process already begun. Hence Luther and Calvin could speak of the cross as one "moment" in the larger movement of Christ's solidarity with his people.[138] (If one radically divorces Christ's life and crucifixion, where does one make the cut off? Gethsemane? Trial before Pilate? Carrying the cross? The actual moment of nails piercing his wrists and/or feet?) Furthermore, an em-

---

135. Boersma, *Violence, Hospitality, and the Cross*, 122.
136. E.g., Boersma, *Violence, Hospitality, and the Cross*, 18–19, 177–78.
137. For this terminology, see Richard Gaffin, "Atonement in the Pauline Corpus," in *Glory of the Atonement*, 145.
138. See the discussion in Packer, "What Did the Cross Achieve?," 84–87, who distinguishes four "moments" in the "larger mystery" of Christ's ontological solidarity with his people (the incarnation, the cross, receiving Christ by faith, and the second coming).

phasis on the notion of substitution (both inclusive and strict) as the centerpiece of the work of atonement enables us to hold together not only Christ's earthly life and death but his ascended work as well, as Christ continues to function as intercessor and mediator in his heavenly session and final return.[139]

Some worry that an emphasis on the incarnation as itself a saving event will necessarily entail universalism and/or an Eastern conception of salvation along the lines of *theosis*. But this overlooks the fact that only those who are united to Christ receive the benefits of his incarnate work; the transformation of human nature entailed at incarnation and triggered at resurrection does not spread to all those in Adam but all those in the second Adam (cf. 1 Cor. 15:42–49). And if *theosis* simply means the transformation of human nature into incorruptibility through shared union with the divine nature, this is not an exclusively Eastern conception but belongs to Augustine[140] and Calvin[141] as well—and indeed, arguably to the New Testament (2 Pet. 1:4; 1 John 3:2).

2. Holding Together the Events and the Meaning of the Atonement

Our exploration of the complementary nature of recapitulation and satisfaction may further serve to remind us that the events and the meaning of the atonement do not have an arbitrary relationship. If atonement is reducible to Christ's death (as is conceivable if recapitulation is altogether removed), then the vast majority of Christ's earthly

---

139. Herman Bavinck, *Reformed Dogmatics: Sin and Salvation in Christ*, 4 vols. (Grand Rapids, MI: Baker, 2006), 482, acknowledges differences in the Reformed tradition on how to construe Christ's continued mediatorial role in the eschaton, offering as a solution that in the eternal state Christ's "mediatorship of reconciliation" will end, but his "mediatorship of union" will continue. An intriguing point of further exploration here would be how our emphasis upon substitution as the centerpiece of atonement would cohere with the Pauline doctrine of union with Christ in not only his death and resurrection but also his second coming.

140. Augustine declared in a sermon, "In order to make gods of those who were merely human, one who was God made himself human; without forfeiting what he was, he wished to become what he himself had made." Quoted by Rosenberg, "Interpreting Atonement in Augustine's Preaching," in *Glory of the Atonement*, 238.

141. John Calvin, *Institutes of the Christian Religion*, ed. John T. McNeill, trans. Ford Lewis Battles, 2 vols. (Louisville, KY: Westminster John Knox, 2006), 1.12.2: "He took our nature upon himself to impart to us what was his." Earlier (1.12.1) he spoke intriguingly of the incarnation happening "in such a way that his divinity and our human nature might by mutual connection grow together." For a fuller exploration of deification in Calvin's thought, see Carl Mosser, "An Exotic Flower? Calvin and the Patristic Doctrine of Deification," in *Reformation Faith: Exegesis and Theology in the Protestant Reformations*, ed. Michael Parsons (Eugene, OR: Wipf & Stock, 2014), 38–56.

incarnate existence seems rather unimportant. If atonement is reducible to recapitulation, then the exact brutality of Christ's death, and its climactic significance, seems difficult to explain. Thus if we take it as presuppositional that nothing of Christ's incarnate life was wasted, that in fact the events and meaning of the atonement hang together in close relationship, then it is legitimate for us to ponder questions like these:

- Why did Christ have to develop in the womb as a zygote and then embryo and then fetus, be born as a baby, and then pass through infancy and childhood in the ordinary human manner? Supposing the Son of God had beamed down more directly from heaven as a full-grown (but real) man, or at least a ten-year-old who continued to grow from that point—what would have been lost with respect to his saving work?

- Why did Christ's atoning death come only after several years of public ministry, including teaching, leading the disciples, healing the sick, casting out demons, and getting locked into an escalating conflict with the religious and political powers of the day? Supposing Christ had left Joseph and Mary as a young teen to live the solitary life of a desert monk, suddenly to reenter society just in time to be crucified—what would be lost with respect to his saving work?

- Why crucifixion? Supposing Christ had been hanged, drowned, or beheaded—what would be lost from the meaning of his saving work?

- If it must be a cross, why *death* on a cross? Supposing Christ had hung for several hours on the cross, agonizing through the asphyxiation, the blood loss, the crown of thorns, the abandonment and mockery, etc., but then, in approaching the moment of actual death, skipped over this experience to be translated immediately into glory and resurrection—what then would be lost from the meaning of his saving work?

- If Christ had to die, why must he suffer the ignominy of burial—and why for so many long hours, presumably decomposing in the normal manner? Supposing Christ had endured death but then, at the exact moment his heart stopped beating, he is resurrected into glory and the cross is shattered into a thousand pieces? This could conceivably have constituted a dramatic illustration of his making a "public spectacle" of the powers (Col. 2:15). But what would be lost with respect to the meaning of his saving work?

- Why must forty days elapse between Easter and Pentecost? Supposing the resurrection and ascension had been one singular event, and Christ's victory over the grave had immediately issued forth into his entrance into heaven; or supposing the two events were separated by, say, 45 minutes—what would be lost from the meaning of his saving work?

Many other such questions could of course be formulated (extending into Christ's ascension, session, intercession, etc.), and our retrieval of Irenaeus, Athanasius, and Anselm should sensitize to their legitimacy, even where we cannot fully provide an answer. To this extent the narratival concreteness of the atonement will continually surpass our most eloquent systematic expressions of it. We will be driven again and again to metaphor, to partial explanation, and to questions of synthesis, rapprochement, and integration. For no interpretation of a story's meaning can ever fully contain the weight and wonder of the story itself.

3. Holding Together the Central and Peripheral Aspects of the Atonement

But recognizing the multifaceted complexity of the atonement should not be taken (as it too often is) to flatten out its meaning, as though it had no center of gravity. It is an error to eclipse the periphery; it is equally an error to diminish the center. To the extent that we follow in the tracks of our historical survey, we might detect the notion of substitution as at the heart and center of the atonement, as is also common in some of the leading contemporary accounts of atonement.[142] At the same time, it would be a mistake

---

142. Cf. Roger Nicole, "Postscript on Penal Substitution," in *Glory of the Atonement*, 445, who calls substitution the "linchpin" of the atonement, and Stott, *Cross of Christ*, 203, who claims

to allow the strictly penal element of the atonement to exhaust the meaning of the substitutionary element. By putting substitution at the center rather than penal substitution per se, we signify that in the phrase "penal substitutionary atonement," the word *substitutionary* has a more expansive, wrap-around meaning than the word *penal* (though both words are very important). One might say: *All that is penal is substitutionary, but not all that is substitutionary is penal.*[143] This broader focus helps us not displace Christ's active obedience as our federal head and covenant representative, together with the broader recapitulative aim of the entire incarnate work of Christ. Using Gaffin's terminology, the strict substitution ("for us") flows from, but does not exhaust, the representative substitution ("in him").

In parsing out the importance of both Christ's substitutionary death and his broader incarnate work, we must take special care not to give the impression that they are in competition, as though each were fighting for our attention. This is a persistent error in much atonement theology, the danger of false dichotomy: divorcing Christ's life and death, or—what often leads to this—setting the legal dimension of the Creator/creation relation against its other dimensions. In truth, a deeper understanding of the various "moments" of Jesus's saving work will lead to an expanded, not diminished, view of the cross, because all these other moments find their deepest meaning in relation to that great moment. So long as the peripheral is seen *as peripheral*, it can only enhance the visibility of the center, just as—to put it in terms of our earlier metaphor—understanding the broader narrative of a novel only enhances the understanding of that novel's climax. Thus recapitulation at Bethlehem, rightly understood and emphasized, *enhances* the significance of the cross; satisfaction at Calvary, rightly understood and emphasized, *enhances* the significance of the manger. Ultimately, Jesus's great saving work is a unity (as much as his person is a unity) whose components can be distinguished but never divided.

---

that the substitutionary principle of the atonement is "the essence of each image and at the heart of the atonement itself."

143. Cf. Packer, "What Did the Cross Achieve?," 77, who puts it a bit more strongly, stipulating that the qualifier *penal* anchors the term *substitution* "not exclusively, but regulatively."

Excursus: Atonement in Narnia

This common error in contemporary atonement theology of pitting central and peripheral aspects of the atonement against one another can be seen somewhat anecdotally through a discussion of the meaning of Aslan's atoning death in C. S. Lewis's *The Lion, the Witch, and the Wardrobe*.[144] Lewis's presentation of atonement in Narnia is worth engaging because it is often referenced as a "mere Christianity" version of the atonement and thus as a litmus test of acceptability; a presentation of the atonement that has helped millions of children understand the gospel has a kind of street-level credibility. Hence the strongest critiques of penal substitution frequently appeal to Narnia to strengthen their case. Thus, in a follow-up volume to *Recovering the Scandal of the Cross*, intended to address more practical concerns regarding how the atonement should be articulated and preached, Mark Baker lists C. S. Lewis's portrayal of atonement in Narnia as the first in the whole book because, in his view, "unlike stories that paint a picture of penal substitution, Lewis does not portray Aslan as suffering a punishment from God that another person (in this case, Edmund) deserved. The conflict is with the Witch."[145] Similarly, in his response to Tom Schreiner's articulation of penal substitution in a *Four Views* book on the meaning of the atonement, Greg Boyd spends much of his response engaging with Lewis as an alleged proponent of his own *Christus victor* view.[146]

But is atonement in Narnia really closer to *Christus victor* than penal substitution? While certainly some of its themes are present (as they are in practically any understanding of atonement), a closer read suggests that atonement in Narnia is quite friendly to classical objective models. On the whole, it is probably

144. C. S. Lewis, *The Lion, the Witch, and the Wardrobe* (Grand Rapids, MI: Zondervan, 2005), 141–42.

145. Baker, *Proclaiming the Scandal of the Cross*, 37.

146. Gregory A. Boyd, "Christus Victor Response," in *The Nature of the Atonement: Four Views*, ed. James Beilby and Paul R. Eddy (Downers Grove, IL: IVP Academic, 2006), 100–105.

best represented by some combination of the ransom and satisfaction theories, with perhaps the governmental theory also
impinging. Boyd, like Baker, argues that in Lewis's allegory, it is
Satan, not God, who demands Christ's sacrifice:

> Who demanded that the deep magic of the law be satisfied
> with "a kill"? For Schreiner, it is God. For Lewis (and most
> advocates of the Christus Victor view) it is the devil. Here is
> where the rubber meets the road in terms of the difference
> between these two views. . . . The demand for "a kill" does
> not come from God . . . it comes from the cosmic accuser.[147]

But here Boyd is pitting law and lawgiver against each other in a
way that Lewis does not. During her claim on Edmund's life, the
witch bases her claim upon the concept of "Deep Magic." When
Aslan permits the witch to tell of the Deep Magic, she says:

> Tell you? . . . her voice growing suddenly shriller. Tell you
> what is written on that very Table of Stone which stands
> beside us? Tell you what is written in letters deep as a spear
> is long on the firestones on the Secret Hill? Tell you what is
> engraved on the scepter of the Emperor-beyond-the-Sea? You
> at least know the Magic which the Emperor put into Narnia
> at the very beginning. You know that every traitor belongs
> to me as my lawful prey and that for every treachery I have
> a right to kill. . . . Unless I have blood, as the Law says, all
> Narnia will be overturned and perish in fire and water.[148]

From this passage it is clear that the Deep Magic is a good
creation of Aslan's father, the emperor across the sea, i.e., God the
Father. It was put into Narnia at the beginning by *him* and stands
engraved upon *his* scepter. While it is certainly true that the witch
insists upon sacrifice, her insistence derives its power only from the
emperor's magic, which is acknowledged by Aslan as well as the

---

147. Boyd, "Christus Victor Response," 103.
148. Lewis, *The Lion, the Witch, and the Wardrobe*, 141–42.

witch. It is clear that Aslan regards the Deep Magic as both good and inviolable—he acknowledges the truth of the witch's claims, and later when Susan suggests to Aslan that they work against the Deep Magic, Lewis writes: "'Work against the Emperor's Magic?' said Aslan, turning to her with something like a frown on his face. And nobody ever made that suggestion to him again."

It is therefore untrue to Lewis to portray Aslan's death as oriented more toward the witch (the devil) than the emperor (God). While circumstantially Aslan's death comes in response to the witch's demands, it is more fundamentally a satisfaction of the emperor's Deep Magic so that Narnia is not overturned in fire and water. Indeed the very reason that the witch's claims upon Edmund are undermined by Aslan's death is that his substitutionary fulfillment of the Deep Magic removes the *basis* of her accusation. In addition, under a *Christus victor* model, in which the primary aim of atonement is the destruction of evil forces, Edmund's role in the whole transaction becomes secondary. In the book, however, the substitutionary character of Aslan's death is front and center. It is a story not first and foremost of victory and conquest but of redemption and love *through* that victory.

4. Holding Together the Clarity and Mystery of the Atonement

Finally, our retrieval of the atonement theologies of Irenaeus, Athanasius, and Anselm reminds us of the vital importance of the atonement but also its simultaneous mysteriousness and grandeur. Its importance is difficult to overstate. Emil Brunner went so far as to say that atonement "is the Christian religion itself; it is the main point; it is not something alongside the center; it is the substance and kernel, not the husk."[149] Or as Gustav Aulén put it, "each and every interpretation of the Atonement is most closely connected with some conception of the essential meaning of Christianity, and reflects some conception of the Divine nature."[150] In other words, how one understands

---

149. As quoted in *Glory of the Atonement*, 18–19.
150. Aulén, *Christus Victor*, 12–13.

atonement reflects how one understands both God and Christianity. To miss atonement is to miss at the center, not at the fringes.

At the same time, the atonement is a mysterious, difficult, even unsettling doctrine. It is not a formula that can be mastered but a divine working that must be received by faith. It is vitally important to remember, as Packer puts it, that we are seeking to expostulate the *meaning* of the atonement, not its exact mechanics.[151] At the end of the day, we do not know how it all works, and we must be comfortable with this. Nor must we try to drain the offensiveness out of it. Nothing could be more offensive, in fact, to human pride, reason, and ability than the thought of God incarnate crucified. No interpretation of this event can be more earth shattering than its actual occurrence. Why should the meaning of an event be calm and easy when the event itself is unimaginable? The death of Christ is like a wild animal that can save us but not be tamed by us. It is well, to this end, to conclude with the devastating words of James Denney:

> If the Atonement . . . is anything to the mind, it is everything. It is the most profound of all truths, and the most recreative. It determines more than anything else our conceptions of God, of man, of history, and even of nature. . . . It is the inspiration of all thought, the impulse and the law of all action, the key, in the last resort, to all suffering. . . . It is that in which the *differentia* of Christianity, its peculiar and exclusive character, is specially shown; it is the focus of revelation, the point at which we see deepest into the truth of God and come most completely under its power. For those who recognize it at all, it is Christianity in brief; it concentrates in itself, as a germ of infinite potency, all that the wisdom, love and power of God mean in relation to sinful men. . . . The Atonement is a reality of such a sort that it can make no compromise. The man who fights it knows that he is fighting for his life, and puts all his strength into the battle. The surrender is literally to give up himself, to cease to be the man he is, and to become another man. . . . The cross of Christ is man's own glory, or it is his final stumbling block.[152]

---

151. Packer, "What Did the Cross Achieve?," 78–80.
152. Quoted in J. I. Packer, "The Atonement in the Life of the Christian," in *Glory of the Atonement*, 414–15.

Cultivating Skill in the "Art of Arts"

Gregory the Great on Pastoral Balance

Wherever you go, let the pastoral book of St. Gregory be your companion. Read and re-read it often, that in it you may learn to know yourself and your work, that you may have before your eyes how you ought to live and teach.

—Alcuin to Archbishop of York, 796 AD

Since at least the ninth century, Gregory I has been called "Gregory the Great."[1] But what was it that made him *great*? For many historians of church and doctrine, it is certainly not his theology. Frederick Dudden, for instance, in his dated but influential biography, describes Gregory as "destitute of originality," a man who "has neither freshness of thought nor depth of insight," a thinker who is "extremely uncritical, and in his exegesis often puerile and absurd."[2] In Dudden's

---

1. John Moorhead, *Gregory the Great*, The Early Church Fathers (London: Routledge, 2005), 1.
2. Frederick H. Dudden, *Gregory the Great: His Place in History and Thought*, 2 vols. (New York: Russell & Russell, 1905), 2:286. Dudden's work has now been replaced by the more recent and more comprehensive work of R. A. Markus, *Gregory the Great and His World* (Washington,

analysis, Gregory "is careless in his definitions, slipshod in his formulas, disorderly in his treatment of subjects."[3] This account of Gregory's theology is all the more striking in light of Dudden's general sympathy for Gregory. For Dudden, Gregory is "by far the most important personage of his time,"[4] a man without whom "the evolution of the form of medieval Christianity would be almost inexplicable."[5] What makes Gregory "great," in Dudden's estimation, is his ecclesiastical accomplishments and influence; he is fundamentally "a man of action, a great practical genius."[6]

A feeling of dissonance arises in attempting to regard one individual as, on the one hand, the greatest churchman of his time and, on the other hand, "slipshod," "puerile," and "absurd" in his theology. Yet Dudden's portrait remains a common way of understanding Gregory.[7] George Demacopoulos notes that even the most sympathetic interpretations of Gregory tend to regard him as a "derivative thinker" and that "the majority of twentieth-century commentators, in fact, see Gregory as little more than a monastic sieve between Augustine and the Middle Ages."[8] A contributing factor

---

DC: Catholic University of America Press, 1997), though Markus acknowledges that Dudden's work, particularly Books I and II, remains the best narrative account of Gregory's pontificate available at the time of Markus's writing (*xi*). Dudden's work is thus worth engaging despite its age, particularly because, as we shall see, its account of Gregory's significance coheres with continuing trajectories in Gregorian scholarship.

3. Dudden, *Gregory the Great*, 2:289–90.

4. Dudden, *Gregory the Great*, 1:*v*.

5. Dudden, *Gregory the Great*, 1:*vi*.

6. Dudden, *Gregory the Great*, 2:285.

7. More recent studies tend to share Dudden's account of Gregory's greatness, although they are more balanced. E.g., G. R. Evans, *The Thought of Gregory the Great*, Cambridge Studies in Medieval Thought and Life (Cambridge: Cambridge University Press, 1986), *xii*: "Gregory the Great was not a thinker of Augustine's sort. His mind was practical." And later: "We do not find him struggling with a problem as Augustine does. There is a calmer air, an air of exposition rather than investigation" (8). At the same time, Evans resists denigrating Gregory's intellectual ability and draws attention to some of his more original insights, e.g., his treatment of the life of the soul in the world to come in Book IV of the *Dialogues* (13). Similarly, Moorhead, *Gregory the Great*, 26, argues that "in the history of Christian theology his place is secondary." So also Bernard Green, "The Theology of Gregory the Great: Christ, Salvation, and the Church," in Matthew Dal Santo and Neil Bronwen, eds., *A Companion to Gregory the Great*, Companions to the Christian Tradition (Leiden: Brill, 2013), 135: "Though at times capable of unexpected subtlety of thought, his was not a mind much given to speculation." A more careful account is offered by Carole Straw, *Gregory the Great: Perfection in Imperfection*, Transformation of the Classical Heritage 14 (Berkeley, CA: University of California Press, 1991), 13, who suggests that "in many ways, Gregory only articulates what is latent in earlier Christianity" but also acknowledges his own distinctive contributions.

8. George E. Demacopoulos, *Gregory the Great: Ascetic, Pastor, and First Man of Rome* (Notre Dame, IN: University of Notre Dame, 2015), 21. Demacopoulos notes that this is changing in the early twenty-first century, particularly in French, German, and Italian scholarship.

may be the embarrassment of modern interpreters (most memorably Adolf Harnack) over Gregory's seemingly superstitious appeal to the miraculous.[9]

In addition to relying on often inaccurate claims (such as the charge that Gregory knew no Greek theology), this impression of Gregory as intellectually simple suffers from a more basic vulnerability: namely, the assumption that innovation and creativity are an essential criterion for theological ability.[10] In this chapter I will proceed on the view, ably articulated by George Demacopoulos, that this whole approach to interpreting Gregory does not assist us to appreciate the context and aims of Gregory's theological work. As Demacopoulos puts it:

> Gregory was a unique and nuanced theologian, whose subtlety is often missed by scholars who wrongly assume that theological originality must be of a dogmatic nature or who fail to see the ways in which his particular theological commitments to asceticism and pastoral ministry informed his approach to administrative and diplomatic tasks.[11]

Of course, Gregory *was* a skillful administrator, and it is not unreasonable to emphasize this aspect of his contribution to church history. Nonetheless, we must be wary of divorcing his thought and life, such that the wholeness of his legacy and person is punctured. Gregory's theology, rather than being slipshod and puerile, reflects a kind of depth and shrewdness that cannot be isolated from the practical skills that made him great.

This chapter approaches Gregory's pastoral theology as prime material for retrieval among a modern evangelical audience. With Demacopoulos, it sees Gregory's pastoral vision as at the heart of theology and life, blending together his deeply felt monastic ideals with his practical gifts of leadership.[12] It is hoped that even a brief and

---

9. See the discussion in Straw, *Gregory the Great*, 7–8.

10. On Gregory's knowledge of Greek, see the discussion in Dal Santo and Bronwen, *A Companion to Gregory the Great*, *xxii*, who suggest that Gregory's knowledge of Greek was limited but not so much that he was ignorant of the larger world of Greek thought and theological discussion, as often implied.

11. Demacopoulos, *Gregory the Great*, 16.

12. Demacopoulos, *Gregory the Great*, 10–11: "If there is any single axiom that explains Gregory as both theologian and papal actor, it is that he felt ever conflicted between his inclination for ascetic ideals (namely humility and retreat) and a Ciceronian-like compulsion to public service."

somewhat summative engagement with Gregory in this area will encourage greater familiarity and appreciation for Gregory among contemporary Protestants (especially evangelicals), while perhaps serving as a kind of case study of the larger method for which this book has argued. To that end we will focus our attention on three ways that Gregory develops the motif of *balance* throughout his *Book of Pastoral Rule* and then conclude with some reflections regarding evangelical engagement with this book.

Balancing Aspiration and Unworthiness for the Pastorate (*Book of Pastoral Rule* 1, 4)

In *The Book of Pastoral Rule*'s introductory letter to John, one of Gregory's fellow bishops, Gregory makes the purpose of his writing plain: "I write the present book to express my opinion of the severity of [the burdens of pastoral care], so that he who is free of these burdens might not recklessly pursue them and he who has already attained them might tremble for having done so."[13] Gregory's aim in *The Book of Pastoral Rule* appears here as something other than mere practical instruction—it is not primarily a "how to" book, assuming an agreed-upon target and supplying suggestions on how to reach it. Rather, Gregory is concerned with his readers' *view* of the pastoral office. Strikingly, he does not write to help his audience desire, love, or pursue the pastoral office. He wants to help them *tremble* before it. This high view of pastoral office is sustained throughout the book. Again and again, Gregory wants to pierce the heart with fear and humility before the awesome weight of responsibility that is assumed in spiritual leadership in the church. Ultimately, Gregory feels himself unworthy to even give an account of pastoral ministry, lamenting in the final paragraph of the book, "I am like a poor painter who tries to paint the ideal man."[14]

This emphasis on the height and difficulty of the pastoral office is particularly evident in the early chapters of *The Book of Pastoral Rule*, where Gregory discourages the inexperienced and those who do

---

13. Gregory the Great, *The Book of Pastoral* Rule, introductory letter, trans. George E. Demacopoulos, Popular Patristics 34 (Crestwood, NY: St. Vladimir's Seminary, 2007), 27. In this chapter I rely upon Demacopoulos's helpful translation and introduction.

14. Gregory, *Book of Pastoral Rule* 4.

not put into practice what they study from seeking the role of pastor and then warns of the burdens and anxieties that are associated with the pastoral office.[15] Later Gregory warns that the person in spiritual leadership must be "a model for everyone,"[16] since no one can cleanse others from their sins if he is still consumed by his own sins.[17] Gregory's concern about qualifications for pastoral office throughout this section concern godliness, skill, and experience, but his emphasis is above all on the pastor's possessing preeminently godly character, particularly of an ascetic variety. For instance, Gregory's elaboration on what being a "model for everyone" entails focuses on such qualities as being devoted to good living, putting to death the passions of the flesh, disregarding worldly prosperity, forgiving quickly (but nonetheless "never so far removed from righteousness as to forgive indiscriminately"), deploring evil, suffering the afflictions of others, praying fervently, and so forth.[18] Gregory's language here recalls "ascetic ideals as reflected in the works of Cassian, Benedict, or the writings of the Christian East,"[19] and often throughout *The Book of Pastoral Rule* the ideal pastor will appear as tantamount to the ideal ascetic.

At the same time, Gregory balances his concern about the ungodly taking up of the pastoral office too hastily with an opposite and corresponding concern about the godly being *unwilling* to take up the office. Addressing those who have both the godly character and skill to help others, Gregory warns, "To be certain, if they refuse to accept a position of spiritual leadership when they are called, they forfeit the majority of their gifts—gifts which they received not for themselves only, but also for others."[20] The temptation in view here is not forsaking spiritual leadership for the sake of worldly benefits but forsaking it for the sake of personal contemplation and study. This temptation might seem to be somewhat understandable, given Gregory's recurrent emphasis on the value of personal contemplation and study. Nonetheless, Gregory regards it as a very serious sin, such

---

15. Gregory, *Book of Pastoral Rule* 1.1–4.
16. Gregory, *Book of Pastoral Rule* 1.10.
17. Gregory, *Book of Pastoral Rule* 1.11.
18. Gregory, *Book of Pastoral Rule* 1.10.
19. George E. Demacopoulos, "*Gregory's Model of Spiritual Direction in the* Liber Regulae Pastoralis," in Dal Santo and Bronwen, *A Companion to Gregory the Great*, 213.
20. Gregory, *Book of Pastoral Rule* 1.5.

that those who succumb to it are acting contrary to the example of Christ and indeed demonstrating a lack of love for Christ: he who "refuses to feed the flock of God is found guilty of having no love for the supreme Shepherd."[21]

Gregory acknowledges that the avoidance of pastoral office can occasionally spring from genuine humility. But if a calling to the pastoral office is clearly God's will, the refusal to take it is not humility but just the opposite—disregarding divine decrees rather than submitting to them.[22] This, too, springs from failing to properly reverence the office. Gregory appeals to the examples of Isaiah and Jeremiah to demonstrate that sometimes the calling to preach is sought (as in Isaiah 6:6), while other times it is taken under compulsion (as in Jeremiah 1:6) Both circumstances can reflect a genuine calling, but both also reflect a corresponding danger. Specifically, Isaiah should see that his willingness does not cause him to rush past being cleansed by a coal from the altar while Jeremiah must take care that his reluctance does not induce him to reject God's calling.[23] Gregory thus balances the danger of hastiness against the danger of self-interest. While many seek the pastoral office when they should not, it is also possible to fail to seek the pastoral office when we *should*, and *both* errors ultimately stem from failing to tremble adequately with reverence before the office.

This balance of the need for both a willingness and a sense of unworthiness for the pastoral office is primarily developed in part 1 of the book, but the inclusion of the very brief part 4 adds something important in the same direction. Here Gregory warns that after the preacher has done everything that has been required of him, he should "return to himself" so that he does not take pride in his life or teaching.[24] Thus, the four sections of *The Book of Pastoral Rule* reflect a clear logical order: the first pertaining to a pastor's qualifications before he carries out his duties, the last pertaining to the pastor's responsibilities after he has carried out his duties, and the middle two pertaining to the duties themselves (his life and teaching, respectively). In his introductory letter Gregory has stipulated that the four parts of

---

21. Gregory, *Book of Pastoral Rule* 1.5.
22. Gregory, *Book of Pastoral Rule* 1.6.
23. Gregory, *Book of Pastoral Rule* 1.7.
24. Gregory, *Book of Pastoral Rule* 4.

the book are ordered "so that the reader might advance by an orderly succession, as if step-by-step."[25]

What comes through in the fourth section most forcefully is the danger in pastoral leadership of spiritual pride. Precisely because it is such a great weight of responsibility, the effective execution of the pastoral office often produces a state of elation in the heart of the pastor.[26] The antidote, for Gregory, is to remember our infirmities and humble ourselves in light of them. The eye of our mind "should not look at the good things that it has done, but at those things that it has neglected, so that when the heart reflects upon its infirmity, it will be all the more strongly established before the Author of humility."[27] Indeed, God often leaves little flaws in great leaders for this very reason, that they may "never take pride in their great achievements while they continue to labor against minor things."[28] Ultimately, therefore, Gregory wants his readers to tremble before the pastoral office not just before they have taken it up but after they have laid it down. In all this, Gregory balances his emphasis on the height and glory of the pastoral office with a corresponding emphasis on the pastor's need to lower himself in humility and remember his sins. We must be neither unwilling to ascend to "the highest things" nor unaware of our unworthiness to do so.[29]

Balancing Contemplation and Action in the Pastorate (*Book of Pastoral Rule* 2)

In part 2 of *The Book of Pastoral Rule* Gregory transitions from the qualifications of pastoral leadership to the life of a pastor during the course of his leadership. This section also is characterized by a calling to balance, but the balance this time is between the *active* and *contemplative* components of pastoral leadership. This aspect of *The Book of Pastoral Rule*'s teaching is related to Gregory's own personal struggle to live spiritually amidst the burden of administrative responsibilities associated with church leadership, and it may be useful to note how

---

25. Gregory, *Book of Pastoral Rule*, introductory letter.
26. Gregory, *Book of Pastoral Rule* 4.
27. Gregory, *Book of Pastoral Rule* 4.
28. Gregory, *Book of Pastoral Rule* 4.
29. Gregory, *Book of Pastoral Rule* 4.

this motif crops up in his other writings before discussing *The Book of Pastoral Rule*. It would not be unreasonable to regard this tension between the practical and the spiritual as the deepest theme of Gregory's life and thought (and perhaps the clearest rubric by which they can be integrated).

Gregory was the first monk turned pope.[30] When his pontificate began in 590, he was extremely reluctant to take the office, and the intensity of his longings to remain in the monastery can be detected from his letters around this time. While the strong desire to leave the pastoral office is a theme in patristic writings (e.g., in Gregory of Nazianzus's *Orations* or John Chrysostom's *On the Priesthood*), Gregory's protestations should not be regarded on that account as insincere, and his expressions throughout his personal correspondences make it very difficult to interpret him that way.[31] This struggle at his administrative load is the great theme of his letter to the emperor's sister Theoctista soon after his appointment as pope, for instance, where he laments that he has been dragged back to the world and thus "lost the high joys (*alta gaudia*) of quiet."[32] In both this letter and another from the same month to his friend Narsus, he compares becoming Pope to tumbling downward in the darkness; he has, paradoxically, attained the highest external office possible, only to plummet down to the deepest places internally. As a result, his grief is so thick that he complains he is almost unable even to speak.[33] Later letters written soon after *The Book of Pastoral Rule* was completed testify to the experience of a gloomy cloud of depression (*caligo moeroris*) at considering how unfit he is to bear the weight of pastoral care.[34] Similarly, he opens his *Dialogues*, written just after this, by referencing how depressed the pressures of public office have made him.[35]

The nature of Gregory's struggle with the administrative weight of leadership is not merely circumstantial or reducible to a personality

---

30. Barbara Müller, "Gregory the Great and Monasticism," in Dal Santo and Bronwen, *A Companion to Gregory the Great*, 83.
31. This comparison to Gregory and John is observed in Evans, *Thought of Gregory the Great*, 24.
32. Gregory, Ep. 1.5, Oct. 590 (PL 77:448B), my translation. Evans, *Thought of Gregory the Great*, 24–25, has drawn my attention to several of Gregory's letters in this connection.
33. Gregory, Ep. 1.6, Oct. 590 (PL 77:450C).
34. Gregory, Ep. 1.25, Feb. 591 (PL 77:468B).
35. Gregory, *Dialogues* (PL 77:149B).

trait. Rather, it reflects his theological vision of the pastoral office and the paradoxes that necessarily plague the one who occupies it—the need for simultaneous humility and boldness, for instance, or the necessity of balancing both kindness and correction.[36] But the deepest paradox of pastoral leadership is that the responsibilities inherent to the office require attention to many details that inevitably distract one from spiritual solitude and vitality; and yet the effective oversight of those very details requires the spiritual well-being that can come only from quiet and solitude. To be effective in their office, every pastor must therefore find an effective balance between the active and contemplative sides of spiritual leadership.

In considering the nature of the pastoral office in terms of the *active* life and *contemplative* life, Gregory is not introducing an innovation. Rather, he is drawing on categories that are ultimately rooted in classical thought (especially Seneca and Cicero),[37] and then take on a particular focus in the patristic era (particularly through Augustine, and also Cassian and Ambrose of Milan), and become common throughout medieval theology.[38] Specifically, the active/contemplative distinction was employed in the interpretation of the story of Mary and Martha in Luke 10:38–42 such that the "active" life of earthly labors is typified by Martha ("many things"), and the "contemplative life" of heavenly rest/enjoyment of God is typified by Mary ("one thing"). Gregory defines this typology at greater length in his sermons on Ezekiel and in his commentary on Job.[39] On occasion he will also involve Rachel (contemplative) and Leah (active) to make the contrast.[40]

In *The Book of Pastoral Rule*, then, Gregory takes the categories of this broader tradition of interpretation and employs them in the context of his own struggles enduring the strain of administrative responsibility. Indeed, this balance between the active and the contemplative in the life of the pastor is arguably the driving theme that occupies

---

36. Gregory, *Book of Pastoral Rule* 2.6.

37. Evans, *Thought of Gregory the Great*, 19–20, 108–9.

38. I trace this construct from Augustine through Gregory and Bede all the way up to Aquinas in Gavin Ortlund, *Ascending toward the Beatific Vision: Heaven as the Climax of Anselm's Proslogion*, PhD diss. (Fuller Theological Seminary, 2016), 224–28.

39. E.g., Gregory, *Moralia* 37, rec. 17 (PL 75:764C–746D); Gregory, *Homilies on Ezekiel* 2.2.8–9 (PL 76:953A–954A).

40. Gregory, *Ep.* 1.5, Oct. 590 (PL 77:449B).

part 2 of *The Book of Pastoral Rule*. Gregory opens this section of the book by arguing that the pastor's life must be characterized, above all, by righteousness—he must "transcend that of the people in proportion to how the life of a shepherd outshines that of his flock."[41] He then fleshes out what this exemplary righteousness should look like in terms of the pastor's thought, speech, conduct, etc., topics that he will then develop throughout 2.2–2.7. The climactic statement on pastoral qualification, which is picked up in the lengthy chapter 2.7 and then bridges into the various topics treated in 2.8–2.11, is that "he must not relax his care for the internal life while he is occupied by external concerns, not should he relinquish what is prudent of external matters so as to focus on things internal."[42] Thus, for Gregory, the pastor's righteousness comes to ultimate expression in the appropriate balance between the active and contemplative life.

Although it is not until 2.7 that Gregory will explicitly advance the pastor's need for balance between the active and contemplative life, this theme is already involved in the various other exhortations he makes throughout 2.2–2.6. When expressing the importance of charity, for instance, Gregory warns that contemplating high things may lead the pastor to despise the infirmities of his neighbors, but he immediately balances this warning with the opposite warning that when the pastor adapts himself to those infirmities, it can lead to the abandonment of high things.[43] Similarly, when it comes to the use of spiritual authority, Gregory counsels that the pastor should downplay his high position to godly laypeople and think of himself as their equal. But to those who persist in sin, he should not hesitate to wield his authority to correct them.[44] The effective pastor will therefore function with a balance of both kindness and discipline— he must be "as a mother with respect to kindness and as a father with respect to discipline."[45] He quotes here from his own *Moralia in Job*: "Either discipline or kindness is lacking if one is ever exercised independently of the other."[46]

---

41. Gregory, *Book of Pastoral Rule* 2.1.
42. Gregory, *Book of Pastoral Rule* 2.1.
43. Gregory, *Book of Pastoral Rule* 2.5.
44. Gregory, *Book of Pastoral Rule* 2.6.
45. Gregory, *Book of Pastoral Rule* 2.6.
46. Gregory, *Book of Pastoral Rule* 2.6; cf. *Moralia* 20:15.14.

Gregory develops the notion of pastoral balance throughout this section with his characteristic rich use of imagery. In 2.3 he offers an extended discussion regarding how the materials of the priestly ephod robe are symbolic of pastoral integrity.[47] Gregory correlates various materials of the priestly garments with different aspects of pastoral integrity, concluding with a connection between the twice-died scarlet on the robe and charity, which must adorn all other virtues. Strikingly, the consequence that Gregory draws from this association is that "whoever, therefore, pursues so completely the beauty of his Maker as to neglect the care of his neighbors or, conversely, whoever attends to the care of his neighbors so as to grow listless in divine love (whichever of these two he neglects), he does not know what it means to have twice-died scarlet in the adornment of the Ephod."[48] Another image is employed to this same end in 2.5, where Gregory draws attention to the angels ascending and descending the ladder in Jacob's vision in Genesis 28, which he argues "signifies that true preachers do not only aspire through contemplation to the holy head of the Church (in other words, to the Lord), but they also descend to the needs of the members through compassion."[49] He then draws similar connections with Moses's entering and exiting the tabernacle, and with Christ's retreating into solitude and prayer during his incarnate life. Both of these provide an example to pastors, who must balance their retreat into secret contemplation with their return to deeds of compassion.[50]

The reader is thus well familiar with the content of *The Book of Pastoral Rule* 2.7 before she reads its title: "The spiritual director should not reduce his attention to the internal life because of external occupations, nor should he relinquish his care for external matters because of his anxiety for the internal life."[51] Now in 2.7, the central chapter of this section, Gregory unpacks this theme at length. The vital importance Gregory attaches to maintaining this balance between the internal and the external can be detected in how he describes the consequences when a pastor becomes too focused on

---

47. Gregory, *Book of Pastoral Rule* 2.3.
48. Gregory, *Book of Pastoral Rule* 2.3.
49. Gregory, *Book of Pastoral Rule* 2.5.
50. Gregory, *Book of Pastoral Rule* 2.5.
51. Gregory, *Book of Pastoral Rule* 2.7.

either just one or the other. He compares the pastor to a head and the laity to a body, warning that if the head becomes preoccupied with only worldly affairs, the entire congregation will lose its way. "How can a leader of souls employ his pastoral dignity among the laity if he is himself engaged in the very worldly affairs that he is supposed to correct in them?"[52] In the other direction, when a pastor takes no interest in external matters, the laity are equally unfruitful.[53] Thus the pastor's balance between the active and the contemplative life is essential to the health of the flock he oversees. Throughout the end of this section, 2.8–2.11, Gregory will continue to unpack various ways that pastoral balance is essential to the health of the whole church.[54]

The significance of the balance of the active and contemplative life can be further observed in the vivid allegorical imagery employed in 2.7. Gregory references the destruction of the temple in Lamentations 4:1 and particularly the scattering of the stones of the temple throughout the streets, with the resultant loss of gold and color. He then builds an extended metaphor in which gold represents sanctity, "finest color" represents reverence for religion, spiritual leaders represent the stones, and the streets represent the breadth of this life, which leads to destruction (Gregory quotes Matthew 7:13 in this regard).[55] The impatience with which modern interpreters often regard this kind of allegorical hermeneutic, which occurs throughout *The Book of Pastoral Rule* and is common in Gregory's context, may discourage reflection on the rich theological understanding of the pastorate that it presupposes. But Gregory's purpose is to emphasize the tragedy of when a pastor becomes preoccupied with worldly affairs: such an occurrence is like the holy stones being scattered in the streets and the sacred gold and color being trampled in the streets and losing its luster. That Gregory would use this particular imagery—the desecration of the temple!—to describe pastoral imbalance reveals how essential he believes it is to pastoral integrity.

---

52. Gregory, *Book of Pastoral Rule* 2.7.
53. Gregory, *Book of Pastoral Rule* 2.7.
54. E.g., in *Book of Pastoral Rule* 2.10, he spends considerable space arguing that in order to edify his people, a pastor should sometimes use open correction and other times disregard a vice, and similarly that when a correction is needed, it should sometimes be given fervor and other times with gentleness.
55. Gregory, *Book of Pastoral Rule* 2.7.

Balancing Encouragement and Exhortation in Preaching (*Book of Pastoral Rule* 3)

Gregory considered preaching to be the highest duty of the bishop, and part 3 of *The Book of Pastoral Rule* is devoted to how different kinds of people need different kinds of preaching.[56] The significance of this section of the book is suggested from the fact that it is roughly twice the length of the other three combined, and from the fact that it is the only one with a prologue. At the start of the prologue Gregory quotes a statement from Gregory of Nazianzus to the effect that the same exhortation will not suffice for all people, because not everyone has the same character.[57] Then in 3.1 Gregory lists roughly three dozen contrasts of different kinds of people, e.g., young and old, healthy and sick, lazy and hasty, "those who bewail their sins but do not cease in committing them, and those who cease but do not bewail past sins," and so forth.[58] Throughout 3.2 to 3.35 Gregory provides instruction on how to teach differently in each case, with each chapter beginning with the same sentence: "The ____ and ____ should be advised differently."[59] The section closes with several final practical considerations pertaining to the pastor's preaching, again seemingly occasioned by the challenge of the diversity of people in the preacher's audience.[60]

The dominant concern throughout this section is thus the balance required for effectively teaching different kinds of people. This concern has already surfaced in the previous sections of the book. In describing the pastor's speech in part 2, for example, Gregory calls for a balance between recklessness and timidity, because both can leave a sinner in error by failing to correct them.[61] Later, as already noted, he advises pastors to distinguish when a sin should be "gently amended" from when a sin should be "vehemently rebuked," because different kinds of sins must be handled differently.[62] Gregory acknowledges the difficulty of acquiring this balanced approach, warning that a minister

---

56. On Gregory's view of preaching, see Evans, *Thought of Gregory the Great*, 80.
57. Gregory, *Book of Pastoral Rule* 3, prologue.
58. Gregory lists each different contrast in *Book of Pastoral Rule* 3.1.
59. Gregory, *Book of Pastoral Rule* 3.2–3.35.
60. Gregory, *Book of Pastoral Rule* 3.36–3.40. Gregory is also concerned here with the diversity of struggles that can be present within *one* person (3.37).
61. Gregory, *Book of Pastoral Rule* 2.4.
62. Gregory, *Book of Pastoral Rule* 2.10.

who lacks zeal in his correction will forfeit his own salvation but also exhorting a minister who has spoken overzealously to repent with lamentation.[63]

But it is here in part 3 of *The Book of Pastoral Rule* that this concern is fully borne out. Gregory's treatment of the humble and the proud directly in 3.17 may provide a useful sample as an entry point into the text, as it is illustrative of both his copious use of Scripture and his persistent insight that different appeals must be balanced against one another:

> Let the humble hear how the things they strive for are eternal, and the things that they despise are transitory; let the proud hear that the things that they pursue are transitory, and the things that they abandon are eternal. Let the humble hear from the authoritative voice of the Truth: "everyone who humbles himself will be exalted." Let the proud hear: Everyone who exalts himself will be humbled." Let the humble hear: "Humility precedes glory." And let the proud hear: "The spirit is exalted before a fall." Let the humble hear: "Whom shall I respect if not the humble, the quiet, and those who tremble at my words?" Let the proud hear: "Why are earth and ashes proud?" Let the humble hear: "God respects the humble"; and let the proud be told: "And the proud he knows from afar." Let the humble hear: "Because the Son of Man did not come to be served, but to serve." And let the proud learn: "Because pride is the source of all sin."[64]

The scriptural quotations continue further, with Gregory eventually appealing to the fall of the devil and the incarnation of the Son of God as the ultimate expressions of pride and humility, respectively, and therefore the chief causes of both pride and humility among human beings. Those who exalt themselves thus imitate the fall of the devil, and those who humble themselves thus ascend to the likeness of God.[65]

Many of the other contrasting character traits addressed by Gregory boil down to the more basic contrast of pride and humility, with

---

63. Gregory, *Book of Pastoral Rule* 2.10.
64. Gregory, *Book of Pastoral Rule* 3.17. Some of these quotations are from the apocryphal *Sirach*.
65. Gregory, *Book of Pastoral Rule* 3.17.

the corresponding pastoral needs of boldness and gentleness. Thus the rich are to be more readily rebuked than the poor because they are more likely given to pride, as are the wise more than the dull, the healthy more than the sick, and so forth. At the same time, Gregory recognizes exceptions to this tendency and nuances his exhortation to account for the possibilities (for instance) of the humble rich,[66] or for those who are hardened but nonetheless may be won over by "sweet admonitions" more than by "harsh punishments."[67] The overall emphasis, however, is that pastoral exhortation must function with great sensitivity and balance, recognizing the different needs among the people in the congregation and not allowing the kind of exhortation needed for one particular vice to drown out the kind of exhortation needed for another. There must even be balance in the commendation of different kinds of virtue: "The greatest good should be praised in a way that does not ignore lesser goods; lesser goods should be acknowledged, but not in a way that compromises the greatest goods."[68] In the other direction, Gregory advises that sometimes lesser vices must be tolerated in order to deal with greater ones.[69]

Some of the contrasting behaviors in view throughout this section are two different kinds of vices, and thus the instruction pertains simply to how different vices require different kinds of instruction. Thus the lazy must be warned against missed opportunities, while the hasty must be warned against incautious haste.[70] Those who misinterpret Scripture must consider the damage that their errors causes, while those who understand it but do not speak about it with humility are exhorted to apply the Scripture to their own hearts before they do anything else with it.[71] Those who commit minor sins frequently must be warned about the cumulative effect of sin, while those who commit grave sins only occasionally must be warned that when the heart is elated with pride, sin can devour them in but a moment.[72]

---

66. Gregory, *Book of Pastoral Rule* 3.2.
67. Gregory, *Book of Pastoral Rule* 3.13.
68. Gregory, *Book of Pastoral Rule* 3.36.
69. Gregory, *Book of Pastoral Rule* 3.38.
70. Gregory, *Book of Pastoral Rule* 3.15.
71. Gregory, *Book of Pastoral Rule* 3.24.
72. Gregory, *Book of Pastoral Rule* 3.33.

But more commonly the contrasts that Gregory sets up function more subtly such that a vice is contrasted with a virtue, but—surprisingly—both are still admonished. In fact, often the virtuous are admonished more forcefully than those stuck in some vice. Thus, for instance, the impatient are warned against pride, but the patient are not commended but rather warned against the danger of self-pity that often plagues a patient disposition.[73] Similarly, after Gregory warns the gluttonous that their gluttony often leads them into excessive speaking, laziness, and lust, he does not praise the abstinent but rather warns them that "the sins of impatience and pride often accompany abstinence."[74]

Gregory's insight into fallen human psychology is evident in his emphasis on the deceitfulness of sin, such that those who possess certain virtues are perceived as all the more vulnerable to other vices. He warns, for instance, that those who are quiet often avoid sins of the mouth but harbor malice in their hearts.[75] Additionally, the pursuit of a virtue often makes one susceptible to a particular vice. For instance, those fleeing gluttony must take care that "even worse vices are not produced through this one virtue. . . . There is no virtue in conquering the flesh if the spirit of wrath emerges."[76] Similarly, one who attains abstinence often forsakes unity with those who persist in gluttony, thus yielding to the greater sin of discord.[77] Related to this, there are certain vices that often masquerade as virtues, such that sinful wrath often sneaks into the heart more readily under the guise of spiritual zeal,[78] and sinful fear often masquerades in the false pretence of humility.[79] The upshot of all this is that those who possess a particular virtue are never simply affirmed. Instead, they are usually exhorted to pursue additional virtues that may protect their integrity. For instance, the sincere are advised to "add prudence to the goodness of sincerity" so that these virtues will secure one another.[80]

---

73. Gregory, *Book of Pastoral Rule* 3.9.
74. Gregory, *Book of Pastoral Rule* 3.19.
75. Gregory, *Book of Pastoral Rule* 3.14.
76. Gregory, *Book of Pastoral Rule* 3.19.
77. Gregory, *Book of Pastoral Rule* 3.22.
78. Gregory, *Book of Pastoral Rule* 3.16.
79. Gregory, *Book of Pastoral Rule* 3.17.
80. Gregory, *Book of Pastoral Rule* 3.11.

Throughout this section, Gregory displays a shrewd sensitivity to the danger of self-righteousness. He often warns the virtuous not to look down on others, such as those who are ignorant of the sins of the flesh must not consider themselves better than the married.[81] More intriguingly, when two different kinds of people are contrasted, it is often surprising which one receives the stronger rebuke. In 3.25 Gregory treats "those who are able to preach with dignity but fear to do so out of humility, and those whose lack of skill or age prevents from preaching but who nevertheless rush into preaching."[82] One might think that the former fault would be more forgivable since it springs from humility, and the latter springs from pride. But Gregory is quite forceful in his condemnation of this first flaw, heaping up metaphors in which to show how wicked it is when a person is able to help his neighbor but fails to do so. In contrast, his warnings against the overzealous/young preachers are relatively tame.[83]

Similarly, when Gregory treats "those who give generously and those who steal," his admonishments to the generous come first and are lengthier than his admonishments against theft. He first of all warns those who give generously to take care that "they not consider themselves to be greater than those upon whom they bestow earthly goods; in effect, that they not assume that they are better than those whom they themselves . . . support."[84] Gregory observes that God appoints among his people some to receive and others to give, and then he suggests that it is typically those who give who incur offense through pride. As a result, they should humble themselves under God and acknowledge that all they have has been given to them by God.[85] He goes on at length to warn further that those who give should take care that they not distribute unworthily what has been given to them, that they should not give hastily or sorrowfully, that they not rejoice immoderately at their giving, that they should not desire fleeting praise for their giving, that they give without expecting anything in response, that they not give too late or too little, that they neither give to the

---

81. Gregory, *Book of Pastoral Rule* 3.28.
82. Gregory, *Book of Pastoral Rule* 3.25.
83. Gregory, *Book of Pastoral Rule* 3.25.
84. Gregory, *Book of Pastoral Rule* 3.20.
85. Gregory, *Book of Pastoral Rule* 3.20.

202 Case Studies in Theological Retrieval

unworthy nor withhold from the worthy, and that they be careful to avoid sin in their giving.[86] Gregory's warnings about the spiritual dangers associated with generosity attest again to his profound insight into the deceitfulness of the human heart and the elusiveness of true virtue. It is this emphasis on the danger of vices accompanying (and even masquerading as) virtues that drives much of Gregory's appeal to balance throughout this section.

Conclusion: What Have Evangelicals to Do with Gregory?

Having explored the motif of pastoral balance in Gregory's *The Book of Pastoral Rule*, it may be useful to conclude by reflecting on how contemporary Protestants, particularly evangelicals, might benefit from this emphasis of Gregory's. Historically, evangelicals have not placed much emphasis on appropriating Gregory's theology. We often regard him (if we have heard of him at all) as a suspicious figure, representing much of the theology that separates us from contemporary Roman Catholicism. After all, Gregory was himself a pope, and he played a critical role in the development of medieval Roman Catholicism.[87]

Admittedly, there are significant differences between certain strands of Gregory's theology and modern evangelical theology, and these differences should not be muted. It does not follow from this point, however, that evangelicals have nothing to learn from him, and we must be wary of exaggerating the differences by focusing too narrowly on Gregory's role in the development of Roman Catholic institutions such as the papacy. As we argued in chapter 1, he was an enormously respected figure throughout the medieval church; Chris Armstrong goes so far as to suggest that "throughout [the Middle Ages] he was the most read of all the Western fathers."[88] It seems unwise to reject wholesale a figure so highly revered in the church for nearly a millennium, and not even the Reformers took this approach. While criticizing many of his views (such as his affirmation of purgatory), Calvin

---

86. Gregory, *Book of Pastoral Rule* 3.20.
87. As Dudden, *Gregory the Great*, 1:v, puts it, "Almost all the leading principles of the later Catholicism are found, at any rate in germ, in Gregory the Great."
88. Chris R. Armstrong, *Medieval Wisdom for Modern Christians: Finding Authentic Faith in a Forgotten Age with C. S. Lewis* (Grand Rapids, MI: Brazos, 2016), 146,

nonetheless called him a "godly man" and dated the decline of the papacy later into the medieval period.[89] Melanchthon also resisted dating the origin of the decline of the church with Gregory, attributing it instead to his successor, Boniface III.[90] Furthermore, as we pointed out in chapter 1, his unique contact with the Eastern church makes Gregory a bridge into several different worlds. In engaging Gregory we find ourselves grappling with ideas touching both the Eastern and Western church at a pivotal time of the church's development from late antiquity to medieval Christendom. Thus here we conclude by articulating three particular benefits that Gregory's emphasis on pastoral balance in *The Book of Pastoral Rule* may provide for modern evangelicals.

First, Gregory's *The Book of Pastoral Rule* can deepen evangelical theology of the nature of virtue and vice. Evangelicals tend to spend significant energy reflecting on spiritual growth and spiritual disciplines in general, but we have often neglected to explore the nature of *specific* virtues and vices. What is the nature of charity? How is envy related to other vices? How does sin work upon the will differently from the mind? These are questions medievals worked over much more carefully than we tend to. C. S. Lewis, strikingly, devoted the largest section of his apologetic of Christianity to this area—Book 3 of *Mere Christianity*, which explores the "cardinal virtues" (prudence, justice, temperance, and fortitude), marriage, various vices (including the "great sin," pride), and theological virtues (hope, faith, and charity). Such a focus is much rarer in popular-level evangelicalism; the closest one comes is often an occasional sermon series on the seven deadly sins. Gregory can help enrich this aspect of our pastoral theology. His book is filled with psychological wisdom into the nature of virtue and vice, for instance, his reflection on the way pride and impatience are often connected,[91] or his insights into envy as the essence of sin and unhappiness,[92] or his warning that sin can be mentally opposed and

---

89. John Calvin, *Institutes of the Christian Religion*, ed. John T. McNeill, trans. Ford Lewis Battles, 2 vols. (Louisville, KY: Westminster John Knox, 2006), 4.7.22. Cf. the discussion on this point in chapter 2.
90. As observed by Ann Kuzdale, "The Reception of Gregory in the Rennaissance and Reformation," in Dal Santo and Bronwen, *A Companion to Gregory the Great*, 381.
91. Gregory, *Book of Pastoral Rule* 3.9.
92. Gregory, *Book of Pastoral Rule* 3.10.

nonetheless inwardly harbored.[93] (Of course, it is Gregory who revises the seven deadly sins to include envy in the first place, and Gregory's revisions became standardized throughout the medieval era.)

Second, Gregory's *The Book of Pastoral Rule* contains much practical and psychological insight that may supplement the more *theological* emphases of Protestant literature in the stream of pastoral theology. There are some profound similarities between Gregory's text and, say, Richard Baxter's *The Reformed Pastor* or Charles Spurgeon's *Lectures to My Students*; for instance, they all begin with a strong emphasis on the personal salvation and godliness of the minister. But throughout his work Gregory tends toward more practical considerations, often related to his struggle with the administrative load of pastoral leadership and often concerned with the challenges and complexities of human psychology. For all the rich insights in the works of Baxter and Spurgeon, they contain nothing comparable to part 3 of Gregory's text, such as where he gives instruction on how to teach different people differently. Protestants need not subscribe wholly to Gregory's vision of pastoral service in order to benefit from the wisdom, shrewdness, and tact that characterize this section of his work.

One example of where we might benefit from Gregory's wisdom is his appeal throughout *The Book of Pastoral Rule* for pastors to be careful and discerning in their speech. In 2.4, Gregory develops his assertion that the pastor should be "discerning in silence and profitable in speech."[94] Gregory's counsel throughout this section contains subtleties such as the following:

> Spiritual directors must be careful not only to guard against saying something wrong, but also to avoid offering the right words too frequently or unprofessionally, because often the virtue of what is said is lost when it is enfeebled in the hearts of the audience since the speech was offered hastily or carelessly.[95]

Such consideration of *how* we speak, as well what we say, is a recurrent emphasis throughout *The Book of Pastoral Rule*, and it re-

---

93. Gregory, *Book of Pastoral Rule* 3.29.
94. Gregory, *Book of Pastoral Rule* 2.4.
95. Gregory, *Book of Pastoral Rule* 2.4.

flects Gregory's insight into the complexities of human motivation and the importance of pastors' cultivating the skills of winsomeness and persuasion. As Dal Santo and Neil Bronwen state, Gregory writes with "the awareness that the human heart is itself no less a maze than the Scriptural mysteries he was so fond of allegorizing and that it requires all the discretion (*discretio*) of the spiritual director, trained in contemplation and perfected in the care of souls, to navigate its secrets."[96]

Gregory's concern for skillful persuasion and winsomeness is evident in his counsel for how pastors should correct the proud. For all Gregory's admonishment to be firmly opposed to human pride, he balances this emphasis with advice for how to win the hearing of the proud. At one point he argues, "It is generally more useful to correct the proud if we combine a measure of praise with our correction."[97] Gregory then develops this thought with metaphor: just as unbroken horses must first be touched gently with the hand before they should receive a whip, so the proud should be given a measure of praise at first so that they will receive correction they would otherwise scorn. Likewise, just as bitter medicine is mixed with sweet flavor so what can heal a deadly illness will not be spit out of the mouth, so our speech to the proud should be initially pleasing so it is met with favor. Gregory is even willing to display a kind of deference to the proud in the hope of winning them over: "It will generally be easier to persuade the proud that amendment is beneficial if we speak to them about their improvement as though it would help us rather than them. . . . We should convince them that their amendment is a favor to us."[98] In areas like these, contemporary Protestant pastors may find a practical wisdom in *The Book of Pastoral Rule* that richly supplements their Protestant literature in this field.

Finally, and most basically, *The Book of Pastoral Rule* may help us grow in our reverence for the pastoral office. Most pastors, according to their disposition and context, will tend to gravitate toward *either* theory or practice, ideas or actions, the intellectual or the practical, otherworldly holiness or earthly wisdom. Of course, this is rarely an

---

96. Dal Santo and Bronwen, *A Companion to Gregory the Great*, xxi.
97. Gregory, *Book of Pastoral Rule* 3.17.
98. Gregory, *Book of Pastoral Rule* 3.17.

206 Case Studies in Theological Retrieval

absolute contrast but instead a matter of emphasis. To this extent, every pastor may benefit from considering Gregory's call to pastoral balance. It is false to assume that Gregory is writing exclusively about the office of bishop in *The Book of Pastoral Rule*. As George Demacopoulos notes, Gregory uses a variety of terms for the kind of spiritual leadership with which he is concerned, including *sacerdos*, *rector*, *praedicator*, and *pastor*—but, strikingly, *episcopus* is not one of them.[99] Gregory's calling for balance in the pastoral office is a perennially relevant insight, applicable across other theological and cultural divides to various roles of spiritual leadership.

Gregory's thesis that effective pastoral ministry requires a delicate balance of both inner and outer qualities entails that pastors, perhaps more than any other vocation, must embrace and grow in their areas of weakness. This is a profoundly humbling consideration, because every pastor has weaknesses that temper and relativize even their greatest strengths. Appropriating Gregory's calling for pastoral balance will therefore help us become more effective in the execution of our office, but, even more profoundly, it will humble us before its difficulty and complexity and help us understand why Gregory called it the "art of arts" before which we all must tremble.[100]

---

99. George E. Demacopoulos, "Gregory's Model of Spiritual Direction in the *Liber Regulae Pastoralis*," in Dal Santo and Bronwen, *A Companion to Gregory the Great*, 211.
100. Gregory, *Book of Pastoral Rule* 1.1.

General Index

Adam-Christ typology, 150–52, 154–55, 159
adoption, 149
Adversus Haereses (Irenaeus), 146–57
Against the Arians (Athanasius), 168
Albigenses, 38
Alcuin, 77, 185
Al-Farabi, 132
Alfred, King, 77n16
Al-Kindi, 132
Allen, Michael, 17–18n3, 18nn5–6, 41n77, 52
Ambrose, 121, 133, 193
American Protestantism, sectarian spirit of, 24–25
Anabaptists, 19, 31, 34, 40
analogical relationship between God and creation, 126, 128–29
Anatolios, Khaled, 161n92, 161n94, 164n102
ancient-future movement, 18
angelology, 69, 72
Anglicanism, 50–51
anhypostatic-enhypostatic distinction, 144
Anselm, 11–12, 13, 46, 77, 118, 141; caricature of, 157n75; on divine simplicity, 124–25, 134–35; doctrine of substitution, 157; on

recapitulation, 160; satisfaction motif of, 146, 170; on uniqueness of God's existence, 129
antidote metaphor (Irenaeus), 165
apophaticism, 121n23, 130n66
Apostles' Creed, 32n33, 33, 36
Arianism, 161
Aristotle, 93, 95
Armstrong, Chris R., 78, 144, 202
artificiality, danger of, 73–74
ascetic ideals, 189
Athanasian Creed, 33
Athanasius, 13, 60, 73, 100n31, 146, 161–70
Athenagoras, 123
atonement, 73, 141–84; and creation, 150, 159; and incarnation, 178–79; as multidimensional, 175; mysteriousness and grandeur of, 183–84; and recapitulation, 157, 175–76
attributes, as privations, 132
Augsburg Confession, 41
Augustine, 19, 100n31, 153, 193; on divine simplicity, 118–19n12, 133–34; as proto-Protestant, 29; sacramentology of, 28; on theosis, 177; on transcendence of God, 129

Scripture Index